Changing L

Scotland and Britain since 1830

CW00547296

Oliver & Boyd

Oliver & Boyd
Longman House
Burnt Mill, Harlow
Essex CM20 2JE

An Imprint of Longman Group UK Ltd

© Oliver & Boyd 1990

ISBN 0 05 0039687

First published 1990
Second impression 1990

Set in 10/12pt Helvetica and Palatino
Produced by Longman Group (FE) Ltd
and printed in Hong Kong

Acknowledgements

The author and publishers wish to acknowledge permission to reproduce the following extracts:

Edward Arnold for C. Harvie, *No Gods and Precious Few Heroes*, J. Pollard, *The Development of the British Economy*; David Bold Associates for Anna Blair, *Croft & Creel, Tea at Miss Cranstons*; Cambridge University Press for B. R. Mitchell & P. Deane, *Abstract of British Political Historical Statistics*, M. W. Flinn (ed), *Scottish Population History*; Century Hutchinson Pub. Group Ltd for L. Derwent, *A Breath of Border Air*; Collins for T. C. Smout, *A Century of Scottish People*, J. Colville, *The New Elizabethans*, C. Booker, *The Neophiliacs*; Curtis Brown for © copyright David Jones, *Chartism and the Chartists*; Robert Gibson & Sons Glasgow Ltd for William Haddow, *My 70 Years*; Victor Gollancz for D. Kerr Cameron, *Cornkister Days*; Gower Publishing Group for N. Gray, *The Worst of Times*; David Higham Associates, for Paul Addison, *The Road to 1945*, Corelli Barnett, *The Collapse of British Power*, Molly Weir, *A Toe on the Ladder, Shoes were for Sunday, Best Foot Forward*, Ralph Glasser, *Growing up in the Gorbals*; International Thomson Publishing Services Ltd for Amy Stewart Fraser, *The Hills of Home*; Lawrence & Wishart Ltd, Abe Moffat, *My Life with the Miners*; Longman Group UK Ltd for E. Royle, *Chartism*, R. C. Birch, *The Shaping of the Welfare State*, P. Adelman, *The Rise of the Labour Party*; Manchester University Press for A. Wilson, *The Chartist Movement in Scotland*; M. Morris for *The General Strike*; Oxford University Press for R. M. Breach & R. M. Hartwell, *British Economy and Society 1870–1970*; Penguin Books for © J. Stevenson, *British Society, 1914–15*, © A. Sked and C. Cook, *Post-War Britain: A Political History*; Peters, Frasers & Dunlop for Arthur Marwick, *British Society since 1945*, R. D. Anderson, *Education and Opportunity in Victorian Scotland*; Pluto Press for H. McShane, *No Mean Fighter*; Polygon for Billy Kay, *Odyssey*; Sidgwick & Jackson Ltd for A. Thompson, *The Day Before Yesterday*; Weidenfeld & Nicolson Ltd for A. Beattie, *English Party Politics*.

They also wish to acknowledge permission given by the following for the use of illustrations on the pages shown.

Messrs Annan, Glasgow: p. 42; Aberdeen Art Gallery: p. 63; Aberdeen Journals: p. 202 (bottom), p. 205 (top right); Aberdeen University Library: pp. 29 (2), 68, 102 (bottom), 103 (top), 166 (right & bottom), 179 (top right); Aerofilms: p. 122 (bottom right), 220; Sir David Baird: p. 10; City of Aberdeen Library: pp. 19, 143 (bottom right); Clydebank District Library: pp. 74, 97, 140, 185 (right), 194, 196 (bottom), 205 (bottom) 215 (bottom); Communist Party Library: p. 203; Cumbernauld District Council: p. 220; Dumbarton District Library: pp. 101 (bottom left), 161 (left), 243; Dundee Art Galleries & Museums: pp. 16 (bottom), 20, 24, 27, 39, 43 (bottom), 78 (right), 91, 93, 96 (right), 99 (left), 100, 114 (right), 118, 124 (right), 160 (top right), 161, 124 (right), 179 (bottom right), 229; Dundee District Library: p 16 (top right), 32 (bottom right), 43 (inset), 44, 46, 96 (bottom), 99 (top), 126 (2) 128 (right), 160 (top right); Dunfermline District Libraries & Museums: pp. 103 (bottom right), 120 (top), 136 (bottom), 163, 178, 206 (bottom), 237 (right); Edinburgh Central Constituency Labour Party: p. 154; Edinburgh City Libraries: pp. 48, 80, 102 (right), 125 (left); *Edinburgh Evening News*: p. 205; E. T. Archives: p. 14 (top left); Falkirk Museums: pp. 22, 23, 90 (bottom), 103 (left bottom), 108; Glasgow District Library: pp. 65, 69 (left), 73, 90 (top), 211; *Glasgow Herald*: pp. 98, 120 (bottom), 156, 157, 202 (top), 212 (top right), 237 (left); John Gorman: pp. 13, 142, 162; Hawick & Jedburgh Co-operative Society: p. 57 (right); Hulton Picture Library: pp. 58 (right), 88, 153, 165, 183, 197, 211 (2), 241; Hunterian Art Gallery: p. 128 (left); Huntley House Museum: pp. 61, 143 (left); *Illustrated London News*: pp. 15 (bottom), 62, 81; Imperial War Museum: pp. 114 (top left), 117 (3), 187, 206 (top left); Inverclyde District Council: p. 122 (left); Norman Johnstone: p. 167; Kirkcaldy District Library: p. 159 (left); Lothian Health Board: p. 215 (top); Mansell Collection: pp. 35, 49 (2), 94; Mary Evans Picture Library: pp. 147 (left), 148; Moray District Council: pp. 6, 7; Motherwell District Council: pp. 189, 213 (left); National Coal Board: p. 36; National Farmers Union: p. 110 (right); National Galleries of Scotland: pp. 10, 18, 23; National Library of Scotland: pp. 25, 35 (right), 37, 78 (bottom); National Museums of Scotland: pp. 32 (top right), 39, 69 (bottom), 109, 110 (bottom), 111, 112, 113 (right), 114 (2), 119, 125, 133 (3), 138, 159 (bottom), 161 (right), 224; North East Fife District Library: pp. 116, 136 (bottom); Paisley Museum & Art Gallery: p. 34; Alex Paulin: p. 235; Peoples Palace: pp. 53, 129 (right), 144, 145 (2), 146, 147 (right), 179 (left); Perth & Kinross District Library: p. 57 (left); Perth Museum & Art Galleries: pp. 14 (right), 129 (left), 170; *Punch*: pp. 60, 85, 137, 143 (top right), 158, 184; Robert Fleming: p. 164; St. Andrews University Library:

3

pp. 7, 45, 71, 124 (right), 129 (right), 167 (left), 181, 233; Scotsman Publications: pp. 238, 244, 245; Scottish Film Council: pp. 175, 177 (2); Scottish Labour History Society: pp. 61, 143 (left); Scottish Record Office: pp. 26 (2), 58 (left), 185 (left); Strathclyde Regional Archives: pp. 99 (bottom), 105, 177; Strathkelvin District Library: p. 216; Strathkelvin District Museum: p. 55; Syndication International: pp. 227, 230; D. C. Thomson: pp. 191, 196 (top), 199 (2), 201, 212 (bottom right), 213, 217 (3), 219, 221, 223, 234, 239, 240, 243 (2); Topham Picture Library: pp. 127, 172, 173 (left), 189; University of Glasgow: p. 95; University of Kent at Canterbury: p. 149; Cover: City Art Gallery, Edinburgh for Robert MacGregor, 'Gathering Stones', The Fine Art Society for William Kennedy, 'Stirling Station' Collection of Andrew Macintosh Patrick.

Artwork and design by Cauldron Design Studio

The publishers have made every effort to trace the copyright holders, but if they have inadvertently overlooked any they will be pleased to make the necessary arrangements at the first opportunity.

Contents

Section A

The Workshop of the World – 1830s–1880s

Introduction

This book explores some of the ways in which life in Scotland has changed over the past 150–160 years. We might ask: how has life changed? Why has it changed? Has it changed for the better? Questions like these are not easy to answer. Look at the following figures, for example.

Source I.1

Number of petitions for divorce in Scotland:-
1901–5 – 181:
1968– – 4803

Letter deliveries in Scotland:
1850 – 35 million: 1925 – 311 million.

Offences known to the police in Scotland:
1869 – 7113: 1896 – 143 684: 1897 – 32 632: 1936 – 59 407.

Do these figures provide any clues as to how life has changed? Notice the sudden drop in crime figures from 1896 to 1897. Why do you think this might have happened? (In fact the kinds of offences included in crime figures were altered in 1897 to exclude very trivial matters. Scots had not suddenly become more law-abiding!)

Source I.2

Source I.3

The photographs of the little village of Archiestown in north-east Scotland provide further clues as to how life has changed over the past 100 years. How many changes can be seen? Do they suggest life in this village has improved?

Source I.4

Photographs that show people's appearances may help us see how life has changed. This photograph was taken in 1910 in St Andrews. How can you tell it is not a modern picture? Would you agree that 'This photo shows life in the past was poorer than life today'?

Comments and observations on life in the past from people who actually lived then can provide further clues. Perhaps you can guess when this was written?

In many homes in Inverness in those days Christmas was a day of more satisfying happiness for the children than it is at present when they are surfeited with Christmas cards and costly gifts. In those days toys and books were much more expensive than they are now and children did not get so many of them. Therefore they prized the few they did get.

Might that have been said by someone living today? In fact the book it comes from (*Inverness before Railways*) was published in 1885. The author, Isabel Harriet Anderson, was recalling life around 1850! The next sentence shows it could not have been written very recently – 'children . . . were quite satisfied with a sixpenny [2.5p] or shilling [5p] book from their parents and no remembrance [gift] from anyone else, except, perhaps, a pen-wiper or pin cushion.' The author believes that, in one way at least, life has not improved.

The author was speaking in her old age, looking back to her youth. Might that make a difference to how she feels about the present?

So far you have looked at three sorts of historical sources – statistics, photographs and reminiscences. But were they all produced by people with actual direct experience of life in the past? If they were then historians call these **primary sources**. But facts and figures and other information that has been gathered since by people who did not themselves directly experience the topics they are studying are also helpful. Such materials are called **secondary sources**. Perhaps you can work out which of the sources you've looked at so far are secondary sources.

Studying the past

As a result of looking at the above sources, you should have gained at least a little more *knowledge* and *understanding* than you had before looking at them. Throughout this book you will be building up your knowledge and understanding of the past. Where questions in the book are asking you to do this they are labelled (K.U.)

However, as you can see from source I.5 you need to think about the source. Was it produced at the time? Did the author really know what he was writing about? Might he/she be biased in some way? Is he/she trying to persuade an audience of something? How? Does the author's view differ from the view of someone else living them? Problems like these mean you must think about – i.e. *evaluate – the source*. Where questions ask you to do this they are labelled (E.1).

As a result of your work you will build up an understanding that will make it possible to say what you think. Why did this happen? What was the result of that taking place? Was that a sensible action to have taken? Questions like these are asking *you to evaluate the past* and are labelled (E.2). These sources are but a few of the many available. You may be *investigating* your own area, too.

1 The Changing Economy

Scottish people lived their lives at this time in a country that was altering very rapidly. There were changes in the work people did, the kinds of places where they worked and the machinery that they used. The size of the Scottish population was changing too. In the eighteenth century the great majority of Scots lived in the countryside, between 1830 and 1880 that was altering. The sources in this chapter explore these changes and some of the main reasons why they took place.

The Scottish People

Search through the following sources for evidence of how Scotland's population was changing.

Source 1.1
The population of Scotland:

1831	2 373 000	1861	3 062 000
1841	2 620 000	1871	3 360 000
1851	2 888 000	1881	3 735 000

Glasgow's population grew especially. In 1831 it was 202 000. By 1861 it was 448 000. In 1841 Glasgow housed 9.75% of Scotland's population: by 1889 it housed 13.69%. In 1870 the *Glasgow Herald* reported:

Source 1.2
During the past few years green paths where cattle grazed and greens where housewives bleached their clothes have been almost covered with houses, there has been much building of late of tenements for workmen's houses. During the past season in the north-west district there have been, or are about to be erected 1069 separate dwelling houses, about 800 of which are suitable for working men. [In the east of the city] whole streets of dwelling houses have been erected within the past few years. Still the supply is insufficient to meet the requirements of the increasing population.

Source 1.3

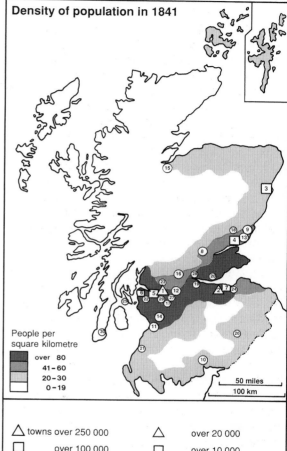

Density of population in 1841

People per square kilometre

- over 80
- 41–60
- 20–30
- 0–19

50 miles
100 km

△	towns over 250 000	△	over 20 000
□	over 100 000	□	over 10 000
○	over 50 000	○	over 5 000

Towns over 5 000 inhabitants in 1841

1.	Glasgow	274 533	16.	Stirling	11 699
2.	Edinburgh	138 182	17.	Hamilton	8 876
3.	Aberdeen	64 778	18.	Forfar	8 362
4.	Dundee	60 553	19.	Falkirk	8 209
5.	Paisley	60 487	20.	Dunfermline	7 865
6.	Greenock	36 135	21.	Girvan	7 424
7.	Leith	26 433	22.	Port Glasgow	6 973
8.	Perth	19 293	23.	Kirkintilloch	6 698
9.	Montrose	13 402	24.	Musselburgh	6 331
10.	Dumfires	13 299	25.	Rothesay	5 789
11.	Ayr	12 746	26.	Hawick	5 770
12.	Airdrie	12 418	27.	Rutherglen	5 623
13.	Arbroath	12 313	28.	Alloa	5 434
14.	Kilmarnock	12 232	29.	Pollockshaws	5 283
15.	Inverness	12 100	30.	Campbeltown	5 028

Source 1.4
Princes Street, Edinburgh, 1825

Percentage of population living in places of 5000 or more

| 1831 | 31.2% | 1871 | 44.4% |
| 1851 | 35.9% | 1881 | 48.9% |

(M. W. Flinn ed., *Scottish Population History from the Seventeenth Century to the 1930s*, 1977)

Source 1.5

The Population of Counties	1831	1881		1831	1881
Aberdeen	177 657	267 990	Lanark	316 819	904 412
Angus	139 606	266 360	Midlothian	219 345	389 164
Argyll	150 973	76 468	Moray	34 498	43 788
Ayr	145 055	217 519	Nairn	9 354	10 455
Banff	48 337	62 736	Orkney	28 847	32 044
Berwick	34 048	35 392	Peebles	10 578	13 822
Bute	14 151	17 657	Perth	142 166	129 007
Caithness	34 529	38 865	Renfrew	133 443	263 374
Clackmannan	14 729	25 680	Ross and Cromarty	74 820	78 547
Dumfries	73 770	76 140	Roxburgh	43 663	53 442
Dumbarton	33 211	75 333	Selkirk	6 833	25 564
East Lothian	36 145	38 502	Stirling	72 621	112 443
Fife	128 839	171 931	Sutherland	25 518	23 370
Inverness	94 797	90 454	West Lothian	23 291	43 510
Kincardine	31 431	34 464	Wigtown	36 258	38 610
Kinross	9 072	6 697	Zetland	29 392	29 705
Kirkcudbright	40 590	42 127			

(Ed. J. Gray Kyd, *Scottish Population Statistics*, 1952)

As early as 1825 Sir John Sinclair, a wealthy landowner and politician who had a very keen interest in collecting information about Scotland offered his reasons as to why the country's population was increasing in number in some places and falling in others. He listed his explanations for population growth, including:

Source 1.6

1. The beneficial effects of inoculation for the smallpox.
2. The improvement of waste lands.
3. Better cultivated soil, a more extensive employment in fishing.
4. The great increase in manufacturers.

. . . causes of decreased population.

1. The increased size of farms . . . There are numerous instances of one person renting a property in the cultivation of which six, eight or ten farmers had formerly been employed.
2. The conversion of large tracts of country into sheep farms. What can be more painful than to see one person living on a property on which formerly 100 inhabitants found a comfortable subsistence?
3. Some of the modern improvements in agriculture.
4. The habits of the lower ranks which make them afraid of marriage and desirous of enjoying the pleasures without the burdens of matrimony.
5. The army and navy carry away numbers of young men.
6. Emigration. The flower of our young men incited by the prospect of making a fortune, go abroad.

(Analysis of the Statistical Account).

Were these changes welcome? Could they be controlled? A number of people in Britain wrote about these questions. In 1798 the Reverend Thomas Malthus argued that a country's population could not grow bigger than the supply of food to feed it would allow. If it got too large then diseases among poor starving people would reduce population again.

QUESTIONS

1 Use the sources to explain:
   a) in which ten years Scotland's population grew fastest;
   b) which two counties increased most in size;
   c) which counties suffered a fall in population? (K.U)

2 Using the sources, especially your views on source 1.6 together with your own ideas, write a paragraph suggesting why the population was changing in size and where it was located. (It will help you to compare source 1.3 with a geographical map of Scotland.) (E.2)

3 How can you tell from source 1.6 that Sir John Sinclair was a member of the upper classes? (E.1)

4 Look through the sources again. List those which are *primary* sources. (E.1)

The Economy

Where people lived, and how this changed from the 1830s to the 1880s, depended very much on where there was work to be found. Evidence of this can be seen in official population details gathered every ten years, called 'census returns'. The early census returns were not very detailed, however.

Source 1.7

1831 Details of the occupations of the Scottish people

Agriculture			Employed in Manufacture, or in making Manufacturing Machinery	Employed in Retail Trade, or in Handicraft as Masters or Workmen	Capitalists, Bankers, Professional and other Educated Men	Labourers employed in Labour not Agricultural	Other Males 20 Years of Age (except Servants)	Male Servants		Female servants
Occupiers employing Labourers	Occupiers not Labourers	Labourers employed in Agriculture						20 Years of Age	Under 20 years	
25 887	53 966	87 292	83 993	152 464	29 203	76 191	34 930	5 895	2 599	109 512

By 1881 the census returns were more detailed and differently organised.

Source 1.8 _____

1881   Details of the occupations of the Scottish people

	Total	Male	Female
Class I – Professional			
1. Engaged in the General or Local Government of the Country	13 235	12 084	1 151
2. Engaged in the defence of the Country	8 310	8 305	5
3. Engaged in Professional Occupations (with their immediate Subordinates)	74 558	45 110	29 448
Total	96 103	65 499	30 604
Class II – Domestic			
4. Engaged in Domestic Offices or Services	176 565	25 292	151 273
Class III – Commercial			
5. Engaged in Commercial Occupations	45 854	43 551	2 303
6. Engaged in Conveyance of Men, Goods, and Messages	86 272	83 192	3 080
Total	132 126	126 743	5 383
Class IV – Agriculture			
7. Engaged in Agriculture	229 008	177 361	51 647
8. Engaged about Animals and Fisheries	40 529	37 854	2 675
Total	269 537	215 215	54 322
Class V – Industrial			
9. Working and Dealing in Books, Prints, and Maps	16 305	12 185	4 120
10. Working and Dealing in Machines and Implements	38 600	38 008	592
11. Working and Dealing in Houses, Furniture, and Decorations	108 539	106 201	2 338
12. Working and Dealing in Carriages and Harness	5 796	5 772	24
13. Working and Dealing in Ships and Boats	18 492	18 470	22
14. Working and Dealing in Chemicals and Compounds	6 038	5 330	708
15. Working and Dealing in Tobacco and Pipes	2 847	1 600	1 247
16. Working and Dealing in Food and Lodging	90 016	67 803	22 213
17. Working and Dealing in Textile Fabrics	201 867	70 796	131 071
18. Working and Dealing in Dress	111 321	48 493	62 828
19. Working and Dealing in Animal Substances	6 678	5 715	963
20. Working and Dealing in Vegetable Substances	30 682	22 590	8 092
21. Working and Dealing in Mineral Substances	181 161	177 761	3 400
22. Working and Dealing in General or Unspecified Commodities	112 647	94 025	18 622
23. Working and Dealing in Refuse Matters	1 664	1 215	499
Total	932 453	675 964	256 689
Class VI – Unoccupied			
24. Persons without Specified Occupations	830 055	39 241	790 814
25. Scholars and Children of No Stated Occupations	1 298 534	651 521	647 013
Total	2 128 589	690 762	1 437 827

The skills needed to work in Scotland at this time varied greatly. Notice the large number of domestic servants. The figures include people working in hotels but the majority (136 098 in 1881) worked in the homes of private families. Furthermore, many men were skilled craftsmen working in small workshops in towns and villages.

Source 1.9

Joiners in Carnoustie

This was a time when Britain could claim to be 'the workshop of the world'. Inventions of earlier years – like steam power and the use of machines to spin and weave cloth – were being used on an ever-growing scale. In 1851 Britain celebrated her importance as a country of inventions with a 'Great Exhibition' in a huge specially-built glass 'Crystal Palace' in London.

Many of the people applying inventions, as well as some of the inventors themselves, were Scots. Steam power owed much to the work of James Watt. The gas industry developed from pioneering efforts by William Murdoch. Though Murdoch died in 1839 he had lived long enough to see his ideas taken up, developed and used to light around 200 British towns.

Moreover, this was a time when goods produced in Britain could be moved about the country to be sold, and could be sent overseas, far more easily than ever before. Better roads, canals, better harbours which

steamships were now beginning to use, all made this possible. During these years there was a surge of railway building that created 21 700 km [13 500 miles] of track in Britain by 1870. The economy of Scotland, therefore, was linked as never before into the economy of Britain and to the wider world as British trade expanded. In 1848 exports were worth £48 millions. By 1860 their value was £136 millions. Scotland's merchants and manufacturers played a big part in these developments. Thomas Lipton, for example, was just 21 when he opened a shop in Glasgow in 1871. He bought what he needed directly from suppliers. He had learned how to advertise effectively in the United States when (after a trip there as a cabin boy) he had worked in a food shop. Lipton's shops spread into most Scottish towns and into England too. By the 1880s he was especially famous for Lipton's tea, supplied from plantations he bought in Ceylon.

Farming

How important do the numbers working in farming (sources 1.7 and 1.8) suggest that this occupation was to the Scottish economy?

1 Read through the following sources to list all the examples of improved farming you can find. (K.U)

2 Find any changes that were taking place in the way farming was being carried out. (K.U)

Source 1.11

Farmworkers in Gannochy

QUESTIONS

1 Use sources 1.7 and 1.8 to show:
 a) which jobs had grown most rapidly by 1881; (K.U)
 b) which were the most important industrial jobs in 1881. (K.U)

2 Why do you think most domestic servants were women? (E.2)

3 Which jobs commonly found in 1881 are rarely found today? (K.U)

4 Using all you have read so far in this chapter write a brief report that Thomas Lipton might have written, on where you are going to open your shops and how you are going to advertise your goods. (E.2)

In 1840, John Kerr noted in his part of Scotland:

Source 1.12 _____
Corn and wheat crops were invariably cut with the sickle and at harvest time crowds of Irishmen appeared with their sickles wrapped up in straw under their arms. Scythes were used only for grass and hay. Reaping machines were unknown.

(J. Kerr, *Leaves from an Inspector's Logbook*, n.d.)

Horses made all sorts of machinery work. They powered mills to thresh grain (separating off the seed head). They pulled ploughs, harrows and carts.

Specialist plough-makers, like Sellars of Huntly, became increasingly important in the 1850s. Very few farmers used wooden ploughs by then.

Source 1.13 _____
Horse mill at Kirkbean, Kircudbright

By 1881 another observer noticed:

Source 1.14 _____
A steam threshing machine in 1881

Source 1.15

'The most improved implements of all kinds are in general used where good husbandry (i.e. farming) is carried on. Within the last 20 years the reaping machine has been introduced and is now almost universally employed and so are grain-sowing machines. Steam cultivation has likewise been carried on. Single ploughs, horse rakes, harrows and rollers, potato diggers are employed generally: a large proportion of the light implements – forks, hoes, etc., are of American manufacture.

(I. Carter, *Poor Man's Country*, 1979)

In 1845 the minister of Crail looked around at the improved farming of the time in Fife and wrote:

Source 1.16

Almost every modern improvement has been tried so as to bring the land to the highest state of productiveness. In few places have the effects of draining been more conspicuous. 115 ploughs are at work in the parish, each drawn by a couple of horses guided by a single man. The sound of the flail is seldom heard as each farmer has his threshing mill. Near the coast seaweed is much used as a manure. Lime and stable dung are, of course, universal: bone dust and guano are also employed [to feed the land]. Great attention is paid to the quality and keeping of horses.

(N.S.A.)

Further improvements included planting trees, building fences, dykes (walls), new farmhouses and farm steadings, and breeding more productive cattle and sheep.

QUESTIONS

1 What reasons can you work out from earlier chapters, and add from your own ideas, as to why farmers were now able to improve the land, and were so keen to do so? (E.2)

2 Use the evidence to design and label a simple plan of an ideal Scottish farm of 1880. (K.U)

Mines and Industries

As the farming section shows, Scottish workers from 1830 to 1880 were increasingly using all sorts of sources of power as well as their own muscles. In workshops and small factories, too, power was needed.

Source 1.17
Watermill at Ardoch

Source 1.18
Windmill at Broughty Ferry, 1860

Coal

It was steam power that was the most modern way to drive machinery at this time. Steam-engines were expensive, however. Wind and water were free; steam needed endless supplies of expensive coal. Coal was also increasingly used to heat homes. By 1881 there were 53 741 coal miners at work in Scotland, supplying the country's needs. They cut coal totalling 20 million tonnes – nearly three times the amount cut in 1851. As a result both new pits and deeper and more extensive workings were needed.

Source 1.19

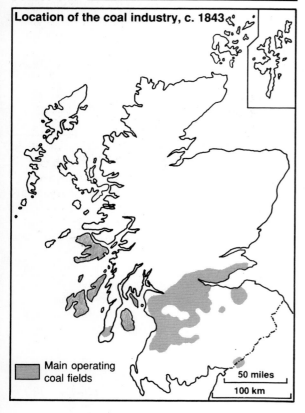

Location of the coal industry, c. 1843

Main operating coal fields

50 miles

100 km

Steam pumps to take water out of mines, steam-engines to haul miners and coal up from the pit, helped improve the mines. In 1871, the **Fife News** reported:

Source 1.20

Till within the last 60 years the coal pits at Lochgelly, as in many other mining localities in Scotland, were sunk on an inclined direction, the coal being hewn and brought to the surface by manual labour. The coal pits have in this century undergone so great a change that, coupled with the extensive railway communication we are left in astonishment as to how trade was carried on by our ancestors. The application of steam has overcome many obstacles in the pursuit of mining. The Eliza Pit is the most extensive in the district. The pumping engine is 100 h.p and the winding engine 40 h.p.

(*Fife News*, 28 October 1871)

Another improvement was the use of pit props to support the roofing of tunnels (instead of leaving pillars of coal). There remained the danger of explosion of dangerous gases, caused by the use of candles to light the gloomy tunnels.

A Fife doctor noted how some miners coped when explosive gases were around:

Source 1.21

One old man told me that he remembered some 60 years ago working below ground by the phosphorescent light of decaying fish heads in a part of the mine where the air was too foul to allow his candle to burn.

(D. Ross, *The Mining Folk of Fife*, 1914)

By 1870 nearly 70% of Scottish coal output came from Ayrshire and Lanarkshire.

Source 1.22
Engraving of a steam engine built in 1830 for Sir John Hope of Craighall, Fife, a coal master

Iron and Steel

Coal also supplied the needs of Scotland's developing iron and steel industry. In 1828 James Neilson developed a process called 'hot blast' that meant that coal, not coke could be used in the furnaces; low grade Scottish coal worked adequately if hot air (at 300°C) was blown onto the furnace. Huge deposits of blackband ironstone were to be found in Scotland, especially in the Lanark area. This stone was a mixture of iron ore and coal. Neilson's invention meant it could be easily smelted into iron. Between 1828 and 1838 iron production increased over 500% and Lanarkshire developed into the most important centre of the industry. In 1835 there were 29 furnaces that produced 76 000 tonnes of iron. By 1869 158 furnaces produced 1.52 million tonnes. It was said that so many furnace fires lit the sky around Coatbridge that there was no need for street lighting! In Monkland parish, an observer noted how the area had changed with:

Source 1.23
. . . the introduction of the hot-air blast and the increasing demand for iron for railway and other purposes. To the burning of ironstone was added works for the manufacture of malleable iron. Everywhere one heard the rattling of machinery, the stroke of mighty hammers and the hissing and clanking of the steam engine. Fortunes have been realised in the iron trade with rapidity.

(*Ordnance Gazeteer of Scotland*)

In 1869 David Bremner found the famous Carron Ironworks near Falkirk was making:

Source 1.24
. . . stoves, grates, cooking ranges, boilers, pots, rain-pipes, etc. The raw material is brought in by railway. For the conveyance of goods to the east and west 16 canal boats are employed. The company employs nearly 2000 men and boys.

(D. Bremner *The Industries of Scotland*, 1869)

Scotland's biggest ironworks at this time was at Gartsherrie, near Coatbridge. Over 3000 worked there, many living in two- or three-roomed company houses. So successful was the iron industry that, in mid-Victorian times, it turned out a quarter of all British iron. The steel industry was much smaller and its products expensive. It was hampered by the impure quality of Scottish iron ores. By 1880 this problem of phosphoric ores had been solved by a Welsh police court clerk who was a keen amateur scientist – Sidney Gilchrist Thomas. He used a limestone lining to eliminate the phosphor.

Shipbuilding

The use of steam power and of iron and steel began to transform Scottish shipbuilding. Sailing ships continued to be built in this

Source 1.25

The *Thermopylae* built in Aberdeen, 1885

period, especially large, fast clipper ships. In 1868 the greatest of all clippers, Aberdeen's *Thermopylae*, was launched. Its greatest rival, *Cutty Sark* left the Dumbarton shipyards in 1869.

But, from 1866, even clipper builders began to use iron frames around which to fit wooden planking. Steam-powered vessels began as early as 1802 with the launch of the *Charlotte Dundas*, a canal and river tug. In 1812 the Scottish engineer Henry Bell launched *The Comet* to carry passengers between Glasgow, Greenock and Helensburgh. Shipbuilding developed in Aberdeen and Dundee but, above all, on the Clyde. By mid-century Clyde yards were Britain's busiest. Between 1851 and 1870 the Clyde produced 70% of all iron shipping tonnage launched in Britain. By 1870 24 000 of Britain's 47 000 shipbuilders worked on the Clyde. The invention of the screw propellor to replace the paddle wheel and James Howden's high-pressure boilers (1862)

seemed to further stimulate Clyde firms. In 1847 the *Glasgow Examiner* reported on one of the most important of them, Napier's at Govan:

Source 1.26

No other foundries in the world are able to compete either for the magnitude or perfection of the work they produce. Mr Robert Napier also does the fitting up of vessels, both wood and iron. There are six smelting furnaces. The heavy castings are moved with cranes. An engine is turning [working] and planing machines. The only noise is that of machines and hammers.

(In S. Berry & H. Whyte, *Glasgow Observed*, 1987)

Napier-trained men, Charles Randolph and John Elder, patented a compound expansion engine that was powerful and effective. They were able to strike out on their own and set up Fairfields shipyard.

Handloom weaving, 1850

In textiles, too, machines began to dominate. In 1840 there were 84 560 handloom weavers and spinners. By 1880 only 8000 were at work. The Scottish cotton industry suffered from the competition of Lancashire, especially in eastern Scotland. Linen, too, declined from the 1840s because of Manchester's competition as well as a shortage of its raw material, flax. But a successful woollen industry developed, particularly in Border towns like Hawick and Galashiels. Above all the jute industry boomed. By the 1870s 72 mills and factories in Dundee employed 42 000. The Camperdown Works alone provided employment for 14 000. The use of whale oil to make jute fibre pliable (developed in 1832) had much to do with this, helped by Dundee's success as a whaling port.

At the same time, banking developed to serve the needs of this growing economy. The leaders of these developments prospered and so did the places where they lived. In 1858 Glasgow impressed James Burn.

Source 1.28

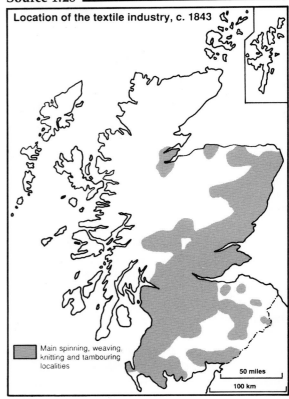

Location of the textile industry, c. 1843

Main spinning, weaving, knitting and tambouring localities

50 miles

100 km

20

Source 1.29

The prosperity of the town is the result of private enterprise, well-directed industry and the application of capital to manufacturing or commercial pursuits. We know no town in the United Kingdom where the trading community have undergone such a change in their manners and habits. A love of finery and an assumption of gentility pervades a large portion of society.

(In Berry & Whyte, *Glasgow Observed*)

QUESTIONS

1 What reasons do you think the owners of the buildings in sources 1.17 and 1.18 might have given for the use of these forms of power instead of steam? What problems might they have faced? (E.2)

2 From the sources provided, list the reasons why the coal industry grew at this time. (K.U)

3 How do you think the evidence in this chapter would affect where most Scottish people would want to live? Would this produce any problems? (E.2)

4 Use the evidence in this section to write a report from Scotland (for an English newspaper) entitled 'The Enterprising Scot'. (E.2)

Travel

Between 1830 and 1880 there were great changes in travel in Scotland. The following sources deal with these changes.

QUESTIONS

1 Search through the sources to write an article for a Scottish newspaper of 1880. Entitle your article 'A Stagecoach Owner Looks Back over a Long Life'.

  a) Describe the main changes. (K.U)
  b) Explain what you think are the reasons for these changes. (E.2)
  c) Describe your feelings about the changes, and whether they are an improvement. (Remember your job! Think about what the changes have done to your work.) (E.2)

(In order to do this question, first read through the whole of this section and note down any useful information.)

2 Your article annoys a director of a railway company. Write the reply such as a person might have sent to the newspaper. In it he would mention all the benefits of railways and all the disadvantages of other ways of travelling. (E.2)

3 Use the evidence provided in these sources to design a poster advertising the opening of either your local railway line or a new tramway. Stress all the advantages they will bring. (K.U)

4 Which source or sources suggest that railway travel did not ruin horse-drawn travel? (E.1)

5 Find a source you think is biased. Quote words and phrases that show the author's point of view and feelings. (E.1)

In 1830 a network of privately paid for 'turnpike' roads covered the country. At 10-kilometre intervals barriers stopped the traveller.

Source 1.30
Toll house near Denny, 1916

Source 1.31

Carts and waggons, including carriers carts (that would take goods and parcels, and even passengers) moved along at a walking pace. Stage coaches often managed 16 k.p.h. They stopped at coaching inns to let travellers rest and to change the horses.

In the Dunfermline area R. S. Mackie remembered these days:

Source 1.32
. . . we knew most of the people who used the roads; they were not very numerous on ordinary days. Only the gentry had carriages of their own in these days; a few of the townsfolk took afternoon drives, but for the most part they used hired carriages. Dunfermline was 'tolled' up to the last degree. There were toll bars at Lady's Mill, close to the old Dunfermline and Charlestown railway; at the Spittal, through which the traffic to the Ferry and the lands beyond the Forth had to pass; at the Town Green; at Grantsbank, a little distance north of Provost Whitelaw's foundry, at Baldridgeburn; and at Pittencrieff, the last being situated in proximity to the Elgin Colliery railway.

(R. S. Mackie, *When We Were Boys*, 1911–13 in E. Simpson, *Auld Grey Toun*, 1987)

Source 1.33

Forth-Clyde canal at Grangemouth, 1870s

A network of canals crossed parts of Scotland, too. Canal building was costly and not suited to hilly areas. Nevertheless, some canals prospered. The canal from Monkland to Glasgow made profits, for example. In 1865 alone it collected in £35 000 which came especially from the traffic in coal.

Source 1.34

Sedan chair

In towns and cities ordinary people walked, the better-off had private horse-drawn vehicles. Some well-to-do folk used a way of travelling described here by J. H. A. Macdonald. When an old man he looked back on his youth in Edinburgh in the 1840s:

Source 1.35

At every corner of the residential streets there was kept the sedan chair, used to convey ladies from house to house. At the corner there sat the chairmen. They were for the most part Highlanders. There were a number of them still in the 1870s. The sedan chair was a very pleasant way for a lady going out, she entering her chair within her own lobby and leaving it in the entrance hall of her friend's house. The chairmen carried their passengers very pleasantly except when there had been too many drams during the day. The sedan chair could not hold its own when the cities grew larger.

(J.H. Macdonald, *Life Jottings*, 1914)

By 1880 a new form of horse-drawn traffic worked the main streets of cities – the horse-drawn tram. In Edinburgh Eleanor Sillar watched these vehicles:

Source 1.36
Horse-drawn tram in Perth

Source 1.37
It was steep going up to the top where the High Street crossed the tram-lines. We watched a pair of tram-horses, poor panting beasts, straining up the hill with a dead weight of car and passengers behind them, and helped by what we knew as a trace-horse hitched on to the centre pole, and ridden by a jovial raggamuffin of a boy, who egged on the team, with yells and whip-crackings. At the top he unhitched his tackle, and went clattering and jingling down the hill again ready for the next load.

(E. Sillar, *Edinburgh's Child*, 1961)

Railways

In 1825 the *Scotsman* newspaper wondered how steam power was going to affect travel overland:

Source 1.38
There is nothing very extravagant in expecting to see the present rate of travelling [16 kph] doubled. We shall then be carried at the rate of 400 miles [644 km] per day. Such a new power of locomotion cannot be introduced without working a vast change in the state of society . . . provincial towns would become suburbs of the metropolis . . . commodities, inventions, discoveries, opinions, would circulate with a rapidity hitherto unknown.

(*Scotsman* 22 December 1825)

It had long been known that wagons ran more easily on rails than over roads. Horse-drawn 'wagonways' were built. Alloa, for example, had such a line in 1766. By 1832 the Monkland & Kirkintilloch line, which had opened in 1826, was mainly using steam power to pull coal wagons. Scotland's first passenger-carrying line, the Glasgow–Garnick, opened in 1831 – just six years after

The opening of the Glasgow to Garnkirk railway,
1831

Stephenson's famous Stockton–Darlington
railway. George Buchanan saw the line open:

Source 1.40
2 engines travelling the line and drawing
behind them long trains of carriages and
wagons amid an immense concourse of spec-
tators assembled to witness so new and
extraordinary a scene. One engine conveyed
the directors and a number of ladies and
gentlemen to the amount of 200: the other
drew a train of 32 wagons loaded with coal,
freestone, lime, grain, iron and other articles.

Railways spread rapidly, built by a whole
number of private companies. As time passed
smaller companies often merged to form larger
ones like the North British and the Caledonian.
The lines were built by hundreds of labourers
called 'navvies'. They often lived in miserable
conditions. Scurvy was so common among
them, because of their poor diet, that it was
known as 'the railway disease'. The coming

of navvies could spread alarm in country
areas. The Minister of Erskine was horrified by:

Source 1.41
The scenes of drunkenness, Sabbath profa-
nation, and horrid blasphemy, with which an
unsophisticated country population has been
familiarised by a residence among them of the
very worst description of English, Irish and
Highlanders, to the amount of 1500–2000
employed on the railways for the last two years
. . . [produced] . . . most blighting and perni-
cious effects . . . which it is to be feared, in
many cases, will never be fully eradicated.

(N.S.A. Erskine VII)

In 1849 the *Edinburgh Courant* newspaper
complained:

Source 1.42
For some years past we have been in the habit
of hearing of severe conflicts in different parts
of Scotland with navvies and police: Men have
been killed and valuable property destroyed
and the majesty of the law set at open
defiance.

(Quoted in A. Gordon, *To Move with the Times*,
1988)

Source 1.43

Steam digger excavating the approach to the Forth Railway Bridge, 1888

The navvies used picks, shovels and barrows, but by 1880 steam power was being used. Their work involved building embankments, hacking out cuttings, and constructing bridges.

Source 1.44

Remains of a steam engine after the boiler has exploded

All sorts of accidents took place. Steam locomotives terrified some of the people who just saw them. It cannot have surprised such people when an engine blew up.

The most famous Scottish railway disaster happened in 1879. During a storm the Tay Bridge, designed by Thomas Bouch, collapsed

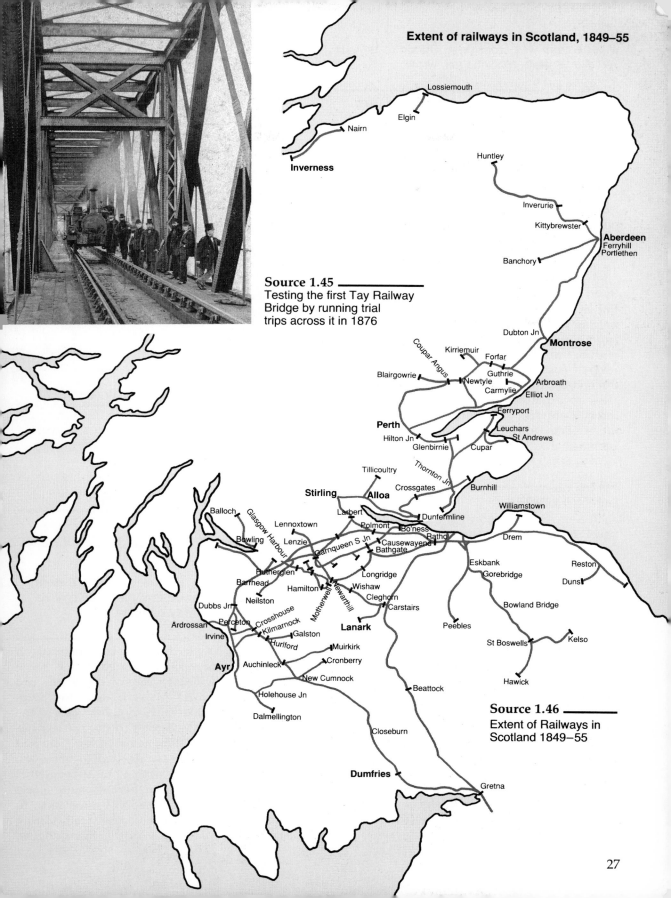

Extent of railways in Scotland, 1849–55

Lossiemouth
Elgin
Nairn
Inverness
Huntley
Inverurie
Kittybrewster
Aberdeen
Ferryhill
Portlethen
Banchory

Source 1.45
Testing the first Tay Railway
Bridge by running trial
trips across it in 1876

Dubton Jn
Montrose

Coupar Angus
Kirriemuir
Forfar
Blairgowrie
Guthrie
Newtyle
Carmylie
Arbroath
Elliot Jn
Ferryport
Perth
Leuchars
Hilton Jn
St Andrews
Glenbirnie
Cupar
Thornton Jn
Tillicoultry
Crossgates
Burnhill
Stirling
Alloa
Williamstown
Larbert
Dunfermline
Balloch
Lennoxtown
Polmont
Bo'ness
Drem
Glasgow Harbour
Lenzie
Garnqueen S Jn
Bowling
Causewayend
Ratho
Eskbank
Reston
Rutherglen
Bathgate
Gorebridge
Duns
Barrhead
Hamilton
Longridge
Neilston
Motherwell
Wishaw
Bowland Bridge
Dubbs Jn
Newarthill
Cleghorn
Peebles
Ardrossan
Perceton
Crosshouse
Carstairs
Irvine
Kilmarnock
Galston
Lanark
St Boswells
Kelso
Hurlford
Muirkirk
Auchinleck
Cronberry
Hawick
Ayr
New Cumnock
Beattock
Holehouse Jn
Dalmellington
Closeburn

Source 1.46
Extent of Railways in
Scotland 1849–55

Dumfries
Gretna

27

whilst a train was crossing it. Dundee's famous versifier, William McGonagall, wrote:

Source 1.47

Beautiful Railway Bridge of the Silv'ry Tay
Alas I am sorry to say
That 90 lives have been taken away
On the last Sabbath day of 1879
Which will be remembered for a very long
  time.

Not all Scots felt railways were welcome. They put many stage-coach operators out of business. They injured the traffic on some canals. The lawyer Henry Cockburn wrote in 1845:

Source 1.48

Britain is at present an island of lunatics, all railway mad. The outrages of [railway] speculators are frightful. Their principle is that nothing must obstruct their dividends – a revered ruin, a noble castle, a glorious wood, the cottage where Burns was born – what are these to a railway? In addition to our Princes Street Gardens, the South Inch of Perth and the College of Glasgow are almost under sentence.

(*Memorials*)

Yet the opening of a new line was usually a time of celebration.
John Kerr remembered what it was like to travel on the early passenger trains in Scotland:

Source 1.49

The comforts, or rather the discomforts, of railway travelling in the middle of the century, were very different from those of the present day. Third-class carriages were often little different from cattle-trucks. For a considerable time they were open and had no seats. First and second-class carriages were covered, and on the top the luggage of the passengers was packed, for there was no luggage-van. The old stage-coach was to a large extent the model for the railway carriage. There was no shelter for the guards [there were usually two], who, exposed to the weather, occupied seats on the top, one on the first and the other on the last carriage of the train. The drivers also had little or no protection against the weather.

(Kerr, *Leaves from an Inspector's Logbook*)

Source 1.50

NORTH BRITISH RAILWAY COMPANY.

OPENING OF THE FORTH BRIDGE
FOR
PASSENGER TRAFFIC
BETWEEN
EDINBURGH & DUNFERMLINE
ON
WEDNESDAY, 5th MARCH 1890.

The Public is respectfully informed that the Forth Bridge will be opened for Passenger Traffic between Edinburgh and Dunfermline on **Wednesday, 5th March 1890**, on and after which date the present Passenger Service *via* Ratho, Port Edgar, and North Queensferry will be discontinued, and a new Service of Trains will be given *via* Ratho and the Forth Bridge at the following hours, until further notice:—

From EDINBURGH.	Week Days.						Sat. only.
Classes	1 3 A.M.	1 3 A.M.	1 3 A.M.	1 3 P.M.	1 3 P.M.	1 3 P.M.	1 3 P.M.
EDINBURGH (Wav. Station) dep.	6 40	9 30	11 40	2 5	4 48	7 50	10 30
Haymarket	6 44	9 34	11 44	2 9	4 52	7 54	10 34
Corstorphine	...	9 40	...	2 15	4 58	8 0	10 40
Gogar	...	9 45	...	2 20	5 3	8 6	10 46
Ratho	6 58	9 52	11 58	2 27	5 11	8 13	10 53
Kirkliston	7 4	9 58	12 4	2 33	5 17	8 19	10 59
Forth Bridge Station	7 13	10 7	12 13	2 42	5 26	8 28	11 8
Inverkeithing	7 22	10 16	12 22	2 51	5 35	8 37	11 17
DUNFERMLINE (Low. St.) arr.	7 30	10 25	12 30	3 0	5 43	8 45	11 25

To EDINBURGH.	Week-Days.						Sat. only.
Classes	1 3 A.M.	1 3 A.M.	1 3 A.M.	1 3 P.M.	1 3 P.M.	1 3 P.M.	1 3 P.M.
DUNFERMLINE (Low. St.) dep.	7 45	8 30	10 45	1 45	4 25	6 35	9 10
Inverkeithing	7 54	8 39	10 54	1 54	4 34	6 44	9 19
Forth Bridge Station	8 3	8 48	11 3	2 3	4 43	6 53	9 28
Kirkliston	8 12	8 57	11 12	2 12	4 52	7 2	9 37
Ratho	8 19	9 4	11 19	2 19	4 59	7 9	9 44
Gogar	8 25	...	11 25	2 25	5 5	...	9 51
Corstorphine	8 30	...	11 31	2 31	5 11	...	9 56
Haymarket	8 37	9 17	11 37	2 37	5 17	7 22	10 2
EDINBURGH (Waverley Stn.) arr.	8 45	9 25	11 45	2 45	5 25	7 30	10 10

IMPORTANT NOTICE.
Simultaneously with the commencement of the above service, Port-Edgar Station will be entirely closed for Traffic, while North and South Queensferry and Dalmeny Stations will be used only for Goods Traffic.

QUEENSFERRY PASSAGE.
On 5th March 1890, the Sailings on the Queensferry Passage will be altered to the following, which will remain in force until further notice, viz:—

		Week-Days.							Sundays.	
New Halls	depart	A.M. 8 0	A.M. 9 0	A.M. 11 0	P.M. 1 0	P.M. 3 30	P.M. 5 0	P.M. 6 0	A.M. 8 30	P.M. 1 15	P.M. 5 0
North Queensferry (Old Pier)	arrive	8 12	9 12	11 12	1 12	3 42	5 12	6 12	8 42	1 27	5 12
North Queensferry (Old Pier)	depart	A.M. 7 30	A.M. 8 25	A.M. 10 0	P.M. 12 30	P.M. 2 30	P.M. 4 30	P.M. 5 30	A.M. 8 0	P.M. 12 30	P.M. 3 30
New Halls	arrive	7 42	8 37	10 12	12 42	2 42	4 42	5 42	8 12	12 42	3 42

6·30 a.m. Train from GLASGOW (Queen Street High Level) to EDINBURGH.
The 6·30 a.m. Train from Glasgow (Queen Street High Level) to Edinburgh will cease calling at Gogar and Corstorphine, and will be accelerated so as to arrive at Haymarket at 8·27 and Edinburgh (Waverley Station) at 8·35 a.m.

EDINBURGH, *March* 1890.   (2-M)   **J. WALKER, General Manager.**

When railways were established, there were thousands who vowed that they would never put a foot in a railway carriage.

Source 1.51

What many people thought about railways in those early days is illustrated by a scene witnessed when my father, being in bad health, travelled to Malvern, and my step-mother, for his sake only, took her place in the train. I see her still, sitting in the carriage, as we children were taking leave of her. She had her handkerchief tightly pressed to her eyes, so that she might see nothing, and begged us not to make her uncover them. A more abject picture of terror and dejection I never saw. In my childhood's days I remember well hearing the denunciations of railroads – their dangers, their tendencies to injure health, their ruinous effect on trade, their causing all cows within reach of the railway line to refuse to be milked, their ruin of the horse-breeding trade, and many other imaginary calamities.

(Macdonald, *Life Jottings*)

Source 1.52

Callander railway station

However, Railways helped to change life in all sorts of ways. Stations became the bustling centres of trade and travel. The tourist industry expanded. Letters, parcels, and newspapers were able to cross the country speedily.

Railways moved fresh fruit, vegetables, meat and fish. They also shifted countless tonnes of heavy goods – coal, building materials, iron and steel, fertilizers, grain, etc.
When a railway linked Dundee to Newport, William McGonagall pointed out some of the results.

Source 1.53

The thrifty housewives of Newport
To Dundee will often resort
Which will be to them profit and sport
By bringing cheap tea, bread and jam
And also some of Lipton's ham
And if the people of Dundee
Should feel inclined to have a spree
I'm sure 'twill fill their hearts with glee
By crossing o'er to Newport
And there they can have excellent sport.

The railways provided jobs for many Scots – at least 18 000 by 1881. Railways needed iron, steel and coal, too. Workshops developed, especially around Glasgow, to build and repair locomotives, carriages and wagons. The influence of railways seemed, by the 1880s, to be one of the most important features of Scottish life.

Source 1.54

Railway serving the harbour at Leven, 1870

Government Policy

British governments of the 1830s did not do a great deal to manage the economy. The main economic laws placed taxes on many goods coming into Britain and even these had been reduced in recent years. Howevever, one of these taxes became the centre of a political storm – what ought to be done about the tax on corn coming into Britain? Consider these points:

1 Britain's population was growing and more people were living in towns and cities.
2 British harvests were sometimes poor – as in 1836 for example.
3 Many people – especially in Ireland and parts of Scotland – depended very much on potatoes for their food. Yet this crop, too, sometimes failed. In 1845 potatoes were badly hit by blight and thousands starved.

The answer, at the time, was to set up an organisation to work for the ending of the Corn Laws. This 'Anti-Corn Law League' was led by two self-made businessmen, Richard Cobden and John Bright. It raised money, held meetings, published its ideas and tried to persuade Parliament to end the tax. The league was active in Scotland.

One Scottish MP, Joseph Hume, declared

Source 1.55

Every, man who earns his bread by his labour should raise his voice against the corn laws, as producing stagnation of trade, a want of work, and starvation.

(A. Wilson, *The Chartist Movement in Scotland 1970*)

The 1845 to 1846 potato famine and the suffering that it brought persuaded the Conservative prime minister, Sir Robert Peel, to cut the corn duties till they finally vanished in 1849. He also offered farmers loans of money to be used to drain land so that more food could be grown. Scottish farmers were offered £500 000 at $6\frac{1}{2}$%.

Some Scottish voices were raised against the Anti-Corn Law League. Farmers who feared cheap foreign corn would ruin them attacked it. In fact, the 20 years after 1846 proved to be very prosperous ones for farmers.

WORKING MEN!
You Pay a Tax of Tenpence
Upon every Stone of Flour you and your wives and little ones consume.

If there was not the Infamous CORN LAW you and your Families might buy THREE LOAVES for the same money that you now pay for Two.

Upon every Shilling you spend for Bread, Meat, Bacon, Eggs, Vegetables, &c., you pay 4d. Tax for Monopoly.

DOWN, DOWN
WITH THE
Infamous Bread Tax!

Source 1.56

In following years other taxes on trade were cut. In 1853 the Chancellor of the Exchequer, W. E. Gladstone, abolished 123 duties and reduced 133. In 1860 Cobden organised a treaty with France so that each country cut duties on goods coming from the other. The British government believed British industries and British farmers were so successful that they had no need to fear the rivalry of foreign goods. They moved Britain towards 'free trade' (the ending of taxes on imports).

QUESTIONS

1 What sort of speech might an Anti-Corn Law League member have made to an audience? Use the sources and write such a speech. (E.2)

2 Living and Working Conditions

The changing economy, especially the growth of industry, was the result of the labour of many thousands of men, women and children. The way the economy changed had a very big influence on the working and living conditions of these people. The sources in this chapter explore these working and living conditions.

Working Conditions

In the 1830s not only men and women, but children, too, worked in mines, shops, factories, farms and workshops. There were some jobs that children seemed especially well suited to doing. These jobs included cleaning the large chimneys in houses and factories by actually climbing up inside them. This account from 1840 comes from evidence given to an enquiry into why one of these 'climbing boys' died at his work in a tenement building.

Source 2.1

James Fleming's evidence:
Francis Hughes was one of the sweeps and the other a little boy named John. That boy was very ill-clad having only a pair of trousers and a shirt on and he had no jacket or shoes. That day was very cold and wet and the boy [of] five or six years of age was very weakly. There were 42 vents to be cleared out and the boy went up and down till he had cleared out 37. [In] the 38th he delayed and Hughes called to him several times. Hughes began to threaten him and say if he did not come up quickly he would take off his belt and thrash him. They could get no answer from the boy.

Robert Allan declares that the little boy came down the chimney complaining bitterly of cold seemed to be very exhausted, his clothes were in a wettish state. After the boy had got up the chimney Hughes took a stick and put it up the chimney and kept thrusting away, the boy did not cry out.

(In Berry & Whyte, *Glasgow Observed*)

Many children worked in factories and workshops. The children in the next source made nails in the Stirlingshire nail industry.

Source 2.2

A great number of boys are employed at a very early age. The child squares the rod of heated iron, points the nail, which is 'headed' by repeated blows of the hammer; 3 months teaching was sufficient to enable an infant to accomplish the manufacture of 1000 nails per day. The men frequently work till 10.0 or 11.0 o'clock at night assisted by their infant apprentices, who recommence their toil at 5.0 or 6.0 next morning . . . these infant slaves [have] emaciated [very thin] looks, stunted growth, clothed in apparal which few paupers [very poor people] would be found begging in; of these rags they have scarcely any change.

(*Parliamentary Papers*, 1843, Vol. 15)

QUESTIONS

1 From these sources what can you work out about the laws controlling children's work? (E.2)

2 Do you think the author of source 2.1 agreed with children doing this work? Give reasons for your answer. (E.1)

3 Why do you think families allowed their children to do jobs like these? (E.2)

The work of the 'climbing boys' went on. At least 2000 were still being used in the late 1860s in Britain.

Farming

The improvement of Scotland's farmland was the result of the labour of large numbers of ordinary people.

1881 Numbers working in farming

55 183 farmers
91 801 men employed on farms
44 165 women employed on farms
10 281 shepherds

In 1877 the tenant of one Aberdeenshire farm remembered how he and his father had turned 182 hectares of waste land into farmland. They had built 34 kilometres of stone dykes (walls) and laid an almost endless quantity of tile drains.

Clearing stones, so that horses could easily pull machines over the land, was very hard work. Many of these stones were used to build dykes. In 1889 James Milne, a farmer in north-east Scotland, looked back over a lifetime's work on the land. He wrote about his family's rented farm in the 1830s:

Source 2.4
Kingswell Dykes near Aberdeen

Source 2.5
The rent was fixed at £25. My father agreed to this heavy rent. Economy had to be practised. I can remember my father and mother taking but one cup of tea, and that only in the morning. When meal got scarce we had to fall back on potatoes. Everything had to give way to rent and manure. My father began by draining the bogs with stone drains. The labour and the quantity of drains were immense, but at this time we were glad to get rid of those stones. We broke up the hard land, spade trenching the parts which were too stony to plough. My father applied the first crushed bones [as fertilizer] in 1838. We had to apply guano for oats on new land [and] to thresh with flails. In 1856 we were able to put in a threshing mill. We began to lime every field in rotation. We also began to take out boulder stones. We had no mechanical appliances. Once we got them loose we put on a fire which broke them up. We built 1400 yards [1.28 km] of dyke. We made 1000 yards [914 m] of road for farm use. We also built new byres and stables.

(Trans. *Buchan Field Club,* 1889)

Women, too, worked at jobs described in a mid-nineteenth century booklet:

Source 2.6
Peat cutting in Aberdeenshire

Source 2.7
Tayside farmworkers

Source 2.8

On most farms where two or more servants are kept one of them is generally engaged to act as housemaid. The others work on the farm, that is to labour at almost anything the men are employed at with the exception of holding the plough. [They] work on the dunghill, at spreading on the fields, in the threshing mill in bundling straw, besides they drive carts or pull and cart turnips in all sorts of weather.

(Carter, *Poor Man's Country*)

Horses played a vital part in the work of the farm and looking after horses was most important. Alexander Gray, who was born in 1822, was a horseman. When Gray was in his seventies he was asked if a 12-hour day was too long for a horseman. He replied:

Source 2.9

In my days we wrought [worked] longer time. We had no interval of 2 hours at mid-day. We were at it from 5.0 am till 7.0 o'clock pm. We took no fixed time for breakfast and dinner, we just ate our meal, picked our teeth, and at it again. During turnip seed we began work at 5.0 am so that with getting the horses ready in the morning and settling things at night we were engaged from 4.0 am till 7.0 pm.

(Carter *Poor Man's Country*)

QUESTIONS

1 What evidence – if any – of improved technology helping farmwork can you find in the sources? (K.U)

2 Using the sources, briefly list the main tasks that had to be done to develop farmland into a fertile workable condition. (K.U)

3 On the basis of the evidence here, how do you think a farmer might have advertised for farmworkers, including their work and hours? (E.2)

4 Find two examples from source 2.5 and 2.6 of work *not* done by women. (K.U)
Why do you think women didn't do these jobs? (E.2)

Textiles

The census return of 1881 recorded the numbers of people working in textiles. The more numerous were:

Source 2.10

	Male	Female
Woollen cloth making	13 016	14 704
Knitter of woollen goods	–	4 382
Silk and satin making	1 605	1 376
Cotton making	6 261	25 524
Cotton bleaching	6 439	6 197
Flax and linen making and dealing	8 789	19 944
Thread maker and dealer	539	4 702
Jute making	3 672	12 392
Rope and twine maker and dealer	2 077	292
Sacking maker and dealer	163	1 115
Factory work in textiles (undefined)	6 869	21 179
Dyer and bleacher	4 602	3 395
Tailor	20 608	3 220
Milliner and dressmaker	96	43 525
Shirtmaker and seamstress	252	9 903

QUESTION

Which jobs were most often done by women? (K.U)

What was it like to work in the textile industry? The following sources all deal with this topic. This report describes a visit to a cotton mill:

Source 2.11

Deanston Cotton-mill, near Doune, in Perthshire, is one of those admirably regulated great manufacturing establishments which it is a pleasure to see.

The apartments in the mill are clean, well ventilated, and have the machinery well fenced . . . The windows, instead of being constructed in the usual way in many of the mills we have seen, so that only a single pane of glass in each window can be opened, are so hung that the whole of the upper pane of each window may be let down from the top, and a free current of air admitted.

There are here apartments for the females to dress and undress in, and a pipe of water in each storey; sewering arrangement is adopted throughout the work that tends to the convenience of the persons employed.

The workers live about a mile [1.5 km] from the works, with the exception of about a hundred of them, for whom the Company have built houses, let to them. There are bits of garden ground attached to each of the houses, and a drain for carrying off every sort of filth. The whole arrangements about this extensive factory, at which cotton-spinning, power-weaving, iron-founding, and machine-making are carried on, are obviously made with a view as far as possible to the comfort of the people, and a more cheerful, happy-looking set of industrious men and women, and of young people, is seldom, if I am not mistaken, to be found.

(From Mr James Stuart's reports on Scottish factories; *Parliamentary Papers*, 1833, Vol. XX)

Source 2.12 _____
Millworkers at J. & J. Clark's mills at Paisley, 1880

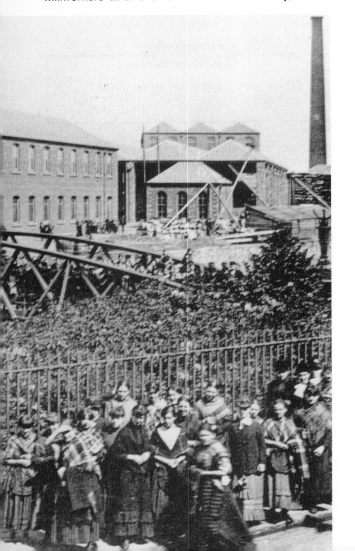

The most famous of employers who tried to give workers decent conditions was Robert Owen. By the 1830s his New Lanark Mills had been operating for many years. He explained in 1831 how in his mill:

Source 2.13 _____
. . . the practice of employing young children of six, seven, eight years of age was discontinued and their parents advised to allow them to acquire health and education until they were ten years old.

(R. Owen, *A New View of Society*, 1831)

Other mill-owners employed young children. In Baxter's Mill, Dundee, an employee reported in 1833:

Source 2.14 _____
. . . he saw the boys when too late of a morning dragged naked from their beds by the overseer with their clothes in their hands, to the mill . . . the boys were stripped naked as they got out of bed.

(*Parliamentary Papers*, 1833, Vol. 20)

A Dundee flax mill worker reported in 1833:

Source 2.15 _____
. . . he obtained his first job at the age of 12 in a flax mill where they worked not less than 17 hours a day, exclusive of meals. Was beaten often. 'I saw one girl trailed by the hair and kicked when she was down'.

(*Parliamentary Papers*, 1833, Vol. 15)

Such evidence led to factory reforms to alter conditions for children, especially, and also for women.

QUESTIONS

1 The sources here differ. From them, list the signs of a 'good' mill. (K.U)

2 'Owners only provided decent conditions so that workers would work better.' Is there any evidence of this in the sources? (K.U)

3 Do you think it is likely to be true? (E.2)

Coal

Coal mining has always been very hard work. In 1840 the minister of a coal-mining area near Edinburgh wrote:

Source 2.16

The collier population is subject to a peculiar disease [commonly] called 'the black spit'. It is a wasting of the lungs occasioned [caused] by the inhaling of the coal dust. Many strong men are cut off by it before they reach the age of 40. Almost all the men are affected by it so as to be rendered unfit for any active exertion for years before they drop prematurely into the grave.

(N.S.A. Newton)

The working conditions in coal mines in the 1830s led Parliament to organise an official enquiry. Perhaps you can think of some changes in the law you would have suggested if you had been faced with evidence like this:

Source 2.17

Ellison Jack, 11-year-old girl coal bearer at Loanhead colliery, Scotland:

I have been working below three years on my father's account; he takes me down at two in the morning, and I come up at one and two next afternoon. I go to bed at six at night to be ready for work next morning: the part of the pit I bear in the seams are much on the edge. I have to bear my burthen up four traps, or ladders, before I get to the main road which leads to the pit bottom. My task is four or five tubs: each tub holds 4¼ cwt [216 kg]. I fill five tubs in twenty journeys.

I have had the strap when I did not do my bidding. Am very glad when my task is wrought, as it sore fatigues. I can read, and was learning the writing; can do a little; not been at school for two years; go to kirk occasionally, over to Lasswade: don't know much about the Bible, so long since read.

(*Parliamentary Papers*, 1842, vol. xv)

Source 2.18

A coal hewer and women bearers from the 1842 Commission on Mines

The memories of a Lochgelly miner noted in 1896:

Source 2.19

It was the custom for the man and his wife to work both. The man digged the coals and his wife carried them to the pit bank on her back. They were called 'bearers' and if anything went wrong with the man she had to be both miner and bearer. Such was the case with my grandmother. She was left a widow with five of a family. She put her two boys in her coal creel, carried them down the pit and laid them at the stoop side till she digged her coals and carried them to the pit bank. Tatties formed their staple living. At the end of the year my grandmother had the highest output of coal in Lochgelly.

(In M. Houston, *Auchterderran*, 1924)

In 1869 David Bremner looked back on this period and observed:

Source 2.20

In the east of Scotland where the side roads [in pits] do not exceed 22 to 28 inches [55–107 cm] in height, females had to crawl backwards and forwards. In them the labour was often continued on alternate days, at least 15 and even 18 hours out of 24. One girl, 17 years of age said, 'I have repeatedly wrought the 24 hours and after 2 hours of rest and my pease soup have returned to the pit and worked 12 hours.'

(Bremner, *The Industries of Scotland*)

The enquiry led to an Act of Parliament. Women and young children were no longer to work underground – though they often worked still at jobs on the surface, near pits.

The act took from the coal worker the extra earnings of his family. For some time a lookout had to be kept for women who went on trying to work underground (and for mine managers who were ready to employ them). It still left miners' wives with plenty to do, however. This account describes homes in the Fife coalfield in 1854:

Source 2.21

The duties of the miners' housewives were hard; their work was never done. In the very early morning they had to see their men out with breakfast and a 'piece' and flask, the latter containing tea but often water. Then the bairns had to be fed and got ready for school; followed by the household chores and shopping for the 'messages'; children back for dinner and the men from the pit following later. Water had to be drawn and carried from the well. Then came the bath for the men folk. For this a tub was stood on the floor filled with hot water, prepared in a boiler or on the fire and carried from the well. In warm weather the pit bath was often outside the back door. Wet and dirty clothes had to be scraped and washed. After the wash and dinner the men folk generally rested from their toil. The kitchen was cleaned up and the bairns attended to on their return from school.

But there was no leisure for the women folk. In the evening they were busy mending and drying the pit clothes, or knitting the heavy woollen underwear and socks that were universally worn.

(*The Jenny Grey Centenary Book*, Lochgelly, 1954)

Source 2.22

NOTICE.

In consequence of the Act of the 5th and 6th Queen Victoria, cap. 99, His Grace the Duke of Hamilton hereby intimates, that from and after the 10th current, no *Females*, under 18 years of age, nor after the 1st of March next, shall any *Females*, of whatever age, be employed in the underground operations at Redding Colliery. He farther intimates, that from and after the 1st day of March next, no *Male* persons, under the age of 10 years, shall be employed under-ground at said Colliery; and he strictly prohibits all his Colliers and Workmen, at said Colliery, from, in any way, taking the assistance of any such in the underground operations which are being performed by them.

(Signed) **JOHN JOHNSTON,** *MANAGER.*

REDDING COLLIERY, 1st November, 1842.

A. Johnston, Printer, Falkirk.

In 1869 the writer, David Bremner, reported on what it was like to go down a mine. The pit he chose to visit was Arniston Colliery:

Source 2.23

The first objects that met our eyes were a number of men engaged in narrow ways about a train of tubs. A number of horses are employed to draw the tubs . . . [In another area] there were no horses, the drawing (or rather 'putting') being done by boys. We advanced into the workings. In a 3 foot [.9144 m] seam a miner can kneel while working, but in thin seams he has to lie on his side and in some cases water pours down on him. As the coal is broken away it is shovelled aside, the putter fills it into his tub and wheels it along the pit bottom. This is very severe toil for boys. The miners enter the pit between 5 and 6 o'clock in the morning. They remain in the pit until 2.0 in the afternoon, the 8 hours spell of work being relieved by a brief interval for breakfast. The miner is in constant danger of a violent death or of injury. The winding gear may give way, he is in danger of being suffocated by foul air and of being scorched to death by the ignition of fire damp. In 1865 in Scotland 12 034 638 tons were raised and 77 lives lost. Previous to 1843 it was no unusual thing to find the [winding] engines in charge of boys of 12, 11 and even 9 years and many lives were lost in consequence. The average wage of miners in Scotland in 1858 was 3 shillings [15p], about 3 pence [1.2p] a day falls to be deducted for light, sharpening tools, etc.

(Bremner, *The Industries of Scotland*)

Reforming working conditions

A number of important people felt that some working conditions, and especially those for children and for women, should be reformed. The reformers included Richard Oastler, Michael Sadler, and Ashley Cooper (later Lord Shaftesbury). Their speeches, writings and pressure for change led to official enquiries that produced such strong evidence of the need for reform that a number of laws were passed.

Source 2.24

REWARD
OF
20 Sovereigns.

WHEREAS late on the Evening of Sunday, or early this Morning, some evil and malicious Person or Persons CUT and DESTROYED the ROPES at one of the Pits of *Wellwood Colliery*; and also DESTROYED part of the Machinery of the Steam Engine thereat; a REWARD of £20 is hereby offered to any Person, who, within fourteen days after this date, shall give such information to the Procurator Fiscal as will lead to the conviction of the Offenders.

DUNFERMLINE, Monday, 1st May, 1837.   J. Miller and Son, Printers.

QUESTIONS

1 Use the evidence in source 2.17 to write out, as a list, 'A Day in the Life of Ellison Jack'. (K.U)

2 The investigators decided to include sketches (source 2.18).
   Why do you think they did this? Was it just to make the situation clearer? Or do you think pictures are more persuasive than words. (E.1)

3 Do you think all collier families would have been delighted by news of the 1842 Act? Give reasons for your answer. (E.2)

4 What dangers do the sources show the miners faced? K.U)

Factory Act 1833

This law applied to all textile mills except silk mills. No child under 9 was to work in such mills, children of 9 to 13 years could work up to 48 hours a week (with no more than 9 hours in a day). 13 to 18 year olds were to work no more than 69 hours a week. Children under 13 had to attend school for two hours a day. Four Inspectors were appointed to enforce the act.

Factory Act 1847

This limited hours of work in textile mills to 58 a week and thus marked the success of those demanding a '10-hour-day' (8 hours on Saturday, Sunday free).

Coal Mines Act 1842

Women, and children under 10, were not to work underground. No child under 15 was allowed to be in charge of winding machinery.

Coal Mines Act 1850

This introduced government inspection of mines.

Coal Mines Act 1860

Children under 12 were not to work in mines unless they had a certificate of educational achievement.
1860 Lace-making workplaces had the same rules applied.

1867 Factory Extension and Workshop Regulation Act

Factory laws were applied to foundries, copper mills, printing and book-binding works, paper and glass-making and tobacco works. Places where more than 50 people worked were to be inspected by the local authority (after 1871 by factory inspectors).

1876 Factory Act

Working days in textile mills were cut by half an hour.

Chimney Sweep Regulations

1834 Sweeps were forbidden from sending boys up chimneys to clean them whilst fires were still lit.
1864 Sweeps were not to employ boys under 10. Only boys of 16 or more could actually clean chimneys.

Some workers tried to stop the spread of machines but this was a hopeless cause. Workers also tried to protect and improve their working conditions by their own actions. However, it was very difficult for local groups of workers to succeed. They did not have the money to stay out on strike or take other sorts of actions that their employers opposed.

Workers had been trying to organise themselves properly to fight for better conditions for many years before 1830. The Trade Union Act of 1834, allowed them simply to bargain peacefully. In 1833 to 1834 Robert Owen helped workers to organise a union that grew to have half a million members – the Grand National Consolidated Trades Union. In 1834 it tried to assist labourers in Tolpuddle, Dorset, who were on trial. The men had tried to resist a wage cut from nine to six shillings

(45p to 30p) a week by forming a society and taking a secret oath to keep its affairs secret. The secret oath-taking was a crime and the labourers were sentenced to be transported to Australia. Such was the outcry that, after two years, they were pardoned and brought home. But the GNCTU failed; it was too difficult to organise. The problem of organising successful action was seen, again, in 1837 in Glasgow. Trading difficulties in cotton led mill-owners to cut wages, the cotton spinners tried to resist this by going on strike. The violence some strikers used against workers brought in to take their place led to arrests, trials and the transportation of union leaders.

The failure of these union efforts led some workers to concentrate on trying to alter the political system. Others worked to set up unions of skilled men that could afford a proper organisation and could build up funds to help members in need.

Source 2.26 _____

1842 Miners Association

1851 Amalgamated Society of Engineers. This union had a full-time secretary and high subscription of a shilling [5p] a week.

1860 Amalgamated Society of Carpenters and Joiners

1866 Tailors Society

1872 Amalgamated Society of Railway Servants. These unions had branches across Britain.

1868 The Trades Union Congress was set up, representing several unions.

1871 The TUC set up a Parliamentary Committee to persuade MPs to do more for unions.

In 1871 a change in the law gave unions legal protection for their funds and in 1875 unions were allowed to carry out peaceful picketing.

Scots were prominent in these developments. The Amalgamated Society of Engineers' first leader was William Allan, who began his working life in a Scottish cotton mill. The Miners Association developed in Scotland and spread to become the National Miners Association. But trade unions, in the 1870s, were still not very strong and did not exist in many workplaces.

QUESTIONS

1 The poster (source 2.24) shows that workers had been attacking machines. What sort of workers might wish to do this? (Think of those whose jobs would be threatened by machines.) (K.U)

2 What would you choose, from the changes listed in source 2.25, as being the most important improvement? Give reasons for your answer. (E.2)

Living Conditions

The people of Scotland lived in farms and villages and, in growing numbers, in towns and cities, too. The sources in this section explore the following questions. What was ordinary life like in these places? Was it pleasanter to live in the countryside, a town or a city? What were the results of living in the conditions of the time? What was done to change these conditions?

Housing

In the countryside

Source 2.27 _____

Aberdeenshire Cottage interior

Many farmworkers lived in bothies which might be separate buildings, but were often rooms in the steading, commonly over the stables. It was male farmworkers who lived in bothies. This account of a typical bothy was written in 1859:

Source 2.28 ——————————————
The walls are rough, bare and dingy. There are three beds, six chests belonging to the men which contain their clothing, and six barrels to hold the oatmeal which is supplied every four weeks, a pot or kettle for boiling water, six wooden bowls, six spoons and a short form or seat. There is no chair and no table. The form can accommodate only four persons. The ashes are never removed nor the apartment swept and cleaned except by the men themselves, nor are their beds made except once in six weeks when a change of sheets is supplied. Only two clean towels are given weekly for the use of six men whose hands and faces would require frequent washing.

(Carter, *Poor Man's Country*)

The bothymen cooked their own meals. In the north-east the 'chaumer' system was common. The men went to the farm kitchen for meals.

Married farm servants lived in cottages on the farm or in villages. This is a description of typical cottages of Buchan, in Aberdeenshire:

Source 2.29 ——————————————
The side walls are scarcely five feet [1.5 m] in height. The door is so low an ordinary sized person, on entering, requires to bend considerably, and the gables are built with turfs. The mason work is composed of undressed surface stone and mortar. The roof is covered with turfs which are over-laid with straw. The floor is the same material as the subsoil of the surrounding area. It is frequently damp. There are two small windows in front each containing four small panes of glass. The rafters [are] covered in soot. One or two bedsteads placed in the middle divide the building, one [end] being used as a kitchen. An air of discomfort pervades the building. Above and beneath the bedstead are huddled various articles of clothing.

(Carter, *Poor Man's Country*)

In the 1850s, 60s and 70s quite a number of cottages were re-built and greatly improved. A writer in 1881 noted in Angus and Kincardine:

Source 2.30 ——————————————
There has been a great improvement in the condition of the ploughman's cottages during the past 25 years. Many of them at that time contained only one big room subdivided by the furniture of two box beds and a chest of drawers and cupboard combined. The floors were generally of earth or clay. The reason for the change – the application of steam to the linen trade and its development drained the population to attend the machinery, even the ordinary workers of the farm could with difficulty be had.

(Carter, *Poor Man's Country*)

QUESTIONS

1. Using the above sources, list the contents of the typical bothy. (K.U)

2. How might the farmer who provided the bothy have justified these living conditions? (E.2)

3. What signs of changing rural living conditions can you find in source 2.27? (K.U)

4. Use source 2.29 to draw a labelled sketch of a cottage. (K.U)

5. Explain in your own words the reason given in source 2.30 as to why cottages were improved. (K.U)

Towns
During this period many of Scotland's burghs grew into sizable towns. New towns also developed, especially near pits, mills, and foundries. The following sources describe life in some of these places. This one is of Dunfermline:

Source 2.31 ——————————————
Our streets are about as bad as ever. One can scarcely walk a dozen steps out of the High Street without having both sight and smell offended in a most disgusting way. Nor is this at all wonderful, when we remember that our town, with a population of 15 000, does not contain a single public urinal or water-closet,

and not a tithe [tenth] of the houses contain such conveniences. True, a cart perambulates the town twice a day to remove the accumulations of offal which may be brought out to the street in pail or bucket; and so far this is a step in the right direction, but till numerous public conveniences are furnished, our sanitary condition cannot be much improved.

(*Dunfermline Journal*, 1854, in Simpson, *Auld Grey Toun*)

In 1842 the provost of Inverness grumbled:

Source 2.32 _____

Inverness is a nice town, situated in a most beautiful country, and with every facility for cleanliness and comfort. The people are, generally speaking, a nice people, but their sufferance of nastiness is past endurance. Contagious fever is seldom absent.

There are very few houses in town which can boast of either water-closet or privy, and only two or three public privies in the better part of the place exist. Hence there is not a street, lane, or approach to it that is not disgustingly defiled at all times, so much so as to render the whole place an absolute nuisance. The *midden* is the chief object of the humble, and though enough of water for purposes of cleanliness may be had by little trouble, still as the ablutions are seldom, MUCH filth in-doors and out of doors *must* be their portion. When cholera prevailed in Inverness, it was more fatal than in almost any other town of its population in Britain.

(*Parliamentary Papers*, 1842, Vol. 26)

The next report describes coal-workers' homes in 1842 in Tranent. Its author was a doctor keen to see living conditions reformed:

Source 2.33 _____

A few of the colliers houses are good, but the great mass of them is very bad. In the worst the windows [are] only partially supplied with glass and its place supplied with paper, rags and old hats. In the better houses the furniture is ample and in some is kept with great neatness. In some the females are so lazy and so filthy they carry their ashes and cinders no farther than to a corner of the apartment. The floors of the cottages are composed of beaten earth. These floors are very dirty and so

uneven as to make a stranger almost fall. The odour is most offensive and sickening from the long-continued presence of human impurities.

(*Parliamentary Papers*, 1842, Vol. 27)

Greenock was one of Scotland's rapidly growing towns. According to a contributor to the *Greenock Advertiser* in 1857:

Source 2.34 _____

The most prominent feature is the overcrowding of the people. The population has increased from 22 000 in 1821 to 39 000 in 1851, chiefly by large additions from Ireland and the Highlands, little has been done in the way of building new houses of a suitable description. This special [type] of property has never enjoyed the favour of the moneyed men . . . as the requirements of the working population increased, the accommodation for them did not increase in anything like the same ratio. Almost all the houses in Greenock fitted to accommodate the working class are very old.

(*Greenock Advertiser*, 1–5, 1857)

In 1842 a doctor in Greenock reported:

Source 2.35 _____

In one part of Market Street is a dunghill. It is never removed: it is the stock-in-trade of a person who deals in dung. There is a land [block] of houses adjoining and in the summer each house swarms with flies. Food and drink must be covered, if left exposed for a minute the flies attack it and it is rendered unfit for use from the strong taste of the dunghill left by the flies.

(*Parliamentary Papers*, Vol. 26, 1842)

QUESTIONS

1 'What's wrong with our towns'.
Use this heading to write a newspaper report of the 1860s. Look through the sources to make a list of all the points to be included before writing your (E.2) report.

2 Do you think the owner of the cottages (source 2.33) would have written a similar report? Which parts might he have altered? (E.1)

In the cities

Source 2.36
Glasgow close, 1860s

In 1857 Nathanial Hawthorne explored Glasgow:

Source 2.37
. . . my wife and I walked out, and saw something of the newer portion of Glasgow; and really I am inclined to think it the stateliest city I ever beheld. The Exchange, and other public buildings, and the shops, especially in Buchanan street, are very magnificent; the latter, especially, excelling those of London. There is, however, a pervading sternness and grimness, resulting from the dark gray granite, which is the universal building material. Later we again walked out, and went along Argyle street, and through the Trongate and the Saltmarket. The two latter were formerly the principal business streets, and, with the High-street, the abode of the rich merchants and other great people of the town. The High-street, and still more the Saltmarket, now swarm with the lower orders, to a degree which I never witnessed elsewhere; so that it is difficult to make one's way among the sallow and unclean crowd, and not at all pleasant to breathe in the noisomeness of the atmosphere. The children seem to have been unwashed from birth, and perhaps they go on gathering a thicker and thicker coating of dirt till their dying days. Some of the gray houses appear to have been stately and handsome in their day, and have their high gable-ends notched at the edges, like a flight of stairs.

(In Berry and Whyte, *Glasgow Observed*)

By the 1870s Glasgow had a medical officer of health – Dr J. B. Russell. He described the city's slums:

Source 2.38
They consist of ranges of narrow closes, only some four or five feet [1.2 or 1.5 m] in width, and of great length. The houses are so lofty that the direct light of the sky never reaches a large proportion of the dwelling. The cleansing, until lately, was most inefficient. There are large square midden-steads, some of them actually under the houses, and all of them in the immediate vicinity of the windows and door of human dwellings. These receptacles hold the entire filth and offal of large masses of people and households, until country farmers can be bargained with for their removal. There is no drainage in these neighbourhoods, except in a few cases; and from the want of any means of flushing, the sewers, where they do exist, are extended cesspools polluting the air. So little is house drainage in use, that on one occasion I saw the entire surface of a back yard covered for several inches with green putrid water.

The overcrowding and wretchedness of late years has brought typhus with it, a disease that not long ago was almost as rare in the large cities of Scotland as ague now is; and wherever typhus has prevailed, there cholera now prevails, or has done so recently.

(In R. Cage *The Working Class in Glasgow*, 1987)

The Clyde flowed through the city. Into it, the city's sanitary inspector reported in 1874, went:

. . . the sewage from 101 368 dwelling-houses, and from shops, warehouses, manufactories, and workshops, numbering 16 218; and the urine from 121 urinals, 5288 ashpits, 935 privies, 2304 stables, and 311 cow-houses, and discharge the same direct into the Clyde from 42 outlets.

In addition, 20 manufactories discharge their waste outflow by private drains direct into the Clyde – consisting of 7 dye-works, 1 confection manufactory, 5 cotton-mills, 1 paper mill, 5 weaving factories, and 1 spinning-mill; 480 of the manufactories contribute to the sewage as follows: 120 manufacture waste outflow, 262 water at various degrees of heat, 89 steam and water, and 9 blow steam only into the sewers.

(In Berry & Whyte, *Glasgow Observed*)

An Edinburgh doctor described homes in his city:

Source 2.40

The dwellings of the poor are generally very filthy . . . Those of the lowest grade often consist only of one small apartment, always ill-ventilated, both from the nature of its construction and from the densely peopled and confined locality in which it is situated. Many of them, besides, are damp and partly underground . . . A few of the lowest poor have a bedstead, but by far the larger portion have none; these make up a kind of bed on the floor with straw, on which a whole family are huddled together, some naked and the others in the same clothes they have worn during the day.

(*Report on Sanitary Conditions of the Population of Scotland*, 1842)

The better-off moved away from areas like these. Scotland's cities expanded with pleasant suburbs growing on the outskirts of city centres. There, large houses were built for families and their servants.

Source 2.41

The impressive frontage of Hazel Hall, 1897
Late nineteenth-century interior of Dunalistair House, Broughty Ferry

Source 2.42
A slum child

But the 1861 census showed how most people lived. The Registrar General reported:

Source 2.43
34% of the families in Scotland lived in one room with a window . . . there ought to be added those living in one room but without a window. This would make the proportion of families living in one room 35%.

246 601 families occupied houses of two rooms – being 37% of the families in Scotland. It thus appears 72% of the families in Scotland live each in either one or two rooms. This is a much larger proportion of families crowded into one or two rooms than even the wildest dreams of social reformers thought credible.

Only 11% live in houses of three rooms, only $5\frac{1}{2}$% live in houses of four rooms, only $\frac{1}{2}$% live in houses of 10 rooms.

(Census, 1861)

Moreover, many poor families had a lodger staying in their rooms. In Edinburgh in 1871 one-fifth of families living in two rooms had a lodger. Even inhabitants of one room might have lodgers, yet the average size of a one-roomed Edinburgh home was 4 metres by 3.5 metres.

QUESTIONS

1 Use source 2.36 to write a description in your own words of what this close looked like. (K.U)

2 Look through the written sources and list the sort of people who wrote them. Who seems to have written the most favourable report? Why? Who seems to have written the most critical report? Why? What sort of person might have written reports that disagreed with these very critical reports? (E.1)

3 What would you say were likely to be the main causes of these housing conditions? What sort of sources might help you find out whether your ideas are correct? (E.2)

Health and Disease

QUESTIONS

You have been asked to write a report that explains why Scots of this time suffer from so much illness. You have also been asked to suggest what reforms should be carried out.

In order to write your report:
- think about all you have read so far and list any reasons you can work out
  (E.2)
- look through the next sources and list all the points you can find   (K.U)
- suggest the changes that should be carried out and what will be needed to make them work   (E.2)

Source 2.44 _____

Annual mortality per 100 000 alive from certain infectious diseases:

	1861–70
Tuberculosis	361
Respiratory diseases	308
Typhus group	106
Scarlet fever	66
Whooping cough	66
Diphtheria and croup	64
Measles	40
Smallpox	17
Total	**1053**

(Flinn, *Scottish Population History*)

Many doctors reported on the diseases in their areas. In Greenock Dr Buchanan described a serious outbreak of typhus fever, from 1864 to 1865:

Source 2.45 _____
Typhus fever appears to be always present in Greenock, it is in the old town that it has been intensely epidemic. In ordinary times the fever affected the poorer classes only. The cause of the great epidemic is essentially the one condition of over-crowding together with the dirty habits of the people. The common method of getting rid of refuse in houses is by de-positing the contents of chamber vessels with ashes and other filth in the roadway.

(*Greenock Advertiser*, 22 June 1865)

In 1857 a group of officials studied the food eaten by Scots to see if it caused illnesses. (This particular group were the Commissioners of Lunacy. They suspected a poor diet might cause madness.)

Source 2.46 _____
The diet of the poor in Scotland varies considerably in different districts. In the Highlands it principally consists of oatmeal and potatoes with the occasional addition of fish; but on the west coast and in the Western Isles the supplies, even of this food, are scanty, and the people are often bordering on starvation. On the whole, the Highland population must be considered as poorly fed. In the rural districts of the Lowlands, also oatmeal and potatoes constitute the chief part of the diet of the peasantry, with the addition of milk and garden vegetables. Bread is occasionally used, but butcher-meat very seldom forms part of the living. The cottars, generally, both in the Highlands and Lowlands, have small patches of potato or garden ground.

In the manufacturing villages and country towns, bread and tea have, to some extent, especially with the women, taken the place of porridge; but, with the men and children, porridge and buttermilk still constitute the general morning and evening meal. Broth and potatoes, with fish when it is plentiful, or perhaps bread, form the usual dinner of the manufacturing classes in such localities. In the large towns, such as Glasgow, the consumption of butcher-meat has latterly greatly increased, and the high wages of the mechanics are frequently entirely expended on their living.

(T. C. Smout, *A Century of the Scottish People*, 1986)

Dr Buchanan, in Greenock, also wondered if a poor diet helped cause the frequent outbreaks of disease:

Source 2.47 _____
The usual food of the very poor people in Greenock is bread and tea and coffee. Oatmeal is not considered so economical as bread, but is largely used. Treacle and potatoes, and a

little fish are the articles first added to the staple diet of bread, as they can be afforded. Then bacon, and broth made of hocks and bones are provided. Eggs, which are got cheap from Ireland, butter milk and skimmed milk are common articles of food. Butcher's meat is not eaten much by any under good class labourers. The Sunday dinner is not, as it so commonly is in England, an extra good meal.

A writer of 1859 explained what bothymen usually ate:

Source 2.48 _____

Their breakfast and dinner consist of brose only. At supper, when there is more time, each man acting as cook in his turn makes strong well-boiled porridge. A Scotch pint of milk is supplied to each man daily. If they have potatoes at supper they are poured on a sack spread on the floor and eaten with salt. There is no-one to keep alive their fire so that the first thing that needs to be done when they come home from toil, often drenched and cold and hungry and weary is to kindle their fire and prepare their hasty meal.

(Carter, *Poor Man's Country*)

From Argyll one minister reported:

Source 2.49 _____

There are many, it is feared, much in the predicament of a little boy of the parish, who, on being asked on a certain occasion of what his three daily meals consisted gave the same unvarying answer, 'mashed potatoes', and on being further asked by his too inquisitive inquirer 'what else' replied with great artlessness but with evident surprise, 'a spoon'.

(N.S.A., Vol. 7)

Better-paid skilled workers might be able to afford food like this diet described in 1843 by a Dumbartonshire textile worker:

Source 2.50 _____

It is to be borne in mind, also, that the occupation of the calico printer is exhausting, and requires a better diet than that of the common agricultural labourer. I myself generally have for breakfast some porridge and milk, a little tea, a slice of bread and ham, and, as far as I can afford it, a little steak. For dinner I gener-

ally have broth; sometimes potatoes and milk; and I generally take tea at night, with bread and cheese, or bread and butter, with a slice of toast. This is a fair specimen of what calico printers would like to have; but I should say that a great number of them do not live quite so well.

(Poor Law Appendix)

Source 2.51 _____
Slum children in late Victorian Dundee

Investigators looking for the causes of ill-health also commented on the clothing worn by many ordinary people. In 1842 Dr Arnott visited many homes in Glasgow:

Source 2.52 _____
We saw half-dressed wretches crowding together to be warm; and in one bed, although in the middle of the day, several women were imprisoned under a blanket, because as many others who had on their backs all the articles of dress that belonged to the party were then out of doors in the streets. This picture is so shocking that, without ocular proof, one would be disposed to doubt the possibility of the facts.

(In Smout, *A Century of the Scottish People*)

In Glasgow, another observer noted:

Source 2.53

No man could pass down the Trongate last winter with the snow frozen fast to the pavement and meeting the cutting piercing east wind without his heart aching. Scores of children were to be seen scuffing along the snowy streets with feet either quite naked or only protected by the remnants of a slipper and mere rags over the rest of the body, the girls with a bit of sack-cloth over their heads, sometimes clothed in a large woman's gown cut short, with the original sleeves like bags at the sides.

Reforming living conditions

Parliament passed a number of laws that were intended to reform living conditions. Several laws were especially aimed at developing stronger local authorities able to tackle the improvement of their own areas. Henry Cockburn wrote of the first of these changes:

Source 2.54

2nd December 1833. A few months ago Scotland saw for the first time a popular election of members of parliament; and it has within these few weeks seen the first popular election of town-councils. These two reforms have changed, and will permanently change, the whole country.

Reforms of Living Conditions

Source 2.55

1833 Burgh Reform Act:

Scottish burghs had been ruled by councils who were not elected by townspeople, but, when there was a vacancy, themselves chose a replacement. Now burgh councils were to be elected by £10 householders. The voters could by-pass the council by electing a separate body of 'police commissioners' (or the council themselves could act as police commissioners). Money from the rates was to be used for 'policing', i.e. not only for keeping law and order, but also for paving, lighting and cleaning, preventing disease, regulating slaughterhouses, arresting vagrants, naming streets and numbering the properties in them.

1847 these 'policing' powers were made available to parliamentary burghs, in 1850 to places of over 1200 and in 1862 to places of over 700.

1845 Poor Law Amendment Act

The problem of poverty was to be tackled in each parish by a 'Parochial Board' of people representing the kirk and the heritors (landowners) together with others elected by ratepayers. The Boards could raise money from rates, employ inspectors to visit the poor, and use the money to help people in their homes (outdoor relief) and by building poorhouses. Able-bodied unemployed were not entitled to help.

1853 Public Houses Act

Public houses were to close on Sundays (though travellers could go to hotels for drinks) and a final closing time in the evening of 11.00 pm was introduced.

1855 The Nuisance Removal Act

The power of police commissioners to clean, or even close insanitary properties, was increased.

1867 Public Health Act

Further power was given to police burghs — and to parochial boards in the areas outside these burghs — to regulate lodging houses, remove filth from streets and houses, lay sewers and drains and provide hospitals.

1872 Education Act

Locally elected school boards for cities, burghs and parishes, were to oversee education, improve it, and make it compulsory.

1875 Artisans and Labourers Dwelling Act

The Conservative Minister Richard Cross brought in this law to allow local authorities to carry out large-scale clearances of slums. They could compulsorily purchase properties their medical officers condemned as unhealthy.

Many of the improvements were the result of local authority work. In 1859 Queen Victoria opened Glasgow's new water supply from Loch Katrine. It had taken four years to build and cost £1.5 millions, but when cholera next came to Scotland between 1865 and 1866 only 53 Glaswegians died of it. The tiny Fife burgh of Methil, where people still drank foul

Lamplighter at work in Edinburgh

water, lost 63! Other towns and cities, too, laid on supplies of pure water, dug drains and sewers, and organised regular scavenging services to keep filth off the streets.

It was the work of local authorities that ended the menace of cholera. Dr John Snow had shown by his work in London that it spread from drinking foul water.

Private companies produced gas and sold it to councils for lighting the streets. In 1867 Glasgow Council took over the private companies in its area – and was able to halve the price of gas!

Local authorities also began to develop new hospitals, or improve old ones. In 1869 Glasgow opened a municipal fever hospital and a new Western Infirmary in 1874. The nurses in these hospitals were, by the 1870s, much better than those seen by Dr Bell in Edinburgh in the 1850s. He wrote that they were:

Poor old useless drudges, half charwoman, half fieldworker, absolutely ignorant, almost invariably drunken, sometimes deaf, occasionally fatuous [simple-minded].

(*Working Women in Stirlingshire*, 1986, WEA)

After Florence Nightingale's magnificent work, nursing soldiers during the Crimean War, a grateful nation presented her with £44 000 to set up a Nursing School in London. Her ideas were copied in other parts of the country and nursing became a skilled and respectable profession.

The work of local authorities was greatly helped by the appointment to them of medical officers of health. Edinburgh's first officer began his duties in 1862, Glasgow's in 1863. These men gathered evidence, organised improvements, and persuaded councils to tackle all sorts of problems.

Victorian doctors charged private patients for their services, commonly asking at least five shillings (25p) for a consultation. Ordinary people, therefore, tried to treat themselves rather than pay such fees. All sorts of remedies were on offer including Beechams Pills (first marketed in 1847) and Godfrey's Cordial, a mixture that had opium in it. Working mothers often gave this mixture to their children to keep them quiet.

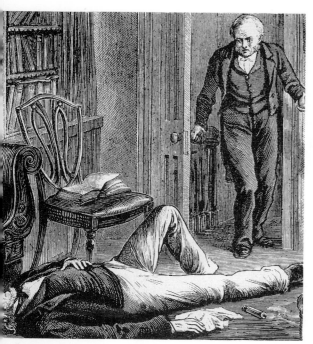

Source 2.58

James Young Simpson on the floor after experimenting with chloroform

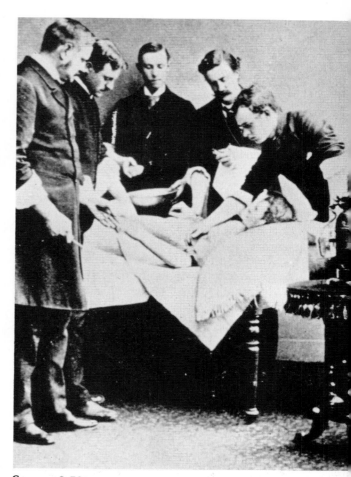

Source 2.59

The Lister carbolic spray in use in Aberdeen Infirmary

Medical care in hospitals improved too. In the early nineteenth century surgeons used brandy to drug their patients and operated as fast as possible since the shock of the operation itself was likely to kill the patient. They usually wore ordinary clothes and worked on rough wooden tables with sawdust on the floor to soak up the blood. From 1846 dentists began to use ether. In 1847 James Young Simpson in Edinburgh introduced the use of chloroform during operations. People's suspicions of this treatment were eased when, in 1853, Queen Victoria accepted chloroform during the birth of one of her children. Chloroform gave surgeons more time to operate properly. But many still died from infections they picked up during operations. In 1856 Joseph Lister used carbolic during his work in Glasgow Royal Infirmary. In 1869 he moved to Edinburgh and developed a carbolic spray that filled the operating theatre with a protective mist. His results showed that the spray cut deaths from operations by 66%.

Despite these developments terrible diseases continued to flourish. Diphtheria, measles, whooping cough, scarlet fever and tuberculosis remained common.

QUESTIONS

1 Henry Cockburn thought the 1833 Burgh Reform Act 'will permanently change the whole country' (2.54). What evidence can you find of that in the sources? (K.U)

2 What sort of workers would an 'improved' burgh need? Design an advertisement for suitable workers for your town. (E.2)

3 'Going into hospital'. Write an account by an elderly person living in the 1870s telling a young person about to go into hospital how lucky they are. (K.U)

Poverty

In the 1830s the Scottish population included people too old, young or ill to support themselves. If the relatives of such people could not care for them then the duty of looking after them belonged to the kirk. Between them, kirk session members and heritors were supposed to raise money from church collections and from money for the poor left in people's wills. If this was not enough they could impose an assessment on local property holders. This was not popular and collecting such money was not easy.

In 1834 the Poor Law in England was reformed. Workhouses were built to house many of the poor. In Scotland a great deal of discussion took place as to whether such a law was needed. By 1843 an official enquiry – a Royal Commission – was looking into the question.

QUESTIONS

1 Look through the following sources and list the arguments in favour of changing the Scottish Poor Law. (K.U)

2 List the arguments against any change. (K.U)

3 Why do you think care of the poor had become such an important issue by the 1840s? (E.2)

Source 2.60 ———————————

Facts and figures

In 1840 236 parishes had a legal assessment: 642 had none. The average amount paid a year to each poor person was
- in crofting parishes   £0.3.4 [£0.16p]
- in large industrial towns   £1.8.4 [1.42p]
- in farming parishes   £1.6.4 [£1.32p]

Poolewe parish, 1837, population 2581, raised £4 and spent it on 45 people.

Source 2.61 ———————————

1831, help to the poor in Edinburgh, noted by Dr Alison:

Societies	Number of poor
Destitute Sick Society	10 500
Strangers' Friend Society	1 900
House of Refuge	1 200
Night Refuge	600
Royal Infirmary	2 000
Society for Incurables	100
Female and Old Man's Societies	200
Society for Clothing Industrious Poor	200
Subscriptions raised last winter for relieving the most destitute of the poor	5 000
Total relieved not less than	**21 700**

(R. Cage, *The Scottish Poor Law*, 1981)

In 1843 Henry Cockburn wrote:

Source 2.62 ———————————

At present I [support] the principles of [the old] system, if they be rightly applied. But whether under the stinginess of the heritors wishing to give nothing and the negligence of the kirk sessions anxious to avoid trouble whether they have been so rightly applied is a different question. Of all the features of society none is so frightful as the hordes of strong poor always liable to be thrown out of employment by stagnation of trade. There have been 10 000 of them in Paisley for more than a year. What answer can be made to 10 000 who simply stand on the street and say 'We have no work'? I see no ground [reason] for expecting, so long as we are a nation of manufacturers, we can ever be uncursed by these heart-rending [events]. The question is whether we adhere to our ancient poor system or abandon it for the poor-rates, workhouses, outdoor relief as a matter of right to the unemployed and able-bodied.

(Cockburn, *Memorials*)

(Cockburn was writing about events in Paisley which so worried the government that they, and the Queen, found £2000 from their own private accounts to help deal with the crisis.)

The Poor Law Amendment Act (1845) gave

Scotland a new sort of system. The Royal Commission collected so much evidence that the old system was failing that the law had to be changed. But the able-bodied without work still had no right to help. Only the disabled, widows and deserted wives with children, orphans under 12 (girls) or 14 (boys) and the old and sick had a right to help. The parochial boards soon introduced poor rates to pay for their work. The new law, therefore, still left the problem of what to do for people who had no work. In Glasgow a committee to help the unemployed organised work for them:

Source 2.63

The work consisted of stone-breaking for the roads, earthworks at the Public Parks, and scavenging in the streets, and never, in any case, yielded a return sufficient to recoup the outlay in wages; but continuance at it was generally found an effective test of the applicant's destitution and willingness to work.

Part of the wages was given in Benevolent Society's tickets, which procured food at certain selected provision shops throughout the city, and part in cash. The relief given to applicants' dependants, and those unable to work, was invariably by these tickets.

The subscriptions raised in these years fortunately more than met the required outlay, leaving balances in the Committee's hands sufficient, at least, to begin a distribution of relief at each returning demand, until new collecting arrangements were made.

(Cage, *The Working Class in Glasgow*)

Where possible the poor were helped in their homes with money, food, fuel or clothes. But many parishes, or groups of parishes, began to build poorhouses too.

Source 2.64

Rules and Regulations for the Inmates of the Black Isle Combination Poorhouse 1860

1. The inmates are to conduct themselves civilly and respectfully to the Governor and Matron, to regard themselves as their servants, are cheerfully and diligently to attend to their instructions and to engage as they are able in any work.

2. The daily arrangements of the House will be as follows:-

   1st, from 1st October to 1st March – Rise at 8.0. Worship at half past 8. Breakfast at 9.0. Work from 10 till 2.0. Dinner at 2.0. Work from 3.0 to 7.0. Worship at 8.0. Bed at half past 8.0.

   2nd, from 1st March to 1stOctober. Rise at 7.0. Worship at 7.30. Breakfast at 9.0. Work from 10 till 2.0. Dinner at 2.0. Work from 3.0 till 6.0. Supper at 7.0. Worship at 8.0. Bed at 9.0.

3. While in the House the Paupers shall remain in their respective Wards, the men in the Men's Ward, the women in the Women's Ward and the boys and girls in the Wards severally appropriated to them and no one shall leave the Ward without having previously obtained the permission of the Governor or Matron.

4. No inmate shall smoke within the Poor House Yard, or any building beyond that, nor have any matches.

6. All healthy Paupers, whether young or old, are to wash their faces and hands every morning and to have their entire person thoroughly washed once a week.

7. Should any Pauper be charged with incivility or rudeness to the Governor, or be observed to swear or quarrel or act in a disorderly manner or be found guilty of dishonesty or drunkenness or of attempting to bring spiritous liquors, the Governor is authorised to punish such Pauper by solitary confinement not to exceed 12 hours for the first offence or 24 hours for the second.

Source 2.65
Kincardine Poorhouse now used as a hospital

The East Linton Poorhouse, its Governor reported, was:

Source 2.66
. . . designed originally as a home for the aged and friendless poor, and for those who from weakness of mind, or by reason of dissipated and improvident habits, are unable to take charge of their own affairs, it has to some extent – from necessity – become a workhouse on the English model, with a system of deterrent administration, intended to eliminate, as far as possible, the element of imposture from applications for relief.

(14 November 1865) Of the twelve men, three from infirmity are incapable of doing any kind of work, one man works at net-making, one acts as porter, one assists in the kitchen. The others are employed working in the ground, pumping water for household purposes, and when the weather is unfavourable for outdoor work they are employed teasing hair in their sitting rooms.

A large proportion of the women are old and infirm persons, some of them however are able to attend to the children whose mothers assist in washing the clothes and cleaning the wards of the house, two are engaged in making and mending stockings, one assists in the kitchen and two act as nurses in the wards. Three of the boys are at the parish school in the village,

six are children under two years of age, four of the children whose ages are between four and six years, could now be sent for a few hours each day to the infant school in connection with the parish.

The continued problem of poverty seemed to some people to be due to the alcohol Scots drank in such quantities.

Alexander Brown described a typical Glasgow public house of the 1850s:

Source 2.67
One can scarcely realise the enormous number of these houses, with their flaring gas lights in frosted globes, and brightly gilded spirit casks, with the occasional mirror at the extreme end of the shop reflecting at once in fine perspective the waters of a granite fountain fronting the door, and the entrance of poor broken-down victims, who stand in pitiful burlesque in their dirty rags, amid all this pomp and mocking grandeur.

(Alexander Brown, *The Streets and Wynds of Glasgow*, 1858)

In 1853 an 11.00 pm closing time was enforced. In 1855 the police were given more powers to enter and search places suspected of being unlicensed drinking places. A strong 'temperance' movement tried to persuade Scots to drink less. It does not seem to have been very successful.

WINE IS A MOCKER STRONG DRINK IS RAGING

HIGHLAND TEMPERANCE LEAGUE

FORMED 29TH JANY 1880

BOND OF UNION

I promise by Divine assistance to abstain from all INTOXICATING LIQUORS as beverages and to discountenance all the causes and practices of INTEMPERANCE.

Signed ....

Was Admitted a Member .... 18...

S. F. Sim Secy.

AND WHOSOEVER IS DECEIVED THEREBY IS NOT WISE

Source 2.68

QUESTIONS

1 What kinds of work were the unemployed required to do? Did the money they received come from the rates or from some other source? What reasons for asking the unemployed to work can you find?   (K.U)

2 Using the sources, write an account of 'A visit to a poorhouse'. Mention clothing, food, work, rules and regulations.   (K.U)

3 Using the sources, design a poster advertising a temperance meeting.   (K.U)

4 The written sources are all the work of people who are not, themselves, very poor. Choose quotations that show how authors felt about the poor. Do you think such authors could really know what it was like to be poor? (Give reasons for your answer). Why do we not have plenty of evidence from the poor themselves?   (E.1)

3 Political Change

Between 1830 and 1880 the way the country was governed changed. There were alterations in the rules that decided who had the right to vote for MPs. To some people, these changes did not seem satisfactory. They demanded far bigger changes than were actually introduced at the time. The sources in this chapter deal with the political changes, and with demands for even more changes.

The Reform of Parliament in 1832

In 1830 only 4500 Scots – all men – had the right to vote for the people who became their 45 MPs. In Scotland, as in Britain, a small number of wealthy people controlled political power often using bribery to get their way, since voting was open, not secret. But, by 1830, a large number of people were no longer ready to tolerate this system. The leaders of the Whig Party, one of the main political groups, decided that some reform was essential. Otherwise, they feared, people might turn to violence. In 1789 in France this is exactly what had happened. Moreover, Britain's growing trade and industry meant there were an increasing number of better-off educated middle-class people – often living in large towns without MPs. These people brought money and good planning to the demand for a change. They offered arguments like this.

Source 3.1

The House of Commons in its present state is too far removed in habits, wealth and station from the wants of the lower and middle class of the people. The interests of Industry and Trade have scarcely any representatives at all. These, the most vital interests of the nation, the source of all its wealth and of all its strength.

(*Declaration of the Birmingham Political Union*, 1830)

In 1830 the Whigs, led by Lord Grey, were elected to power. One of them was the Scots lawyer, Henry Cockburn. He wrote about the feeling in Scotland when the Whigs planned a reform of Parliament. He claimed that even Scottish burgh councils supported it, even though reform would end the control over choosing MPs that their members enjoyed.

Source 3.2

It is impossible to exaggerate the ecstasy of Scotland where it is like liberty given to slaves. Many town councils, though their political monopoly is to be extinguished, and Radicals whose expectations the measure falls short of, have all abated [stopped] their separate claims. There have been meetings everywhere and a universal outburst of popular feeling.

(Cockburn, *Memorials*)

The Whigs had difficulties getting their Reform Bill through Parliament. Their Tory opponents controlled the House of Lords. In some places rioting began to break out. A new election took place in 1831. Under the threat that 50 new Whig members of the House of Lords would be created by King William IV, the Tories gave way and the bill passed.

Source 3.3

Parliamentary Reform, 1832
Separate acts dealt with England and Wales, Ireland, and Scotland.
1. MPs were taken from small places, 56 burghs of under 2000 lost both and 30 with under 4000 lost one.
2. 22 new burghs gained two MPs and 20 more gained one.
3. The Counties gained 62 MPs.
4. In Scotland eight extra burgh MPs were awarded.
5. In burghs all men owning a house, shop, warehouse, etc. with an annual value of at least £10 could vote.
6. In counties the voters were forty shilling

[£2] freeholders, copyholders with land worth at least £10 a year, leaseholders who had long leases and land worth at least £10 a year and tenants with leases of at least 19 years who paid £50 a year or more in rent.

7. Voting was done openly, not by secret ballot.

8. Parliaments could last seven years before an election was required.

9. The act spread the vote to many of the middle class. The total electorate in Britain grew from 435 000 to 652 000. In Scotland the electorate grew from 4500 to 65 000 i.e. about one in every eight adult males. (In wealthier England the figure was one in five.)

Source 3.4

Weaver's banner showing the French cap of liberty and the scales of justice

Lord Cockburn expressed his delight at:

Source 3.5

. . . the limited effect of the Reform Act in promoting that rise of low radicals with which we were threatened . . . I suppose we shall have a houseful of good sound aristocratic Whigs . . . It is quite clear that Toryism is over, that Radicalism is on the rise; and that but for the Reform Bill they would have taken all the institutions of the country by storm. Whether they are to be permanently repressed remains to be seen.

(Wilson, *The Chartist Movement in Scotland*)

Henry Cockburn soon found that many people in Britain were not satisfied. Perhaps he had seen posters like this one advertising a meeting in July 1833 in Edinburgh:

Source 3.6

The Reform Bill is, as regards the diminution of Public Burdens and relief of General Distress, a mere Mockery; the House of Commons consists of the same all monopolising aristocratic body ignorant of and insensible to the Conditions, Interests and Feelings of the People.

The Committee of the Working Classes deeply regrets the Compromise of their Political Rights into which the People entered in favour of the Whiggish Paltry [small] Measure of Parliamentary Reform for the Sake of obtaining the early removal of all Monopolies, Corruptions and Abuses. Still more do they regret that such conditions should be so shamefully forgotten by Earl Grey. Let all unfurl the Flag of Public Liberty and call for Universal Suffrage and for Triennial Parliaments and Vote by Ballot.

(I. Macdougall, *Labour in Scotland*, 1985)

Source 3.7

Chartist Poster

1. A vote for every man 21 years of age of sound mind and not undergoing punishment for crime.
2. The ballot – to protect the elector.
3. No Property Qualification for MPs, thus enabling the constituencies to return the men of their choice, be they rich or poor.
4. Payment of MPs, thus enabling an honest tradesman working man to serve a constituency.
5. Equal constituencies – instead of allowing small constituencies to swamp the votes of larger ones.
6. Annual parliaments, the most effectual check to bribery, a constituency might be bought once in seven years, no purse could buy a constituency in each ensuring twelve month and since members when elected for a year only would not be able to defy and betray their constituents as now.

(G. D. H. Cole and A. W. Filson, *British Working Class Movements*, 1967)

QUESTIONS

1. Why was Lord Cockburn pleased that the Reform Act was not bolder? (K.U)

2. What do you think Lord Cockburn would have thought of the views expressed in source 3.6? (E.1)

3. The people who made the banner (source 3.4) probably had views that would have alarmed both Whigs and Tories. What evidence of this can you find in the banner? (E.1)

4. Design a banner that might have been carried by the authors of source 3.6. (K.U)

Source 3.8

Chartist Associations in Scotland

Chartism

In 1832 the right to vote in Scotland went to more people as Scotland was swept along on a demand for change that affected all Britain. In the following years Scots took part in another British movement that demanded more political reform – Chartism. What the Chartists wanted can be seen in this poster.

RULES
OF THE
PERTH
Chartist Association.

T a Meeting of the Committee, held in the *Chronicle* Office, on *Friday, the 19th Nov.* 1841, the following RESOLUTIONS were unanimously agreed to :—

1st,—That the Name of the Association shall be "THE PERTH CHAR-ST ASSOCIATION."

2d,—That the object of the Association shall be to obtain the enactment the CHARTER, which they pledge themselves to endeavour to effect by all gal, Peaceful, and Constitutional means, and by these alone—holding mselves entirely aloof from, and discouraging all persons or parties who vocate or adopt illegal and violent measures themselves, or countenance em in others ; and for this purpose, the Association shall consider every mber who either himself advocates illegal and violent measures, or coun-ances their advocacy or adoption by others, as no longer belonging to Association—his expulsion following as a matter of course ; and in order t this provision may be more generally known, and better attended to, y resolve that this rule shall be read over at all Meetings called by the sociation.

3d,—That the Association shall consist of all those who agree to its Regu-ions, and receive a Ticket of Membership, for which they shall pay the of Threepence.

4th,—That the business of the Association shall be conducted by a Presi-t and Managing Committee of Thirty, to be appointed by the Associa-n at their Annual Meeting in December, and of Two Vice-Presidents, a asurer, and Two Secretaries, who shall be chosen by the Committee from ir own numbers.

☞ *TICKETS of Membership may be had by applying at the* CHRONICLE *Office.*

C. BAXTER, PRINTER, PERTH.

Working men's associations and political clubs in Scotland rallied to support the Charter. In 1840 the *Glasgow Argus* noted:

Source 3.10
One of the most remarkable features of Char-tism in this part of the country is the number of places of worship which are opening in the various localities where their numerical strength is greatest. They have sermons regularly on Sabbaths in Glasgow, Hamilton, Lanark, Paisley, Greenock, Eaglesham, Kilbarchan and other towns in the neighbourhood.

(Wilson, *The Chartist Movement in Scotland*)

One of the leaders of these Scottish 'Chartist churches' was the Rev. Brewster. He preached that:

Source 3.11
The Son of God came especially to the poor. He taught and fed the poor. He healed their diseases and comforted their sorrows, he directed all the force of his rebukes against those who deceived and oppressed them, their wicked rulers, exposing their real character in all its naked selfishness.

(D. Jones, *Chartism and the Chartists*, 1975)

Source 3.12
Sketch of the first Chartist co-operative store in Silver Street, Hawick, 1839

Scottish Chartists also began to try to improve their own living standards. They not only wanted to reform Parliament because they thought the 1832 system was not fair, they also had other reasons. Chartists hoped a reformed Parliament would carry out changes that would help ordinary people. One of their leaders, Joseph Rayner Stephen, declared in 1838:

Source 3.13
This question of Universal Suffrage was a knife and fork question after all; this question was a bread and cheese question, and if any man ask him what he meant by Universal Suffrage, he would answer, that every working man in the land had a right to have a good coat to his back, a comfortable abode in which to shelter himself and his family, a good dinner upon his table, and no more work than was necessary for keeping him in health, and as much wages for that work as would keep him in plenty, and afford him the enjoyment of all the blessings of life which a reasonable man could desire. (Tremendous cheers).

(E. Royle, *Chartism*, 1980)

EXTRAORDINARY MEETING.

NATIONAL STRIKE
FOR THE
CHARTER.

At the GREAT DELEGATE MEETING, held in the School-Room, Pullar's Close, on the evening of Friday the 19th instant, it was decidedly ascertained that the vast numbers of workmen, of all the Trades in Dundee, represented by the assembled Delegates, with the exception of a very few workmen, agreed to **STRIKE** for the **PEOPLE'S CHARTER.—In accordance with the will of the Delegates,**

A PUBLIC MEETING
WILL BE HELD
ON THE MAGDALEN YARD GREEN,
THIS EVENING, AT HALF-PAST SIX O'CLOCK,

For the purpose of consulting the whole of the people in regard to the means which ought to be adopted for carrying their will into operation.

THE VOICE OF THE PEOPLE IS THE VOICE OF GOD.

A Collection will be made to Defray Expenses.

BY ORDER OF THE DELEGATES.

Dundee, August 20, 1842.   PRINTED AT THE CHRONICLE OFFICE, DUNDEE.

Certainly the number of active Chartists rose when trading difficulties led to widespread unemployment. Scots workers (like handloom weavers) in jobs that were in decline, or were overcrowded, were likely to have been supporters of Chartism.

Source 3.15 ———————
Feargus O'Connor

The Chartists had clear proposals, but how could they persuade Parliament to agree to them? All sorts of approaches were tried. The Chartists tried to persuade Parliament by gathering petitions. They also ran newspapers, including the *Northern Star*. It was controlled by one of the most important of all Chartist leaders, Feargus O'Connor. O'Connor was an able journalist. At its height his paper sold 50 000 copies. He toured the country, lecturing, and his meetings were usually crowded. O'Connor was a powerful and persuasive speaker.

He believed that Chartists must (if compelled to) be prepared to use force. His 'physical force' views had support from some Scots. Dr John Taylor, A Scottish Republican, declared:

Source 3.16 ———————
He approved of what O'Connor said, that moral force could produce no result except to make the people think. They had thought long enough and what better were they if they only thought themselves worse off than before. If a revolution got by blood, and after twenty battles, were good in 1688, it could not be bad in 1838.

(Wilson, *The Chartist Movement in Scotland*)

Other Scots preferred the 'moral force' views of William Lovett. Lovett believed:

Source 3.17

The whole physical force agitation is harmful to the movement. Muskets are not what are wanted, but education and schooling of the working people. Stephens and O'Connor are shattering the movement . . . Violent words do not slay the enemies but the friends of the movement. O'Connor wants to take everything by storm, and to pass the Charter into law within a year. All this hurry and haste, this bluster and menace of armed opposition can only lead to premature outbreaks and to the destruction of Chartism.

(K. Dawson and P. Wall, *Parliamentary Representation*, 1968)

Source 3.18

Chartism – The Main Events

1835 O'Connor helped organise several workers associations to seek political reform, especially in Scotland and north England.

1836 The London Working Men's Association was founded by a cabinetmaker, William Lovett.

1837 The LWMA drew up the Charter. O'Connor's newspaper the *Northern Star* appeared.

1838 Large meetings in Birmingham, Manchester and on Glasgow Green – in support of the Charter.

1839 More meetings. Drafting of petition to Parliament in support of the Charter. 1 280 000 signatures gathered. Parliament rejected the Charter by 235 votes to 46. Chartists in Newport, Wales, led by John Frost, organised a rising and clashed with troops. Frost was transported. The government sent troops under General Napier to control the north.

1840 Chartist leaders arrested and tried after unrest in Sheffield and Bradford. Lovett set up the National Charter Association.

1842 A National Convention of Chartists met in London. A new petition with 3 317 752 names was presented to Parliament and rejected by 287 votes to 49. In parts of northern England, especially Manchester, there were strikes in support of the Charter. The strikes failed. Further trials of Chartist leaders took place.

1842–3 O'Connor proposed a land company to collect subscriptions, buy land, and (by ballot) settle ordinary people on their own plots of land. The Chartist Convention accepted it.

1846 Land acquired.

1847 First settlers established at 'O'Connorville'. O'Connor elected MP for Nottingham.

1848 A revolution took place in France, overthrowing the government. Trade slumped. In London, Manchester and Glasgow there were riots. A large Chartist rally took place on Kennington Common, London. A New Chartist petition was drawn up. The Government enrolled 70 000 special constables and put the Duke of Wellington in charge of troops to protect London. The petition turned out to have 2 million signatures, not the 5 700 000 claimed by O'Connor. A Commons Committee found 'on numerous sheets the signatures are in one and the same handwriting. Your Committee observed the names of Her Majesty, the Duke of Wellington, Sir Robert Peel, 'Pug-Nose', 'Flat-nose', etc.' Parliament rejected the petition. Riots in London and Bradford.

1851–2 Chartist Land Company ended. O'Connor declared insane (died 1855).

1853–8 Revival of Chartist activities. Last Convention in 1858. Chartists now tried to reform the existing system.

A PHYSICAL FORCE CHARTIST ARMING FOR THE FIGHT.

Source 3.19 _____

QUESTIONS

1 List the six Chartist demands. Explain in your own words why reformers were in favour of each of them. (K.U)

2 From all you have read so far, how would you explain the support Chartists got? Why was it not steady, but tended to rise and fall? What sort of groups and places especially supported it? (E.2)

3 Find and list the different ways in which Chartists tried to win reforms. (K.U)

4 Which do you think was the most sensible way to try and win reform? Give reasons for your answer. (E.2)

5 Look at source 3.19. Do you think the cartoonist supported Chartism? Explain your answer. (E.1)

6 Why do you think the Chartist movement failed? Have any of its demands been successful in the long run? (E.2)

Reforms in 1867 and 1872

After the failure of Chartism people eager to see Parliament reformed turned to trying to win more limited changes. The Liberal Party offered them the best hope. By the mid 1860s Liberal leaders like Lord John Russell and William Gladstone all supported the further reform of Parliament. The Chartist leader Ernest Jones persuaded many of his followers to support the Liberals. He argued:

Source 3.20 _____

They should meet the middle class half way, if the working classes could get the universal manhood suffrage then they would for a time waive [set aside] the other points of the charter. If they could obtain the ballot it would be sufficient for a time and if they could get these two points it would throw the balance of power into the hands of the working classes and other points would soon follow.

(Jones, *Chartism and the Chartists*)

Liberal supporters were very numerous in Scotland. Until 1900 the party held a majority of Scottish seats in Parliament. Between 1832 and 1886 Glasgow only once elected a Conservative for one of its seats. In Edinburgh Duncan McLaren, the MP from 1865, was the brother-in-law of John Bright. This former Anti-Corn Law leader was now one of the leaders of the demand for political reform. Men like these were busy improving Scotland's towns and cities. As part of their work they created parks and free libraries that ordinary people could use. They supported the improvement of education too. To these Liberals the skilled workers in towns clearly deserved the vote. But the Liberals' attempt to bring in a new reform failed in 1866. A number of Whigs who disliked the way their old party had become a section of the Liberal Party, helped the Conservatives defeat the bill. One of them, Robert Lowe, argued:

Source 3.21 _____

If you want ignorance, if you want drunkenness, if you want impulsive and violent people where do you look for them in the constituencies? Do you go to the top or to the bottom? The working men finding themselves in a majority will awake to a full sense of their power. They will say 'We can do better for ourselves. We have objects [aims], let us unite to carry out those objects'.

The Conservative Government that replaced the Liberals decided to carry out its own reform, hoping grateful voters would, in future, support it.

These events stirred great excitement in Scotland. Many meetings, rallies and processions took place. In Glasgow, for example, in 1866, the different trades all gathered on the Green for a march.

Source 3.22
Reform Act, 1867

1. All male householders, and lodgers paying £10 year in rent could vote in burghs.
2. All paying £12 a year in rates could vote in counties.
3. 45 burghs with a population of under 10 000 were cut from two to one MP each and four large English towns gained an extra MP. 25 extra MPs were given to counties.
4. The total number of Scottish constituencies was thus increased from 53 to 60.

Source 3.23
Banner of the Edinburgh Bookbinders, 1867

The Act greatly increased the number of men living in towns who could vote. The number of voters in Glasgow, for example, rose from 18 000 to 47 000. The table shows how the sort of people who could vote altered.

Source 3.24
People who could vote in Glasgow, before and after 1867

	Before the Act	In 1868–9
(i) Upper-class, rich, business people and wealthy professional people	3170	4360
(ii) Lower middle-class, business and professional people and clerical workers	8600	12 090
(iii) Manual workers		
– skilled	4130	16 590
– semi-skilled	1670	8310
– unskilled	790	6500

(I. G. C. Hutchison, *The Political History of Scotland*, 1986)

In 1872 open voting ended: a secret ballot was introduced. The reforms increased Liberal support in Scotland. A Liberal Government was elected in 1868. However, it did little for Scottish issues. Disraeli seized the chance to work to revive the Conservative Party in Scotland. Lord Rosebery, especially, attacked Gladstone for his failure to pay attention to Scottish matters. In 1881 Gladstone made Rosebery an under-secretary of state to deal with Scottish affairs and be answerable to the Home Secretary. By 1883 the experiment seemed to Rosebery to be such a failure that he resigned. He told Gladstone:

Source 3.25
I confess I think Scotland is, as usual, treated abominably. Justice for Ireland means every-thing done for her. Justice for Scotland means insulting neglect. I leave for Scotland next week with the view of blowing up a prison or shooting a policeman.

(W. Ferguson, *Scotland 1689 to the Present*, 1968)

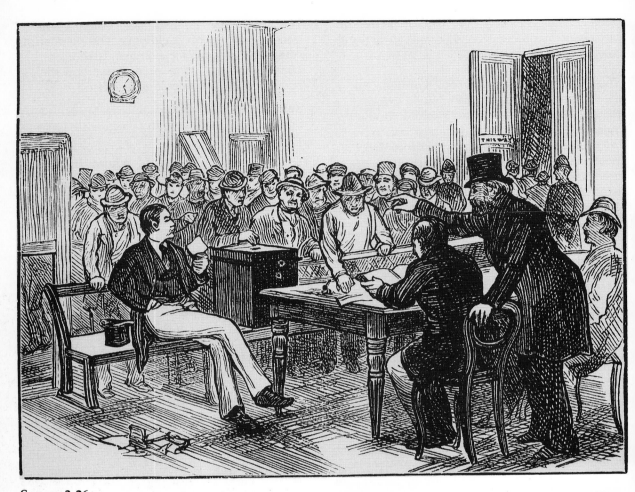

Source 3.26
Secret ballot

1 What did Ernest Jones (source 3.20) think were the two most important reforms of the Chartists' six points? (K.U)

   Why do you think he chose these two? Do you think he was right? (E.2)

2 What social class do you think the author of source 3.21 came from? How can you tell? (E.1)

3 Who else might have been very dissatisfied with the 1867 Reform Act? (E.2)

4 Scottish Culture

Scotland was once an independent country. It had once had its own monarchy and, till 1707, its own Parliament. Even after this date Scotland kept its own legal system, its own educational system and its own church. In many ways Scots thought of themselves as a separate people. In the remoter Highlands and Islands, especially, a distinctive way of life still existed. During this period all sorts of forces were at work, some within Scotland, some coming from outside the country, that were changing the Scottish way of life. The sources in this chapter deal with how this Scottish culture was changing.

From time to time, in his many writings, Henry Cockburn paused to consider what it meant to be a Scot:

Source 4.1

1838: Whisky is certainly one of the curses of Scotland. But in blaming the people for their addiction to it we should recollect we leave them very little other amusements. A Scotchman's weather does not admit of his taking much of his pleasure with only the heavens above him. The tippling house is his natural refuge against a system of moral Calvinism which considers the social, and public recreation of families as dangerous or shameful.

1853: The memory of Old Scotland can only live in the character of its people, and in its picturesque and delightful language. The gradual disappearance of the Scots accent and dialect is a national calamity . . .

But . . . nothing can prevent the gradual disappearance of local manners under the absorption by a far larger, richer and more powerful kingdom. Burns and Scott have done more for the preservation of proper Scotland than could ever be accomplished by laws. How can we retain our language respectably after it has become vulgar in the ears of our native gentility; after scarcely a single Scotch nobleman

will keep a house in a Scotch town and after our soil . . . is passing into English hands? This is all very sad but it is the natural course and foolish associations with their nonsense about Bannockburn and the Union only hastens the progress by bringing the taste for averting it into discredit.'

Source 4.2

Queen Victoria with her servant John Brown (left)

A few years later an English visitor, Edward Bradley, observed:

Source 4.3

What is known as 'the Highland costume' is, of course, not to be met within the Glasgow streets unless we encounter a professional piper and beggar who has donned the kilt as a matter of trade. Neither in Glasgow or Edinburgh did I see the Highland costume except on some dressed dolls in the toy shop window. (1863)

(In Berry & Whyte, *Glasgow Observed*)

QUESTIONS

1 How does Cockburn explain the Scots fondness for whisky-drinking?

(K.U)

2 Why does he think the Scots accent and dialect will fade away? (K.U)

3 How do sources 4.2 and 4.3 show that a 'tourist image' of Scots was developing? (K.U)

People on the Move

Evidence in earlier sources has shown that Scotland's population was increasing. But the changes that were taking place in the countryside, as well as the increase in population there, meant there was not enough work for all. What were people to do? In 1843 an observer gave an example of this sort of problem. He said:

Source 4.4
Take the case of a ploughman. When unable to do his work he is turned off: his cottage is transferred to another. The next best thing he can do is turn carter and for that purpose he comes to town: but such persons do not migrate from the idea that they will be better off or for any other reason than that they expect to get many small jobs which they could not get in the country.

(*Poor Law Enquiry Appendix*)

Irish immigration

Scots from the countryside poured into towns and cities in search of work. So, too, did numerous Irish people. The whole of Ireland was, at this time, part of the United Kingdom. The Irish population was growing, many people were very poor. At times, and especially in the mid-1840s, the failure of the potato crop reduced thousands there to starvation. It was not surprising that so many should cross the Irish Sea to Scotland. A journalist visiting the poorer areas of Glasgow noticed there:

Source 4.5
. . . the poor Irish who have found in this city an asylum from the greater want and beggary in their own country. Between 1811 and 1836 Glasgow doubled its population, it is in great measure caused by a flow of immigrants from Ireland and the Highlands. We are assured that more than a quarter [of Glasgow's population) are Irish Roman Catholics.

(*Midnight Scenes and Social Photographs*, 1858)

Many Irish people came to Scotland to work as navvies building canals and railways. Some of these people stayed permanently in Scotland. Occasionally these men quarrelled and fought with Scots labourers. In 1840, for example, Irish navvies, full of drink, seized control of the town of Hamilton and held it for four days. According to a Scottish newspaper:

Source 4.6
Some hundreds of navigators turned out and, brandishing clubs, picks, etc. broke windows, assaulted every Scotch person they could meet with, jumped, yelled, and altogether frightened for their lives the peaceable inhabitants.

(*Glasgow Herald*, 15 Sept. 1840)

Soldiers recovered control of the town. Other Irish people came across for the corn and potato harvest. According to an inhabitant of Berwickshire, for example, around 2000 Irish helped with the harvesting in the 1840s. These workers were liked by farmers for their ability to labour and the way they accepted harsh living conditions. They, too, sometimes clashed with Scots people. In 1828, for example, a large number of Irish had boarded a steamer in Greenock when:

Source 4.7
A party of idle blackguards on the quay commenced an unprovoked attack upon them, calling them 'Paddies' and throwing stones. A score of the boldest [Irish] sallied [went] forth, flourishing their shillelahs and soon cleared the quay. This brought an increased crowd of townspeople who renewed the assault; stones, pieces of coal flew in every direction, the people on deck throwing back whatever they received.

(*Glasgow Herald*, 15 Sept. 1828)

The 1841 census recorded separately the numbers of Irish-born people in Scotland (but not those actually born in Scotland whose parents were Irish).

Source 4.8
Irish-born numbers in counties

	Male	Female
Lanark	29 343	26 572
Renfrew	9 894	10 523
Ayr	6411	5 624
Edinburgh	3 971	3 129
Forfar	3 024	3 450
Stirling	2 686	1 570
Dumbarton	2 885	2 006
Wigtown	2 964	2 808

These were people who had settled away from their own poor and overcrowded country. Of all Scottish cities Glasgow attracted most Irish. 44 345 lived there at the time of the 1841 census. Since most were Catholics, Irish immigration increased the numbers worshipping in Catholic churches in towns and cities. Witnesses from the time show the sort of work the Irish did, for example, in 1834:

Source 4.9
The Irish in Paisley almost uniformly belong to the poorer classes; I only remember one Irish shopkeeper. They are employed in the more disagreeable and lower descriptions of labour: the employment in the cotton mills is considered of this class. When hands are wanted, the Irish readily obey the call.

(J. E. Handley, *The Irish in Scotland*, 1945)

A further report from the 1830s came from the Catholic Bishop Stott. He explained the Irish in Glasgow, in a few cases:

Source 4.10
. . . have raised themselves to the rank of respectable shopkeepers; there are several who keep licensed whisky shops. The bulk of the male population are weavers or labourers on roads, canals, coalpits, draining, ditching, serving masons, coal porters, etc. and the female population are generally employed at the steam looms or in the cotton manufactories.

(Handley, *The Irish in Scotland*)

Many Irish found themselves attacked –

especially for their Catholic faith – in some news-sheets of the time. The numbers of Irish helped bring about a growth in Scotland of the Orange Order. By the 1830s several Scottish towns were the scene of Orange marches and of counter marches by 'Greens' (i.e. Irish Catholics). Fighting sometimes broke out. Near Edinburgh, for example:

Source 4.11
16 men belonging to the Orange Order were met by a large body of Irishmen armed with sticks, when the conflict began and after a violent scuffle some of them were knocked down and severely hurt.

(*Scotsman*, 23. Sept. 1836)

During the following years these divisions did not go away. The divisions were, perhaps, increased by the number of Irish people from Ulster who poured into Glasgow. Between 1876 and 1883 83% of Irish people coming to settle in Scotland came from Ulster. Some of them were Catholics, many were Protestants. Of these Protestants a number already belonged to the Orange Order in Ulster.

Scottish emigration

Many Scots left their country altogether.

Source 4.12

FREE PASSAGE TO
VAN DIEMEN'S LAND.

Passengers holding Bounty Certificates, issued by the Colonial Government of Van Diemen's Land, will be forwarded by the Undersigned.

Mersey Line of Australian Packets.

THE Undersigned despatch this Regular Line of Vessels with Goods and Passengers, regularly to MELBOURNE, SYDNEY, ADELAIDE, and GEELONG direct, or to each of the last named Ports, *via* Melbourne.

Passengers and their Luggage are Landed on the Wharf at Melbourne, free of expense.

To sail about the 26th August, for Melbourne' direct, the splendid New Clipper Packet Ship,

The local agent for prospective emigrants to Australia was George J Morton, a watchmaker in the Kirkgate: 1853.

The following table explains the numbers who were leaving, between 1840 and 1842. Notice the districts from which most were leaving.

Source 4.13
Numbers of Emigrants leaving Scotland, 1840–2

	Emigrant numbers reported
1. Shetland	40
2. Orkney	139
3. Caithness	239
4. East Sutherland	268
5. East Ross	107
6. NE Inverness	93
7. North-west coast	203
8. Skye and Outer Hebrides	2831
9. West Argyll	382
10. North Argyll	103
11. South Argyll	1144
12. Highland Inverness, Banff, Moray	185
13. Highland Perth, Aberdeenshire	77
14. NW Perth	154
15. Nairn, Lowland Moray	77
16. Lowland Banff	229
17. Buchan	201
18. SE Aberdeenshire	82
19. Inner Aberdeenshire	75
20. Kincardine	31
21. Inner Angus	349
22. Coastal Angus	115
25. East Perthshire	124
25. East Fife	217
26. West Fife	157
27. North Stirling-Clackmannan	136
28. West Lothian, East Stirling	88
29. Edinburgh area	24
30. Dunbarton, Renfrewshire	742
31. North Ayrshire	346
32. South Ayrshire	158
33. North Lanarks	535
34. South Lanarks	86
35. Peebleshire	85
36. Dunbar area	57
37. South Berwick	147
38. Kelso area	96
39. Hawick area	307
40. Inner Dumfries, Kirkcudbright	210
41. South Dumfries	579
42. Sough Kirkcudbright	217
43. Wigtown and south tip of Ayr	94
SCOTLAND	11 707

(I. Levitt and T. C. Smout, *The State of the Scottish Working Class in 1843*, 1979)

Source 4.14

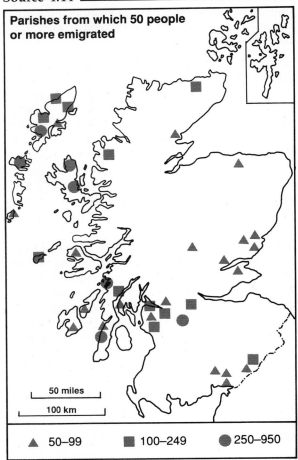

Parishes from which 50 people or more emigrated

▲ 50–99   ■ 100–249   ● 250–950

50 miles / 100 km

Scots who left Britain went, especially to Canada, Australia and New Zealand. In 1854 the *Inverness Courier* included this letter from Simon Fraser, a master mason who had left Inverness for Australia:

Source 4.15
Tell all to come here where they get good wages and not to be starving at home as they do. I was at Melbourne and was offered £10-10-0 per week, but expect to get £12 per week. This is the country to live in. If I am spared for six months I will be an independent man. Everyone that is inclined will do well here.

However, other emigrants letters painted a different picture. This letter came from another emigrant to Australia:

source 4.16
Elizabeth [the daughter] got a place before myself. She is serving with a clergyman, and

her wages are £10 yearly. I could have got her into other places, but I would not allow her, this being one of the most dangerous places for young women . . .

As for myself, I am with a Mr Williams, a Scotsman, belong to Cupar, Fife. He has a flour mill, and I work along with himself in it, which is very hard work, too hard for the wages I get, viz 10s [50p] per week and a house. I work from six in the morning until eight and ten in the evening. I am 180 miles [290 km] from Sydney.

I wear nothing but my trousers, shirt, shoes and my straw hat. The weather here is very hot at present. I was in the bush all day. It was very windy, the sand was like to blind one. I took some water to drink, which was as hot as if it had been on the fire. The people here are wishing for rain as there has been none worth speaking of this seven months past. This country is not what it is represented to be at home; the work is very hard and the wages are not so high as said. I got the offer of £25 a year as a shepherd, that is to say, I was to shepherd the sheep, my wife to be the hut keeper; she and I had to watch the sheep in the night-time, and to be responsible to the master for any sheep that might be destroyed by the natives or the wild dogs.

I was also to have the following rations weekly, viz 40 lbs [18 kg] of flour, 40 lbs [18 kg] of butcher meat, 8 lbs [3.5 kg] of sugar and 2 lbs [900 g] of tea. If I had taken this offer I would require to have gone 600 miles [966 km] up the country to a district called New England, but I could not think of my daughter so far away from us in so wild a country . . .

(*Kinross Advertiser* in N. H. Walker, *A Victorian Countryman's Diary*

Emigrants did not have to pay the full cost of their journey. Some had part of their costs paid, some travelled free. In 1857, for example, the *Inverness Advertiser* announced:

Source 4.17 ⎯⎯⎯⎯⎯⎯⎯⎯⎯⎯
Free Emigration to Van Dieman's Land [now called Tasmania]. For Scottish Emigrants Only. Under the St Andrews Emigration Society and the Government Bounty Scheme. The following

are to be taken by the end of March:

30 experienced ploughmen	20 housemaids and cooks
12 sheperds	12 gardeners
4 tanners	6 grooms

All unmarried.

(*Highland Region, Highland Emigration*)

Not all emigrant ships were well run. In 1850 the behaviour of officers on *The Indian* led to questions in Parliament. It was claimed:

Source 4.18 ⎯⎯⎯⎯⎯⎯⎯⎯⎯⎯
The conduct of the second mate, captain and medical officer had been of such a character that the vessel was made worse than a brothel. A Miss Arnold, who did not chose to yield, was taken on deck where buckets of water were thrown over her and one of the passengers who defended her was knocked down by the cook. No well-conducted female would like to trust herself on board a vessel if she could not be sure of protection.

(*Highland Region, Highland Emigration*)

QUESTIONS

1 Which two districts does source 4.13 say supplied most emigrants, from 1840 to 1842. (K.U)

2 How have the authors of source 4.12 tried to make their vessels sound attractive? (E.I)

3 List reasons why so many Irish people came to Scotland (K.U)

The Highland Crisis

The previous sources show that large numbers of people were leaving the Highlands.

QUESTIONS

1 *Why the Highlanders are leaving*
   Write a newspaper report of 1860, under the above heading.

   In order to do this:
   (i) Look through the following sources to pick out all the reasons you can find. Note them down.   (K.U)
   (ii) Think about the different reasons in order to explain which you think are the most important.   (E.2)
   (iii) Include quotes. As a journalist you would have visited the area and spoken to many eye witnesses. Whom do you believe? Who is biased?

   Say something about whether you really trust each witness to whom you have spoken.   (E.l)

The first witness is Robert Somers. He visited the Highlands in 1846. He noted that blight had badly damaged the potato crop leaving around 100 000 desperate for food.

Source 4.20 ———————————————————
The clothing, furniture and hovels of the people bear every mark extreme poverty, the children are pale and emaciated [very thin]: of the interior of the cottages – they consist for the most part of only one apartment in which the family and cattle find the same accommodation.

(R. Somers, *Letters from the Highlands*, 1848)

In 1850 the *Inverness Advertiser* quoted an official report on suffering in the Highlands being due to:

Source 4.21 ———————————————————
The end of the kelp trade, the failure of the potato crop, joined to the disadvantages of a sterile soil and unfavourable climate.

The *Advertiser* commented on this:

One half of the waste land of Scotland is uncultivated. There is no reason for maintaining there is a surplus population. Why should our people be forced away from their

Source 4.19 ———————————————————
Westbay, Portree on the Isle of Skye

homes? Just go to Glenorchy and there you will find the noble proprietor has this year converted 35 000 acres of excellent land into deer forest. Cross over to Sutherlandshire, that region of sheep, with its tens of thousands of excellent land lying waste and its poor inhabitants perched on barren patches of rocky soil on the sea shore, pining away, and then try if you can tell the tale – no room in the Highlands. If emigration is such a desirable thing, why is it that Highland lairds do not emigrate?

(*Highland Region, Emigration from the Highlands*)

Source 4.22 _____
Highland family leaving their croft

After the potato famine the Government sent Sir Edward Pine Coffin to distribute food and seed corn to the starving. In 1847 the Government set up the Board of Destitution to find work for Highlanders on railways and in road building. They built 'destitution roads' like the one from Poolewe to Ullapool. Certainly the kelp trade – burning seaweed for the alkali of its ash – had slumped badly by this period. For some years landlords had been turning to sheep farming to make money from their estates and some of them had cleared away the Highland crofters' villages that stood in the way of sheep. The uprooted crofters were often moved to the coast.

The geologist Sir Archibald Gieke saw one of these Clearances in 1853 at Suishnish, on Skye, the property of Lord Macdonald. He heard:

Source 4.23 _____
A strange wailing sound. On gaining the top of one of the hills I could see a long procession winding along the road. It was a gathering of at least three generations of crofters. There were old men and women too feeble to walk who were placed in carts, the younger members carrying their bundles of clothes and household effects while the children walked alongside. The long plaintive wail was resumed and after the last of the emigrants had disappeared the sound seemed to re-echo through the whole valley. The people were on their way to be shipped to Canada.

(E. Richards, *A History of the Highland Clearances*, 1985)

Source 4.24 _____
A family whose home has been destroyed

These people lived on poor bleak land. They had already been moved twice. Their homes were destroyed in this final move. It was just one of a whole number of clearances that took place at this time, until the late 1850s. After this date, according to the engineer James Mitchell:

Source 4.25 _____
The evictions are now chiefly for game and deer, the passion for sport having greatly enhanced the value of mountain property in the Highlands. When a deer forest is fixed on such of the inhabitants as remain are unhesitatingly cleared.

Source 4.26 _____
Population of Skye, 23 074 in 1841, 17 680 in 1881
Population of Lewis 17 016 in 1841, 25 421 in 1881

Lewis was bought in 1844 by the wealthy James Matheson. He imported meal, and provided work.

Crofters had no proper rights to their crofts. In Strathaird, Skye, when the laird proposed to clear 620 people to make way for sheep, the local sheriff told the people:

Source 4.27 _____
He was a perfect right to turn you out of your dwellings and possessions and to call upon me and other authorities to aid him. I should have to proceed with constables to turn yourselves, your families and property out of your lands, and to protect the persons employed by your landlord while they unroofed and destroyed your dwellings.

(Richards, *History of the Highland Clearances*)

The local potato crop had failed and the laird offered his tenants – who were now too poor to pay rent – money to emigrate. But Strathaird people – like most Highlanders – were deeply attached to their areas. Their views were published in 1850 in the Glasgow *Daily Mail*:

Source 4.28 _____
Our potatoes have almost entirely failed, the relief given to us by the Highland Relief Fund is discontinued and many of us will suffer severely unless some food is offered to us. We have been prevented from going to any employer at a distance as the proprietor and the sheriff threatened to put [us] away by force. We are very ill-off for clothing and know not what to do.

(Richards, *History of the Highland Clearances*)

In the next few years many Strathaird people, like numerous other Highlanders, emigrated.

The Church

The Kirk played a very important part in life at this time. When John Kerr was a boy living in the 1830s in Scotland he remembered:

Source 4.29 _____
When I was a boy the man who took a walk with his wife and family, to enjoy the fresh air on a Sunday afternoon or evening, was thought to do a very questionable thing, and set a bad example. No music of any kind was tolerated, except the singing of psalms and hymns (and hymns were by many 'suspect' as being 'human') in church or at family worship.

(Kerr, *Life Jottings*)

Writing about the 1870s, William Haddow recalled:

Source 4.30 _____
Sunday at home was a dismal ordeal for the younger generation. All newspapers and books of a secular character were carefully put out of sight. Black clothes were taken from the wardrobe and carefully brushed, boots polished and the whole family was marched to church. After a meal we were marched off again for afternoon service. Sometimes we would read Bunyan's *Pilgrims Progress*.

By 9 o'clock when everybody had to be indoors, Bibles were given to each member of the family. The old man would read a chapter from the Bible, we all knelt down and he would engage in prayer. By 10 o'clock we were all bedded, some of us, I fear, thankful that this dreary [day] was over.

(William Haddow, *My 70 years*, 1943)

For many adults, however, the Kirk was an all-important part of their lives. It was a centre for

Source 4.31

Victorian worshippers outside their church in St Andrews

social life, organising talks, concerts and picnics. Till 1872, it supervised education and it provided Sunday schooling for many children. Some of its ministers played an important part in the campaigns for reforms in living conditions. The Church of Scotland split apart in 1843, giving birth to the Free Kirk. This is the view of a modern historian on this event:

Source 4.32

For Scotland the Disruption was the most momentous single event of the nineteenth century and its repercussions [results] were . . . felt in most departments of Scottish life.

(W. Ferguson, *Scotland 1689 to the Present*, 1968)

The split led to about 40% of the Church of Scotland's ministers leaving for the Free Church. By 1851 the number of worshippers in the two churches were about equal. Thomas Chalmers was elected Moderator of the Free Church.

Thomas Chalmers

The leading churchman of his times. A very powerful speaker and writer. He became the leader of the 'Evangelicals' who wanted religion to dominate the whole of life and were very emotional in the way they preached, worshipped, and tried to convert others to their beliefs. He was not a supporter of trade unions, or political democracy. Instead, he believed that social problems should be solved by the Church, and by the generosity of the wealthy — helped by the State.

The Church split which Chalmers led had a number of causes. His 'Evangelical' followers wanted the Church to change since they could see society was changing. They wanted Church congregations to have more power. Between 1833 and 1843 the 'Ten Years Conflict' took place as the Evangelicals used their power in the General Assembly to try and change the Church. They tried, especially, to reduce the power of landowners as the patrons of their local churches to nominate the ministers. The Church agreed to the 'Veto Act'. The male heads of households could refuse to accept an unpopular minister. The Church also decided to use money it had raised to set up new parish churches. But Scotland's leading judges; the Court of Session, condemned these changes. By 1843 the Evangelicals felt that the reforms they wanted would only come if the Church was free of being the official Church, under the control of the state. They therefore broke away.

In most Scottish towns and cities – and even in villages – the results can still be seen. Free Church congregations had to build their own new churches. They set up a college to train their own ministers. But, after a difficult time, the Church of Scotland began to recover. In 1874 it persuaded Parliament to abolish the lay patron's right to appoint ministers. The Disruption stirred very strong feelings and aroused great arguments, showing the importance of the Church in many people's lives.

QUESTIONS

1 Find and list the activities that were allowed on Sunday.   (K.U)

2 List two reasons why the Disruption took place.   (K.U)

Education
Schools

Many different sorts of schools offered children education in mid-nineteenth-century Scotland.

Source 4.33 _____

Parish Schools. the Church supervised schools in each parish, appointing teachers. A tax on local landowners and fees paid by pupils helped to meet the costs. As the population grew, so the Church added new schools – 'Assembly' schools in rural areas and 'sessional' schools in industrial areas. Thomas Chalmers led the effort to raise money for these: after 1833 more money was added by the state.

Burgh Schools. These were the responsibility of burgh councils. By the mid-nineteenth century they had become very middle class and offered a classical education as well as the reading, writing and arithmetic on which parish schools concentrated.

Religious Denomination Schools. Churches other than the Church of Scotland set up their own schools. The most important were the Free Church Schools but there were Roman Catholic, Episcopalian, Congregational, and other schools.

Adventure Schools. By 1851 around a quarter of children going to school went to schools whose owners had 'adventured' (i.e. risked) their own money in setting up a school. They hoped to make money from the pupils' fees.

Industrial Schools. These were for the very poor, gave practical teaching in subjects like carpentry and sewing. After 1841 'ragged' schools developed along very similar lines.

Factory Schools. The 1833 Factory Act encouraged the development of these. Many children went to them for half a day and worked during the rest of the day.

Sunday Schools. They developed to teach Christian belief. Children were often taught to read so that they could study the Bible.

Endowed Schools. Wealthy people occasionally left money so that a school could be set up, e.g. Heriots in Edinburgh and Robert Gordon's in Aberdeen.

Monitorial Schools. These were the work of Andrew Bell. Bell believed older pupils (monitors) once instructed by their teacher, could then teach younger children. Schools at Cupar and St Andrews (i.e. Madras College) began in this way.

Mechanics Institutes. By 1851 there were 55, with 12 000 members. They encouraged working people to come to lectures and to study in their libraries.

Some Scots were proud of their country's educational arrangements. In 1855 the introduction of the civil registration of births, deaths and marriages meant that people had to show, when filling in the forms, if they could read and write. This event showed 89% of men and 79% of women could cope. (In England only 70% of men and 59% of women were able to reach the necessary standard of literacy.) People educated in Scotland played an important part in British life. The *Edinburgh Review* was one of Britain's most important journals, in the early nineteenth century, indeed one of the magazine's founders, Henry Brougham, went on to lead a campaign in England to provide education for all children.

FREE ST. MARK'S CONGREGATIONAL SCHOOL,

ADJOINING THE NEW CHURCH,

MAIN STREET, ANDERSTON,

Will be RE-OPENED on TUESDAY, the 22d current, at Ten a.m., when Pupils may be admitted into the following Classes, viz.:---

	PER QUARTER.
Reading,	2s. 0d.
Reading, Writing, and Geography,	3s. 0d.
Reading, Writing. Geography, and Arithmetic,	3s. 6d.
Reading, Writing, Geography, Arithmetic, and Grammar,	4s. 0d.
Book-keeping, Latin, and Mathematics,	7s. 0d.

The Deacons' Court, under whose immediate superintendence this Institution is conducted, have great pleasure in recommending to the Inhabitants of Anderston and neighbourhood, the School, and its excellent and experienced Teacher, Mr. FLETCHER, and can assure such Parents and Guardians as may entrust their Children to Mr. FLETCHER'S care, that no effort will be wanting on his part to communicate to his Pupils a first-rate Secular and sound Scriptural Education.

ANDERSTON, July 18, 1850.   *Printed in the Scottish Guardian Office.*

Mechanics' Institution.

Yet many people were not happy with the situation. Between 1854 and 1869 there were five attempts to get bills through Parliament to create a state-financed system of education not tied to any religious group. All failed, even though in 1854 two-thirds of Scots MPs were in favour of the change. In the end, Scotland was swept along by changes in England where demands for reform finally led to an Education Act in 1870.

Source 4.36 ——————

Increasing state interference

1833 The government declared it was prepared to grant money to set up new schools.

1839 An Education Committee of the Privy Council took charge of education. Inspectors visited schools to see if they deserved help with paying for salaries and buildings.

1846 Pupil teachers were introduced. Older pupils could choose to stay on at school, help teachers, study for examinations, and go on to training colleges to qualify as teachers.

1861–2 The Revised Code introduced an annual examination of pupils that would decide how much money a school would receive. It concentrated on reading, writing and arithmetic.

It led to an outcry in Scotland since it neglected other 'higher' subjects. Part of it was suspended while an enquiry – the Argyll Commission – investigated education in Scotland.

1872 *Education Act*

1. The Committee of the Privy Council on Education in Scotland was in overall charge. It worked, in detail, through the Scotch Education Department, based in London, and a feeble organisation.

2. 1872–8 a Board of Education helped set the Act into operation.

3. Local administration was carried out by 984 school boards looking after areas generally the same as existing parishes and burghs.

4. The Board members were elected.

5. Parish burgh and any other public schools were to be handed over to the Boards unless religious organisations (e.g. Roman Catholics) wanted to keep their own schools open.

6. The Boards had to survey their districts to see what needed to be done. They could appoint and dismiss teachers, decide on school fees and salaries. They received money from the government.

7. Parents had 'to provide elementary education in reading, writing and arithmetic for their children between 5 and 13'. School boards had to see this was done and appoint an officer to report on parents who failed in this duty, i.e. education was compulsory.

8. Boards could develop 'higher' schools teaching Latin, Greek, Mathematics, Modern Languages and Natural Science. Such schools got no state or local authority help. (1878 Boards were allowed to use rates money to maintain the buildings of higher schools.)

Source 4.37 ——————

School in Clydebank opened in 1868

'*Investigating our schools*'

If you had been asked to produce a report on Scottish schools and what should be done about them, in 1870, you would have gathered all sorts of evidence. People's memories of schooling would have been helpful, so would the reports of enquiries like the Argyll Commission. The following sources include evidence from which to make up your report. The sources you have already looked at will also be helpful.

(i) Read through all the following sources to see what you can list about the subjects, the hours, the fees. (K.U)

(ii) What were pupil teachers and teachers like? What sort of children might become pupil teachers? (E.2)

(iii) Is the education system properly managed by the government? List any points that will help you answer this. (K.U)

(iv) Are all children going to school? If not, why not? Is the education children are receiving satisfactory? (K.U)

(v) Look back at the 1872 Act. Consider what it actually did. Now write your own views on what sort of reforms you think are needed. (E.2)

In the early 1870s a report on Glasgow children looked at the education of poorer children. The report concluded:

Source 4.38

The parents are of the class who do not in the least care to have their children at school. Besides, many of the children have no parents. Those who have charge of them can hardly be persuaded to send them to the evening school. They will often in preference send them out to beg, to sell matches or blacking or evening newspapers, or, it may be, to pilfer and steal. In a word, scarcely any of the parents of tobacco children care a rush for schools or educa-tion. The wages earned are from 1s. to 3s. 6d. [5p–17p] a week. Their work is pretty easy and regular, from six in the morning till six at night, with two hours for meals. The day-schools in the district are seriously affected by the tobacco-works. It is no uncommon thing, on a Monday morning especially, for the chil-dren on their way to school, as they pass by the tobacco-shops, to ask if any boys are wanted by the journeymen. If there is a de-mand the supply is at once forthcoming, and for weeks or months the children are absent from school

(James Greig and Thomas Harvey, *Report on the State of Education in Glasgow* (1866) in Whyte & Berry, *Glasgow Observed*)

By 1870 even some politicians who had been against a big reform in education were thinking again. One of them was Robert Lowe. He said:

Source 4.39

I suppose it will be absolutely necessary to educate our masters. I was opposed to central-isation [of education]: I am now ready to accept centralisation. I was opposed to an education rate: I am now ready to accept one. From the moment you entrust the masses with power their education becomes a necessity. You have placed the government of this country in the hands of the masses and you must therefore give them an education

(Hansard)

The regulations setting out who could be a pupil teacher show the sort of qualities the authorities wanted:

Source 4.40

At 13 years of age pupil teachers must be able to:

(i) Read with fluency, ease and expression.
(ii) Write in a neat hand, with correct spelling and punctuation, a simple prose narrative read to them.
(iii) Write from dictation the first four rules of arithmetic. Work them correctly, know the table of weights and measures.
(iv) Point out the parts of speech in a simple sentence.
(v) Have an elementary knowledge of geography.

(vi) Demonstrate satisfactory religious knowledge.

(vii) Teach a junior class to the satisfaction of the Inspector.

(viii) Girls should be able to sew neatly and knit.

A number of people who visited, or were pupils at schools, wrote about their experiences. A former Stirling High School pupil remembered:

Source 4.41 _____

I think that much of the time devoted to the ancient languages might have been more profitably devoted to acquiring a knowledge of French or German. History, too, was most imperfectly taught and of science we had practically nothing.

The crowded ill-ventilated rooms, the constant hum and confusion of half a dozen classes being instructed at the same time, was a condition not calculated to improve a naturally irritable temper in a master and it is not to be wondered at if the tawse or cane was laid on with energy.

(A. Bain, *Education in Stirlingshire*, 1965)

The following are all extracts from the Argyll Commission's reports. The first deals with schools in country areas:

Source 4.42 _____

If teachers would only educate their pupils and bring out what is in their minds and teach them to take pleasure and amusement in their lessons, instead of pouring a quantity of knowledge in upon them which they forget as soon as they leave school and which they are too young to find interesting, it would be a great step towards a higher state of education.

The Argyll Commissioners looked at adventure schools:

Source 4.43 _____

The adventure school is maintained wholly upon the wages paid by the pupils. The teacher undergoes no trial of his qualifications. His teaching embraces such branches of knowledge as he may himself think fit to offer. His school is occasionally visited by the clergyman of the parish.

The Commission took a general look at the whole educational system and observed:

Source 4.44 _____

At present there is no competent authority to initiate, administer or to superintend. Schools spring up where they are not required and there are no schools where they are required. The buildings may be good or they may be unsuitable. The school apparatus may be adequate or there may not be a bench to write at or a blackboard or map throughout a whole district. The teachers may be good or they may be utterly incompetent. The children may attend school or they may not attend but grow up in absolute ignorance.

(Bain, *Education in Stirlingshire*)

Universities

Early nineteenth-century Scotland had universities in Glasgow, Edinburgh, Aberdeen and St Andrews. An investigation of 1826 found there:

Source 4.45 _____

Students of every variety and description; men advanced in life, who attend some of the classes for amusement, or in order to recall the studies of early years, or to improve themselves in professional education, originally interrupted; or persons engaged in the actual occupations of business, who expect to derive aid in their pursuits from the new applications of Science to the Arts; or young men not intended for any learned profession, or even going through any regular course of University Education, but sent for one or more years to College, in order to carry their education farther than that of the schools, before they are engaged in the pursuits of trade or of commerce. And all persons may attend any of the classes, in whatever order or manner may suit their different views and prospects. The system of instruction, by a course of elaborate lectures on the different branches of Science and Philosophy, continued daily for a period of six months, is admirably calculated to answer all the objects which such persons may have in view, as well as to afford much useful instruction to regular Students.

(In R. D. Anderson, *Educational Opportunity in Victorian Scotland*, 1983)

Marischal College, Aberdeen

Some pupils from parish schools managed to reach university, helped by the bursaries which were offered to a minority of students to help pay for their fees. Other students came from burgh schools. The main method of teaching was by lecturing: the lecturers were directly paid their fees by the students. Students could study subjects like Latin, Greek, mathematics, logic, moral philosophy and natural philosophy. By this time both Edinburgh and Glasgow had medical schools and teaching in law, chemistry and botany was developing too. Students did not have to pass an examination to enter university and many did not bother to graduate at the end of their course. Even for those who did a certificate of attendance was enough, except in Glasgow.

But universities were having to think about changing. Lyon Playfair, Professor of Chemistry at Edinburgh in 1858, argued that universities must respond to:

Source 4.47

. . . a changed civilisation, which has resulted from three main causes. These are, the rapid advance of science and its numerous applications to industrial life; the free and constant intercommunication of peoples; and the liberalisation of political institutions . . . The youth of our country cannot chain itself to the past, and see the modern stream of thought and action flow swiftly past them. Unless our universities go with the stream, by fitting themselves to the changed requirements of modern society, need they be astonished if society soon get accustomed to look upon them as monuments of a past age?

(Anderson, *Educational Opportunity in Victorian Scotland*)

Scottish universities also had to take account of the introduction of examinations as a way of entering some parts of the Civil Service. The examinations tested literature and history as well as the classics. In 1858 an Act of Parliament reformed the universities. In future they were to be governed by courts led by rectors and including the university principal and assessors chosen by former graduates. Edinburgh's principal believed:

Source 4.48

. . . an entrance examination for the Universities of Scotland is an absolute necessity. The Universities have arrived at a certain pitch of excellence, and they never can advance beyond that without an entrance examination. The schools are in a very usettled and inferior condition, especially the secondary schools, and they can never be improved until an entrance examination is instituted. I think that all persons who know the Universities will agree in this.

(Anderson, *Educational Opportunity in Victorian Scotland*)

Now the universities reorganised their courses, offered entrance examinations and four-year courses leading to degrees.

QUESTIONS

1 List as many reasons for reforming universities as you can find in the above section. (K.U)

2 Which do you think was the most important reason? Explain your answer. (E.2)

Leisure

Most Scots had very long working days and only Sundays wholly free from work. In the 1870s many of them began to get a Saturday afternoon off work, too. Many people were better off by 1880 than the workers of the 1830s. This meant that more of them had time to enjoy a little leisure. For the better off there were even more opportunities. Not only did they have more money, most well-to-do ladies did not work. They needed to find ways to fill their time.

Source 4.50

A street musician

Source 4.49

A musical evening in a wealthy Glasgow home

Children played various games, like these remembered by William Simpson:

Source 4.51

Our games were 'hide and seek' and 'robbers and rangers'. Other games were rounders and 'housie' which was rounders played without a bat. We threw the ball and then ran round the stones forming the 'stations'. We also played cricket, 'bools' – the Scotch word for marbles. 'Peevor' was the girls' game – what is known in England as hopscotch. I was adept at most lassies' games. The 'jumping rope' or 'skipping rope' I was perfect at.

(In Whyte & Berry, *Glasgow Observed*)

Working-class areas contained 'penny theatres' like this one in Glasgow.

Source 4.52

Penny Theatres, half darkened, were crammed every half hour from 10 till 10, with unkept Hizzies, with whom every filthy Joke and Liberty was taken – while coarse Puns and Waggery from the Stage fortified the Depravity which was being carried out. Shameless, pimple-skinned Jades displayed themselves half nude, and capered and kicked up behind and before – ran upon their toes and stood and spinned upon one leg.

(Cage, *The Working Class in Glasgow*)

Until 1843 major theatres in towns and cities often had a monopoly of drama. In that year this monopoly ended.

By the 1870s, new theatres were being built. All sorts of plays, circus acts and spectacular entertainments flourished.

Church leaders and some city leaders did not like the cheaper theatres. They worked to close down the 'penny theatres'. Towns and cities also contained 'free and easies'. A 'free and easy' was a public house with a room where people could gather to be organised for singing by a chairman. Travelling animal shows and waxworks were also popular. So, too, were places like these described in the *North British Daily* in 1871:

Source 4.54

Glasgow literally swarms with cheap, low dancing places, where the youths of both sexes among the lower ranks of society meet regularly once or twice a week to dance, drink and enjoy themselves . . . these dancing parties are got up on the club system. A number of lads in a factory or mill club together to hire a room from ninepence [3.5p] to one and sixpence [7p] a night, if possible in a public house, if not in any building where a room can be had cheaply. They meet . . . every Friday and each brings a partner or partners with them. The music is, if possible, for economic reasons supplied by themselves, there being generally one or two in the society able to play the violin, or failing that the flute or whistle. I have even known cases where a jews harp or trump was the only instrument, and one in (when someone provided) dance music with his lips alone.

(Cage, *The Working Class in Glasgow*)

Source 4.53

A Penny Theatre in Albion Street, Aberdeen

The railways meant that more people could go on day trips (or longer holidays if they were wealthy). In Glasgow there were also trips by paddle steamer from the 1870s. One of these vessels – *The Ivanhoe* – specialised in trips for teetotallers. The leaders of society approved of this entertainment! They were less happy about the large fairs that occasionally took place, especially the fair on Glasgow Green.

Source 4.55

Tom Morris, first winner of the British Open Championship, among professional golfers on Leith Links, 1867

Organised sport emerged during these years. In 1867 Queen's Park Football Club was set up. In 1868 the club secretary wrote to opponents:

Source 4.56

Dear Sir – I have now been requested by the Committee, on behalf of our Club, to accept of the Challenge you kindly sent, for which we have to thank you, to play us a friendly Match at Football on our Ground, Queen's Park, at the hour you mentioned, on Saturday, first proximo, with Twenty players on each side. We consider, however, that Two-hours is quite long enough to play in weather such as the present, and hope this will be quite satisfactory to you. We would also suggest that if no Goals be got by either side within the first hour, that Goals be then exchanged, the ball, of course, to be kicked off from the centre of the field by the side who had the original Kick-off, so that both parties may have the same chance of wind

and ground, this we think very fare and can be arranged on the field before beginning the Match. Would you also be good enough to bring your ball with you in case of any break down, and thus prevent interruption. Hoping the weather will favour the Thistle and Queen's.

> I remain,
> Yours very truly,
> Robt. Garner, Secy.

(Kevin McCarra, *Scottish Football: A Pictorial History*, 1984)

In this year Ayr and Partick Thistle were formed. By 1872 Rangers and Third Lanark had been set up, a year later Hearts were established and in 1875 Hibernians formed.

Scots also enjoyed going to horse races. Betting shops flourished until an act of 1853 in England was extended to Scotland in 1874. This law banned working-class betting shops. There were boxing matches to go to, too – one bare fist fight in 1825 lasted for 44 rounds! To try and lure people from public houses the temperance societies organised concerts, lectures and evening classes and a Band of Hope organisation for children. For those who could afford it there was plenty of entertainment on offer to fill leisure hours.

QUESTIONS

1 How many sports could people enjoy at this time? (K.U)

2 How do the children's games then compare with today's? Are any the same? (E.2)

3 In what ways and for what reasons did leisure activities change at this time? (E.2)

4 Do you think the author of source 4.52 approved of penny theatres? Give reasons for your answer. (E.1)

5 Why do you think Glasgow workers were so eager to support places like those described in source 4.54? (E.2)

6 In what ways has football changed since source 4.58 was written? (E.2)

Troubled Times – 1880s–1939

5 The Changing Economy

If you study this picture you will find evidence that it comes from the late Victorian period.

In 1888 Glasgow was one of the most important cities in the vast British Empire of the times. Around three-quarters of a million people lived in the city. In, and around it, were iron and steel foundries, engineering workshops and shipyards that produced so much of what was needed by customers throughout the world. The Exhibition celebrated

Between 1880 and 1939 great changes took place in Scotland in the kinds of work available for people to do. Some of these changes came about because of developments in Scotland and Britain, others were due to events in the wider world that made an impact on life in this country. The sources in these chapters deal with these changes. Work through them to gather information about the Scottish economy and why it changed.

Source 5.1

the importance of Glasgow and of the whole of Scotland. 5.75 million people visited it. Queen Victoria herself paused on her way to her Scottish home at Balmoral to tour the Exhibition. Tourists and businessmen poured into Glasgow to see the Exhibition's displays of art and science, of ingenious inventions (including 'Royle's Self-Pouring Teapot') and solid engineering. The work of around 40 Clydeside shipyards was especially prominent. The new magic of electric light provided one of the wonders of the Exhibition.

Yet there was little that was really new to be seen there. The River Kelvin wound attractively through the Exhibition site – yet West Glasgow's sewage had to be stopped from flowing into it for as long as the Exhibition was open. The Glasgow Exhibition of 1888 celebrated wonderful Scottish achievements: but it took place at a time when much remained to be done to improve life in Scotland and when all sorts of forces were at work that were to shake the leading world position enjoyed by Scottish industry.

The Scottish People

Some of the features of the changing economy can be seen in figures showing how many people lived in Scotland and which parts of the country they chose to live in.

Source 5.2

The Scottish population

1881	3 735 573
1901	4 472 103
1921	4 882 497
1931	4 842 980
1939	5 006 689

(Census, Scotland 1971)

Source 5.3

The population of major cities

	Aberdeen	Edinburgh and Leith	Dundee	Glasgow
1881	105 000	295 000	140 000	587 000
1901	154 000	394 000	161 000	762 000
1921	159 000	420 000	168 000	1 034 000
1931	170 000	439 000	176 000	1 088 000

(B. R. Mitchell and P. Deane, *Abstract of British Historical Statistics*, 1962)

Source 5.4

In 1881 48.9% of Scotland's people lived in towns and cities (i.e. places of over 5000 people)

In 1901 57.6% lived in towns and cities

In 1921 61.3% lived in towns and cities

In 1939 63.4% lived in towns and cities

(Flinn, *Scottish Population History*)

Source 5.5

Numbers of Scots who moved to other parts of the UK

1881–91	90 711
1891–1901	98 210
1901–11	68 177
1911–21	63 069
1921–31	77 769

(Flinn, *Scottish Population History*)

Source 5.6

Emigration overseas of people of Scottish origin

1880	22 056	1918	1 088
1888	35 873	1920	46 523
1894	14 432	1923	86 584
1902	26 265	1929	42 911
1907	66 355	1931	5 866
1910	79 784	1938	4 474

QUESTIONS

1 Around what time does the growth of Scotland's population start to slow down? (K.U)

2 Which Scottish city grew at the fastest rate between 1881 and 1931? (K.U)

3 Between 1891 and 1931, which Scottish counties experienced a fall in population? (K.U)

4 Look at the sort of areas these counties seem to be. Can you suggest any possible reasons why population in them might have fallen? (E.2)

5 The sources suggest people leaving these areas went to three sorts of destinations. What were they? (K.U)

6 Notice how the figures in source 5.7 vary. Can you think of any possible reasons for this? (E.2)

Source 5.7

Counties (including all Burghs)	Population				
	1891	1901	1911	1921	1931
SCOTLAND	4 025 647	4 472 103	4 760 904	4 882 497	4 842 980
Aberdeen	281 332	304 439	312 177	301 016	300 436
Angus	277 788	284 082	281 417	271 052	270 190
Argyll	75 003	73 642	70 902	76 862	63 050
Ayr	226 283	254 468	268 337	299 273	285 217
Banff	64 190	61 488	61 402	57 298	54 907
Berwick	32 406	30 824	29 643	28 246	26 612
Bute	18 404	18 787	18 186	33 711	18 823
Caithness	37 177	33 870	32 010	28 285	25 656
Clackmannan	28 432	32 029	31 121	32 542	31 948
Dumbarton	94 495	113 865	139 831	150 861	147 744
Dumfries	74 221	72 571	72 825	75 370	81 047
East Lothian	37 485	38 665	43 254	47 487	47 338
Fife	187 346	218 837	267 733	292 925	276 368
Inverness	89 317	90 104	87 272	82 455	82 108
Kincardine	35 647	40 923	41 008	41 779	39 865
Kinross	6 280	6 981	7 527	7 963	7 454
Kirkcudbright	39 985	39 383	38 367	37 155	30 341
Lanark	1 046 040	1 339 327	1 447 034	1 539 442	1 586 047
Midlothian	434 159	488 796	507 666	506 377	526 296
Moray	43 453	44 800	43 427	41 558	40 806
Nairn	10 019	9 291	9 319	8 790	8 294
Orkney	30 453	28 699	25 897	24 111	22 077
Peebles	14 761	15 066	15 258	15 332	15 051
Perth	126 184	123 283	124 342	125 503	120 793
Renfrew	290 798	268 980	314 552	298 904	288 586
Ross and Cromarty	77 810	76 450	77 364	70 818	62 799
Roxburgh	53 741	48 804	47 192	44 989	45 788
Selkirk	27 353	23 356	24 601	22 607	22 608
Stirling	125 608	142 291	160 991	161 719	166 447
Sutherland	21 896	21 440	20 179	17 802	16 101
West Lothian	52 808	65 711	80 161	83 962	81 431
Wigtown	36 062	32 685	31 998	30 783	29 331
Zetland	28 711	28 166	27 911	25 520	21 421

People at Work

Refer back to source 1.8. It lists the main types of work employing Scots in 1881. Compare this with the following source.

N.B.: No. IV = people who made gas, and by-products from coal

No. XX = workers in rubber, bone, horn, celluloid

No. XXI = musical instrument makers, vehicle and shipmakers not already entered as metal or woodworkers, and makers of dental and surgical instruments

No. XXIII = shop owners, shop assistants, salesmen

No. XXVII = chiefly domestic servants (138 679 women and 44 543 men) as well as inn and hotel staff, cleaners, hairdressers and laundry workers

No. XXXI = foremen, timekeepers, watchmen, firemen.

Source 5.8

Year 1931 / Different types of occupations in Scotland	Males				Females			
		OUT OF WORK				OUT OF WORK		
	TOTALS IN OCCUPATION	Total	Per cent. of total in that job	Per cent. of total Out of Work	TOTALS IN OCCUPATION	Total	Per cent. of total in that job	Per cent. of total Out of Work
I Fishermen	18 472	3 111	16.8	1.1	2	—	—	—
II Agricultural Occupations	164 965	6 648	4.0	2.4	15 746	876	5.6	1
III Mining and Quarrying Occupations	124 026	30 514	24.6	10.8	1 227	307	25.0	0
IV Workers in Non-Metalli-ferous Mine and Quarry Products	1 780	128	7.2	0.0	42	13	31.0	0
V Makers of Bricks, Pottery etc	5 108	1 095	21.4	0.4	1 507	365	24.2	0
VI Workers in Chemical Processes	4 589	601	13.1	0.2	1 081	189	17.5	0
VII Metal Workers (not Precious Metals)	189 129	60 644	32.1	21.4	4 610	820	17.8	1
VIII Workers in Precious Metals	813	95	11.7	0.0	130	15	11.5	0
IX Electrical Apparatus Makers: Electricians	16 884	2 497	14.8	0.9	299	36	12.0	0
X Makers of Watches, etc	2 357	266	11.3	0.1	99	4	4.0	0
XI Leather Workers, Leather Goods Makers	3 669	523	14.3	0.2	1 290	216	16.7	0
XII Textile Workers	28 378	5 716	20.1	2.0	81 668	18 497	22.6	24
XIII Makers of Textile Goods, Dress, etc	20 791	2 632	12.7	0.9	39 102	3 610	9.2	4
XIV Makers of Foods, etc.	28 780	3 786	13.2	1.3	16 908	5 278	31.2	7
XV Workers in Wood and Furniture	62 102	12 093	19.5	4.3	1 604	193	12.0	0
XVI Paper, etc., Workers: Bookbinders	7 061	413	5.8	0.1	9 646	1 010	10.5	1
VII Printers and Photographers	13 007	1 175	9.0	0.4	5 158	571	11.1	0
XVIII Workers in Stone: Builders etc	64 664	9 849	15.2	3.5	45	6	13.3	0
XIX Painters, Decorators	21 875	2 833	13.0	1.0	3 213	705	21.9	0
XX Workers in Other Materials	5 404	799	14.8	0.3	4 219	557	13.2	0
XXI Workers in Mixed or Undefined Materials	9 789	3 422	35.0	1.2	500	44	8.8	0
XXII Workers in Transport and Communication	182 178	26 138	14.3	9.2	13 308	1 052	7.9	1
XXIII Commercial Occupations (excluding Clerks)	151 467	10 483	6.9	3.7	95 915	7 593	7.9	10
XXIV Public Administration (excluding Clerks) and Defence Occupations	19 346	212	1.1	0.1	389	8	2.1	0
XXV Professional Occupations (excluding Clerks)	45 580	1 066	2.3	0.4	48 876	1 528	3.1	2
XXVI Entertainments and Sports Occupations	9 356	1 429	15.3	0.5	1 435	336	23.4	0
XXVII Personal Service Occupations	43 630	5 452	12.5	1.9	194 999	18 684	9.6	25
XXVIII Clerks, etc (including Civil Service and Local Authority)	69 272	5 246	7.6	1.9	77 451	4 034	5.2	
XXIX Warehousemen, Packers, etc	23 069	3 143	13.6	1.1	14 767	1 740	11.8	2
XXX Stationary Engine Drivers etc	20 937	4 068	19.4	1.4	49	4	8.2	0
XXXI Other and Undefined Workers	183 775	77 321	42.1	27.3	23 772	6 019	25.3	8
Total	1 542 253	283 398	18.4	100.0	659 057	74 310	11.3	100

The census of 1931 was differently organised from the one in 1881, but you should be able to make comparisons. Notice too that source 5.8 includes the numbers of people who are out of work.

QUESTIONS

1 Compare 1881 (source 1.8) and 1931 (source 5.8) to list:
   a) jobs that have become less important;
   b) jobs that have become more important. (K.U)

2 Look at source 5.8 to list:
   a) the three jobs that had the biggest numbers of people out of work;
   b) the three jobs that had the highest percentage out of work. (K.U)

3 Behind the changes in jobs and the numbers of people with no jobs, lay a number of reasons. The sources that follow explore these reasons. Look through them to:
   a) list all the reasons you can find; (K.U)
   b) explain which you think are the most serious; (E.2)
   c) describe how the author of any one source has tried to use words and pictures to stir up people to take action; (E.1)
   d) use the information you build up to write a report to send to the Prime Minister, in the thirties, explaining what you think is wrong and what you believe should be done. (E.2)

Source 5.9

British merchants have so far failed to adapt themselves to the change going on all around them from monopoly to competition. It pains and surprises them to find that the goods they offer, though acknowledged to be superior are not preferred by the foreign purchaser to the inferior goods offered by their upstart rivals. The purchaser humbly suggests that the article they offer is not exactly to his taste. 'Take it or leave it,' they haughtily answer, 'if you don't know a good British article when you see it, that's your lookout.' The British merchant produces and scatters . . . the most beautifully printed and illustrated catalogues of his goods. But they are printed in a language which the foreigner does not understand, the weights and measures are given in denominations he has never heard of, the prices are quoted in a currency which he cannot readily convert to his own, and they rarely include the cost of freight, duty, and delivery to his own port or railway station. The British merchant, by comparison with his German rival, employs very few commercial travellers abroad, and those he does employ too often speak no language but their own. He despises small orders, and he is uncompromising in the matter of granting credit facilities.

(*The Times*, Leader, 14 November 1898)

Source 5.10

CAUGHT NAPPING!

Source 5.11
Facts and figures

(i) Britain's share of world trade in manufactures
1899 – 33.2%   1913 – 30.2%   1929 – 22.9%
1937 – 21.3%

(ii) British earnings from investments abroad
1880 – £57 millions   1990 – £103 millions
1930 – £220 millions

(iii) In 1922 British cotton exports were ½ those of 1913

In 1922 British coal exports were $\frac{1}{3}$ those of 1913

(iv) British cotton yarn output 1913 – 1982 million pounds [453.6 tonnes] of thread
British cotton yarn output 1930 – 1000 million pounds of thread

(v) British coal production in 1913 – 287 million tons
USA coal production in 1913 – 500 million tons
British coal production in 1931 – 220 million tons

(vi) 1913 Britain produced 10.3 million tons of pig iron
1913 USA produced 31 million tons of pig iron
1913 Germany produced 16.5 million tons of pig iron
Annual output per man in the pig iron industry in the 1900s – Britain 380 tons
Annual output per man in the pig iron industry – USA 599 tons.

(vii) In Britain one operative controlled 4 looms in the cotton industry.
In the USA one operative controlled 20 looms in the cotton industry.

(viii) 1914, Britain possessed just one ball-bearing factory and depended almost wholly on German imports.
90% of optical glass used in instrument manufacture came from Germany.
75% of glass bulbs and tubing for electric lights came from Germany and Austria.

A Royal Commission that investigated technical education in 1900 found that on the Continent there were successful technical evening classes as well as polytechnics:

Source 5.12 ——————————————
. . . the evening science teaching was conducted by professors of higher standing than, and of superior scientific attainments to, the ordinary science teachers who conduct courses in some of the most important of the manufacturing centres of this country. In the case of machine construction, the models and materials for instruction were superior to those found in similar schools at home.

To the multiplication of these polytechnics . . . may be ascribed the general [spread] of a high scientific knowledge in Germany, and the supply of men to take the place of managers and superintendents of industrial works.

In Britain, there is still a great want of this last class of persons . . . In some branches of industry, more especially in those requiring an intimate acquaintance with organic chemistry, as, for instance, in the preparation of artificial colours from coal tar, Germany has unquestionably taken the lead . . .

Your commissioners cannot repeat too often that they have been impressed with the general intelligence and technical knowledge of the masters and managers of industrial establishments on the Continent.

By the late nineteenth century, many people noticed, wrote about and worried about the growing volume of foreign imports that poured into Britain.

In 1904 a report by a group of experts looked for other difficulties facing Britain. It suggested:

Source 5.13 ——————————————
The methods of production, first established in the United Kingdom, have since 1870 extended to foreign countries; and these countries have encouraged national industries similar to those carried on here; thus foreign manufacturers have obtained growing home markets, from which British products have been shut out by import duties. In recent years their policy has been directed to the capture of the home, foreign and colonial trade of the United Kingdom. By attacking our home market, which is open to them without let or hindrance, they have diminished the competitive power of British manufacturers in neutral markets, and they are now threatening our position in British Colonies.

Manufacturers in this country are blamed because they do not show greater enterprise in laying down large capacity plants, such as are common in the United States and in Germany. Some American furnaces, with complete equipment, cost over £200 000 each, whereas the average cost of British furnaces is not probably over £25 000.

British engineers, on visiting American workshops, have been surprised to see so few men about. Automatic machinery is much more largely used there than in this country. The combination of up-to-date plants, economies, and improvements has enabled our American rivals, paying the highest wages known in the trade, to produce plates at a cost of only about 3s. 6d. [17p] per ton for labour, averaging some 225 tons of plates per shift. These results are not equalled in our own mills

(*Report of the Tariff Commission*, 1904, in P. Lane, *Documents on British Economic and Social History*)

The period 1880 to 1939 included times of especial difficulty. From 1914 to 1918 a terrible conflict – the First World War – drew into it huge quantities of British resources and vast numbers of men and women. British traders lost many of their overseas markets, foreign competitors who played a minor part in the War, compared to Britain (such as Japan and the USA) or no part at all (such as the Scandinavian countries) were able to expand their exports at Britain's expense. Britain's older industries produced as much as possible in wartime, instead of modernising and reorganising. This left them in poor shape to fight for a share of peacetime world trade. Moreover, this world trade suffered a very serious collapse between 1929 and 1933.

World trade shrank 35% in these years following the failure of banks and companies in the American 'Wall Street Crash'. Many countries now protected their own economies with high taxes on imports. A Royal Commission reported in 1932:

Source 5.14 ────────────────

The causes of the depression in the industries of exceptional unemployment are easy to understand. There is the class of industry which is still suffering from a war-time expansion in excess of normal peace-time requirements . . . In this class fall iron and steel, shipbuilding and certain branches of engineering, and to some extent, coal mining. There is the class of industry that before the war was dependent to a great extent on exports, and that has suffered since the war a loss of part of its overseas markets, coupled in some cases with an invasion by imports of its home market. This is the largest class.

(*Report of the Royal Commission on Unemployment*, 1932)

Government Policies

Between 1880 and 1939 British governments considered what to do about the problems of the economy. For many years the country's leaders remained convinced that the government ought not to interfere.

Source 5.15 ────────────────

By the early twentieth century, the Conservative Party contained people who did not agree with this Liberal support for free trade. The leader of these 'tariff reformers' was Joseph Chamberlain. In a 1903 speech he explained why he thought foreign imports should be taxed and Britain should try to boost her trade with the Empire:

Source 5.16 ────────────────

You want an Empire. Do you think it better to cultivate the trade with your own people or to let that go in order that you may keep the trade of those who, rightly enough, are your competitors and rivals? . . . we should insist that while we seek free trade between ourselves and all the nations of the world, we will nevertheless recover our freedom, resume that power of negotiation, and, if necessary, retaliation, whenever our own interests or our relations between our colonies and ourselves are threatened by other people. The time has not yet come to settle it; but it seems to me that for good or evil this is an issue much greater in its consequences than any of our local disputes.

(*The Times*, 16 May 1903)

But it was the First World War that first compelled the government to intervene in managing the economy. In 1916 David Lloyd George became Prime Minister. He pointed out:

Source 5.17 ————————————————

a) We are fighting against the best organised community in the world and we have been employing too much the haphazard leisurely go-as-you please methods which, believe me, would not have enabled us to maintain our place as a nation even in peace very much longer.

(Quoted in C. Barnett, *The Collapse of British Power*, 1972)

On another occasion he commented that, before the War:

b) Agriculture was almost completely neglected by the State. During recent years very, very little was done – more, perhaps, than used to be, but very little. It was just like feeding a giant with a teaspoon. In 1913, £300 000 000 worth of the products of the soil were imported from abroad which could have been produced here.

The government increased taxes. In 1914 only 1.2 million paid income tax and the tax was a mere 6d (2.5p) in the pound. By the end of the War 7.8 million paid the tax – which was now 30d (15p) in the pound. Moreover, the government introduced a tax of $33\frac{1}{3}$% on certain imports such as cars, cycles and clocks. The government took control of the coal industry and railways, it allocated space in shipping. In 1917 it gave a guaranteed level of grain prices. But would the War convert the government to playing a bigger part in managing the peacetime economy? By 1918 a Ministry of Reconstruction was at work planning a better post-war Britain. But, by

1921 to 1922 the British economy was in trouble. Low levels of exports, especially, led to a great deal of unemployment. The government responded by cutting its spending, handing back the re-organised railways to four big private companies, and abandoning its policy of supporting farmers against foreign competition. It turned down a proposal to nationalise the coal industry that was put forward by the Sankey Commission (which the government itself had appointed!).

From 1922 onwards, political leaders continued to argue about how best to assist the troubled economy. Then the slump of 1929 to 1933 made it essential to do something. Unemployment rose rapidly, industrial production fell.

Source 5.18 ————————————————
John Maynard Keynes

Lloyd George's Liberals especially argued for the government to do far more. They used the ideas of John Maynard Keynes, a leading economist, and suggested heavy spending on public works like roads. But far too few Liberals were elected in 1929 to make this policy possible. From 1932 Oswald Mosley's British Union of Fascists also urged far more government controls on finance and imports and a great deal more government spending. But the British Union of Fascists stressed the importance of having a great leader and of using force to deal with left wingers: it never really won large-scale support. Falling world trade between 1929 and 1931 split the Labour Government as, once more, cutting government spending was seen as the only answer in a crisis. A few Labour men and some Liberals joined the Conservatives in a new National Government. The government cut the pay of civil servants, teachers and the 'dole' paid to the unemployed. The gold standard was abandoned. In 1932 it introduced protection for certain industries and for farming. The new policy was introduced by the new Chancellor of the Exchequer, Neville Chamberlain, son of Joseph Chamberlain.

Source 5.19

We hope by the use of Protection to encourage our people to render their methods of production and distribution more efficient. We mean also to use it for negotiations with foreign countries which have not hitherto paid very much attention to our suggestions. Last, but not least, we are going to take the opportunity of offering advantages to the countries of the Empire in return for the advantages which they now give, or in the near future may be disposed to give, to us. The basis of our proposals is a duty of 10 per cent. upon all imports into this country, with certain exceptions.

(*Parliamentary Debates*, vol. 261)

The iron and steel industry recovered slowly. The government also organised the Ottawa Conference to encourage trade with the Empire and Commonwealth. Farming, too, benefited from protection. It also obtained extra help from Marketing Boards for milk, eggs, potatoes, bacon and hops. The Boards carried out reorganisation and paid guaranteed prices. By 1937 Scots farmers benefited from guaranteed prices for oats and barley, from restrictions on wheat imports, and from some subsidies. Certain regions – including Scotland – were labelled 'special areas'. In these areas Commissioners used limited amounts of government money to reorganise old industries and develop new ones.

Industries were encouraged to scrap old equipment and merge to make more efficient companies. From 1934, as Britain re-armed to face the threat of Fascist Italy and Nazi Germany; some industries benefited from the orders placed with them by the government.

QUESTIONS

1 What is the point of view of the author of source 5.15? How has the author tried to make his point of view persuasive? (E.1)

2 List all the reasons you can find for and against free trade. (K.U)

3 Explain why the free trade policy was abandoned. (E.2)

The Scottish Experience

During these years Scots shared in the varying fortunes of the British economy. According to the Earl of Elgin, in 1937:

Source 5.20

In the great World Slump which followed the War, Scotland suffered heavily, more heavily than many of her neighbours. The monthly returns of the Ministry of Labour have shown almost consistently a high average of unemployment.

(C. A. Oakley, *Scottish Industry Today*, 1937)

The Earl was introducing a survey of Scottish industry. The survey's author commented:

Source 5.21

There were two outstanding features in the economic life of Scotland during the pre-war years – the large proportion of people employed in the heavy industries and the considerable number of persons emigrating. The proportion in the heavy industries is smaller today. This change has been brought about by a reduced demand for Scottish goods due both to limitations of world trade and to the growth of industry overseas. Scotland's mines, iron works, shipyards, other branches of heavy industry and her jute, linen and cotton factories are unlikely to employ in the future such a high proportion of her workpeople as in the recent past. Her greatest need is, therefore, for new industries.

(Oakley, *Scottish Industry Today*)

The Scottish steel industry faced a lack of good coking coal; few steelworks had blast furnaces nearby; many were too small and were inefficient. The steel firm of Stewarts and Lloyds took the extreme step of abandoning its works near Glasgow and taking most of its workers to a brand new steelworks especially built at Corby in the Midlands of England. Scotland's three remaining major steel firms merged by 1936 in an attempt to become more effective.

Some reforms injured Scottish industry. The merging of the many pre-war private railway companies into four major ones meant Scottish companies were now part of either the London and North Eastern or the London Midland and Scottish Railways. Rolling stock building continued for the moment in Scotland but was under threat of being centralised further south. In the 1920s and 30s Molly Weir lived in Glasgow. Her mother had a job at the Springburn North British Locomotive Company Works. She wrote:

Source 5.22 _____
Springburn depended for its existence on Railways. We children were proud to think that our mothers and fathers had helped to build the wonderful engines. It was a tremendous excitement for us when one of the big locomotives was ready for its journey to the docks, there to be shipped to China or India or some similar far-off land.

(M. Weir, *Shoes were for Sunday*, 1970)

Source 5.24 _____
Locomotive on the way to the docks

Source 5.25 _____

1903	North British Locomotive Co. formed from a merger of three companies
1905	573 engines built
1920	307 engines built
1922	97 engines built
1922–9	183 engines built a year, on average
1933	16 engines built

Source 5.23 _____
The Falkirk Iron Works

The First World War brought temporary relief to Scotland's growing economic worries. Heavy industry picked up wartime orders, indeed almost a quarter of Britain's workers producing military-related goods were to be found in the Clyde area. But by the 1920s many Scottish industries were suffering from the competition of cheap foreign goods and from their own small-scale, labour intensive and poorly managed condition. The £4.9 million spent in Scotland by its Special Areas Commissioner, Sir Hugh Rose, could not seriously alter this situation. Exports worth £53.5 million had flowed from Scottish ports in 1913; £125.6 millions were sent abroad in 1920. By 1933 the figure had collapsed to £29.6 millions.

Source 5.26 ————————————————
Jute workers in a Dundee mill

The Dundee jute industry's fortunes show the problems Scotland faced. During the War demand for goods like sandbags led it to grow rapidly. After the War demand fell and competition – especially from Indian jute mills where wages were far lower than in Dundee – brought depression to the jute industry. By 1932 there were over 37 000 unemployed jute workers in Dundee. Even in 1937 there were still 28 000. Nor could the work of Scotland's cotton industry face up to competition from abroad and from Lancashire. Textiles continued to prosper in Scotland where they

were specialised (like Paisley's thread manufacture) or aimed at wealthy purchasers (like the Borders woollen industry – though even here job numbers fell from 28 000 in 1924 to 24 000 in 1930).

Case Study (i) – Coal in Scotland

Source 5.27 ————————————————

This industry's varying fortunes can be seen through the following figures.

Source 5.27 ————————————————
Coal output in Scotland

1880	18.3 million tons
1900	33.1 million tons
1913	42.5 million tons
1919	32.5 million tons
1926	16.8 million tons
1931	29.1 million tons
1938	30.3 million tons

(Mitchell & Deane, *Abstract of British Historical Statistics*)

Scottish coal lay in Fife, Ayrshire, the Lothians and Lanarkshire. By 1905 the Lanarkshire area faced problems that were described in an official enquiry:

Source 5.28 ————————————————
There is a vast quantity of coal [but] much of it is in seams less advantageously placed than those that have hitherto been worked: it is probable the large export of Lanarkshire coal will gradually cease as the cheaper produced seams get exhausted.

(R. H. Campbell, *The Rise and Fall of Scottish Industry*, 1980)

Before 1914 most coal was cut by hand. New equipment was expensive. It was in the Fife coalfield that companies (like the Fife Coal Company) felt best able to invest in modernising their mines. By 1928 almost 60% of Scottish coal was cut mechanically. Yet the fall in exports of coal, from 1924, hit Fife hard, for nearly a third of its produce was sent abroad. Mine owners tried to meet their difficulties by cutting their costs – including wages. Miners reacted angrily and during the 1920s the industry was repeatedly troubled by serious strikes. The strikes failed to prevent wage cuts, yet these wage cuts did not solve the problems of the industry. Only when demand recovered a little after 1932 did coal's problems begin to diminish.

Coal users had learned to use coal more efficiently. Rival sources of power existed. In 1930 the US Department of Commerce commented on the British coal industry:

Source 5.29 ———————————————
Coal is no longer so supreme as a source of power. Oil and water power have come rapidly to the fore, while invention has made it possible to obtain more power from a given quantity of fuel. Everywhere the growth in demand for coal has been checked. The United Kingdom since the war has lost one third of its former overseas coal market.

(The United Kingdom, An Industrial and Financial
Handbook, 1930)

In 1938 the *Scotsman* reported its concern about:

Source 5.30 ———————————————
. . . the encroachment which continues to be made by our Continental competitors in the export markets. Another feature is the fall in the output per shift worked. In 1935 this amounted to 25.32 cwts [1286 kg] but in 1937 it had fallen to 24.22 cwts [1230 kg]. Strikes have been partly to blame.

(The Scotsman's Trade Review)

The Scottish coal industry's troubles did not end with the thirties.

Case Study (ii) – Shipbuilding in Scotland

Source 5.31 ———————————————

Scottish Shipbuilding outputs		Share of UK output
1882	391 934 tons	28%
1909–13	2 673 000 tons	35.1%
1929–33	1 492 000 tons	39%
1934–38	1 679 000 tons	44.6%

Source 5.32 ———————————————
Fairfield Shipbuilding & Engineering Co. works, c. 1909. The constraints on the maximum size of ships built are obvious

During the years from 1880 to 1920 the Clyde area was one of the world's most important shipbuilding areas. Shipbuilding went on in other places too, but as steam ships replaced sailing ships, so Aberdeen's great clipper vessels were displaced and building them ceased to be worthwhile. Dundee's yards were not helped by the collapse of Dundee's whaling industry. Norwegian rivalry, over-fishing, and the collapse of whale and seal oil prices as mineral oils were developed instead, virtually ended the industry.

But the Clyde area grew between 1870 to 1913. In 1871 a whole new town – Clydebank – emerged when J. & G. Thomson moved their shipyards there from Govan. By 1902 18 000 people lived in Clydebank, John Brown's had taken over Thomson's yards and Beardmore's had established shipbuilding there, too. Harland and Wolff developed yards at Govan (1912), Yarrow moved their naval-building yard from the Thames to Scotstoun. The Clyde seemed to be the centre of inventive ideas and practical skills. A. C. Kirk improved the marine steam engine in 1884, and from 1900

Source 5.34

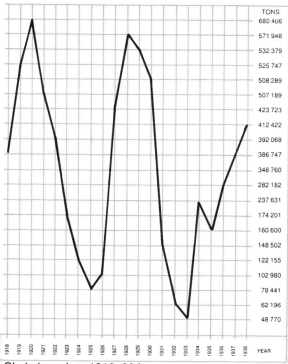

Clyde launches 1918–38 in gross tons

Source 5.33
A Dundee whaler with its catch

Clyde engineers became expert in building the powerful new Parsons steam turbine engines. From the slipways of the area were launched warships, great passenger liners like the *Lusitania*, ferries, dredgers and 'tramp' steamers to carry the world's produce. Orders came from the Empire, from foreign lands, and from British shipping lines. During the First World War, the need to build warships and replace merchant vessels sunk by the Germans, provided plenty of work.

This time of activity made the experience of the years from 1920 to 1939 all the more painful. The contrast seemed so striking. Thomas Bell noticed how the fortunes of the great Clydeside firm of Beardmore's changed:

Source 5.35 ───────────────

With the expansion of imperialism, its ship-building, armaments, etc., Beardmores grew like a mushroom. By the war of 1914 the old puddling process had died out. Electric furnaces, cranes, automatic conveyers and up-to-date methods had wiped out the old conditions. The family concern had become a giant armament ring with its tentacles stretching throughout the minefields and shipyards of the Clyde Valley, and to international concerns. During the Great War over 10 000 workers were employed on munitions and the by-products of the steel plant. It gathered workers from all parts of the country. The village of Parkhead had become a congested cosmopolitan area of many dialects. The economic crash following the close of the War dealt a severe blow to the Beardmore's concern. The works for a time were practically shut down: the poverty and destitution of the workers was unspeakable.

(Thomas Bell, *Pioneering Days*, 1941)

Signs of trouble
(i) Between the Wars the Scottish fishing industry suffered the loss of its East European markets. Few new vessels were needed.
(ii) The Clyde failed to develop its own diesel engines for ships.
(iii) From the 1890s major yards like Brown's & Fairfield's came to depend very heavily on Admiralty orders. Between 1898 to 1913 30 of the 98 ships Fairfield's launched were for the Admiralty. After

1920 there were very few Admiralty orders until the rearmament programme from 1934.
(iv) Brown's also depended on building huge passenger liners. Between 1910 and 1913 they accounted for a quarter of the value of all Brown's launchings. Between the Wars demand for these vessels collapsed.
(v) During the War British yards could not build for export, other countries expanded shipbuilding for their own needs and for export.
(vi) For much of the inter-war period, and especially between 1929 and 1932, world trade was at a low level.
(vii) Rivals like Germany and Japan used subsidies to help their shipbuilding and tariffs to make British ships more expensive.

Source 5.36 ───────────────
A shipyard worker at John Browns

In 1938, Sir Steven Bilsland looked back and said:

Source 5.37 ───────────────
This area over a very long period maintained an organisation to provide warships, etc. Through a change in national policy there was a sudden and complete end of orders, circumstances differing entirely from those of normal ups and down of the trade in which when one market is closed against it an industry endeav-

ours to open another. There was no alternative market . . . The disarmament policy, continued for nearly twenty years after the War, has had a serious effect on the industrial belt.

(Campbell, *The Rise and Fall of Scottish Industry*)

1921, was a time of trade union unrest, the shipyard owner James Lithgow declared:

Source 5.38

Efficient conditions of employment are hopeless when employers are called upon to consult a trade union delegate before an individual workman will agree to work half an hour after the usual stopping time to finish some small but essential job, and where the shift system is surrounded by so many stipulations [rules] as to make it so costly as to preclude the intensive working of the plant.

Why are these absurd obstacles to economy not swept away? Labour clings to these privileges which it has managed to establish in the past.

When labour leaders instruct their members to welcome changes designed to reduce total costs, and to work up to the reasonable capacity of their skill, there will be some real hope of maintaining wages at a higher level.

(*Glasgow Herald*, 1921)

Source 5.39

Constructing the *Queen Mary*

Some improvements took place in the thirties. A government subsidy of £9½ millions helped John Brown's finish work on the Cunard Liner *Queen Mary* and launch the vessel in 1934. In 1938 the yard launched another liner *Queen Elizabeth*. Admiralty orders helped several yards in the late thirties. By then, reorganisation begun in 1930 had closed down a number of yards. In 1938 the *Scotsman's Trade Review* reported:

Source 5.40

Scottish shipbuilding is enjoying a well-deserved spell of activity, a healthy change for the better in world economic conditions developed 2½ years ago. Before this improvement a steady flow of obsolete [out of date] ships had found its way to the shipbreakers. Then came the 'scrap and build' scheme under which two old ships had to be scrapped for each one built with the assistance of Government loans at a low rate of interest. Under this arrangement about 100 vessels were condemned to demolition. One of the most satisfactory features is the amount of tonnage on order for Empire countries.

(*The Scotsmen Trade Review*, 29 April 1938)

Case Study (iii) – Farming

A. G. Bradley visited Scottish farms in the later nineteenth century. He observed changes:

Source 5.41

Suddenly, the grain of the virgin lands from overseas burst upon the country like a flood. Wheat fell rapidly from its old comfortable, consistent figures of fifty [£2.50] and sixty shillings [£3] to thirty [£1.50] odd, with oats and barley to match.

(A. G. Bradley, *When Squires and Farmers Thrived*, 1927)

Investigations by Royal Commissions produced evidence like this:

Source 5.42

(7) *Evidence to the Royal Commission on Agricultural Depression*
1896. Evidence of James Drew, factor to the Earl of Galloway – You have been factor on the Galloway estates for the last 30 years? – I have.

For the last 16 years you have felt the depression more or less severely? – We have.
To what do you ascribe it? – At first to bad seasons, but gradually to foreign competition. The tendency of prices must be downward while the world's productions continue to exceed the world's requirements.
What class of farm has suffered most? – The wheat-growing farms. The fall in the value of wheat having been greater than in other products? – Yes, it is down practically to zero, and it is now impossible to grow wheat at a profit at present prices.
Have the dairy farmers stood the strain comparatively well? – Yes, till this year, when the prospects are not so bright as they have been.
What is the cause of that? – It is owing to the enormous imports of both cheese and butter.
Have they reduced the price of the home-made articles? – Most seriously.
What has been the fall in rents generally in your part of the country? – I put it at 20 per cent, all over, varying according to the different classes of land.

Between 1881 and 1911 the numbers working in agriculture fell by 40 000. The following statistics help to show the kind of farming that suffered most and some of the changes made by Scottish farmers.

Source 5.43
a) Cereal prices per hundredweight

	Wheat	Barley	Oats
1880	10s 5d [52p]	9s 2d [46p]	8s 2d [41p]
1900	6s 5d [32p]	7s 0d [35p]	6s 5d [32p]
1920	19s 0d [95p]	£1 5s 0d [£1.25]	£1 0s 5d [£1.02]
1939	5s 0d [25p]	8s 10d [44p]	6s 10d [34p]

(Agricultural Statistics, H.M.S.O.)

b) Acreages of crops and grasses, in thousands of acres, in Scotland

	Arable	Grass
1880	3579	1159
1900	3491	1408
1920	3380	1359
1939	2935	1623

c) Scottish Livestock numbers

	Cattle	Sheep	Pigs
1880	1 099 000	7 072 000	121 000
1939	1 349 000	8 007 000	252 000

The cereal prices in 1920 were high. The War meant food imports were at risk of attack and Scottish farmers were encouraged to grow as much as possible. In 1917 the government guaranteed the price of cereals, and agreed a

Source 5.44
Changing methods of farming from the late nineteenth century to the 1920s

minimum wage for agricultural workers. But government help to farmers stopped in 1921. World prices fell – between 1920 and 1921 wool prices fell to a quarter of their former value. Between 1919 and 1922 oats fell to a third of their former value. The government was not prepared to meet the cost of continuing to support British farming and it suffered badly until the 1930s. Between 1923 and 1929 agricultural land was freed of rates and in 1925 subsidies for sugar beet led to this industry developing in Fife.

Scottish farmers began to make use of new forms of technology. In 1925 the *Orcadian* newspaper reported:

Source 5.45

Birsay. Power on the farm
Several farmers in this parish are this year installing oil or petrol engines for the purpose of driving their threshing mills. Every year these engines are becoming increasingly popular, and it goes without saying that within the course of the next ten years horse gears for driving mills or machinery will be much more of a rarity than engines.

When, in 1932, the government decided to tax imports, Scottish farming benefited. Guaranteeing wheat growers a minimum price (1932) was of less benefit in Scotland than subsidies to meat producers (1932 and 1934) and oats and barley (1937). The development of Marketing Boards from 1935 benefited producers of milk, potatoes and other items. On the whole Scottish farmers coped better with agricultural troubles than many English farmers – indeed there was a noticeable move by Scots into parts of England to take over the running of farms. Wool from Australia, grain from North America, chilled and frozen meat from Argentina, Australia and New Zealand made many farmers re-think their approach and put more emphasis on poultry, fresh milk, fruit and vegetables.

In 1938, the *Scotsman* reported:

Source 5.46

The prospects for our young farmer are not so gloomy if he is an able man and willing to adapt himself to the new conditions. There will be more Boards that will tend to plan agriculture.

Case study (iv) – 'New' industries

Source 5.47

Workers at the Singers factory in Clydebank, 1890. Notice the number of workers

Between 1880 and 1939 many of Britain's modern industries developed. Before the First World War industries like electricity, car making and chemicals grew especially rapidly abroad. During the War, unable to import from abroad, the government encouraged the growth of these 'new' industries. It set up a Department of Scientific and Industrial Research. It introduced taxes on car imports to help the emergence of a British industry. The needs of war encouraged the growth of certain industries such as aircraft production. Scotland could build on her invention such as this one, reported in the *Scotsman*:

Source 5.48

The first detachable pneumatic tyre was patented in 1896, by W. E. Bartlett, the manager of the North British Rubber Co. It was this patent which has made motoring possible.

(*The Scotsman Trade Review*, 1938)

Scottish factories built both aircraft and airships. The first airship to make a double crossing of the Atlantic (in 1919) was built by Beardmores.

Steam power had been the force driving much of Scotland's industries in the 1880s. The gas industry had developed, too, and, with the invention of a slot meter in the 1890s, spread into working-class homes. In Molly Weir's Glasgow home in the 1920s:

Source 5.50 _____

The tenements were all lit by gas, and on Fridays when Grannie and I were doing the cleaning of all the brasses in the house the mantle had to be removed from the thin brass gas bracket with its swan-like neck, and moved

Source 5.51 _____

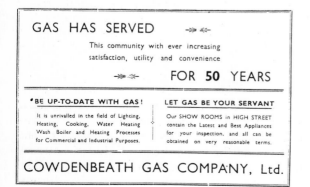

to safety, while we set to with busy polish and cloths and made the bracket and the band which ran round the mantelpiece sparkle like beaten gold.

Sometimes when handing the mantle back to Grannie for replacing on the bracket my fingers would grasp it too tightly and I'd hear a screech, 'My goodness, that's anither mantle awa'. Whit'll your mother say? How often have I to tell you that ye canna handle a mantle like a bool? Awa' doon to the store and get anither ane.'

(Weir, *Shoes were for Sunday*)

Source 5.52 _____

New forms of power developed, too. Electric light was one of the wonders of the 1888 Glasgow Exhibition. Its use spread to shops and industries, to the homes of the wealthy and to street lighting. Dundee's Commercial Street had electric light in the eighties. The first Scottish village to be electrically lit was Wormit (Fife) in 1897.

At Bowhill Colliery, Fife, the *Dunfermline Journal* reported in 1902:

Source 5.53 _____

Electric light has been introduced into every department of the offices and pithead and the glare is such the work is carried on as effectively at night as in the noonday sun.

Opening of Dundee Municipal power Station, 1910

Source 5.55

Power station at Bonnington

William Haddow worked for a pioneer Scottish electrical power station:

Source 5.56

In 1890, the Glasgow Corporation Electric Lighting Order was confirmed by Parliament. This Order authorised the Corporation to supply electricity for all public and private purposes within the city then existing. An up-to-date generating station was built. Within four years of the opening of the station in 1893 it was operating at full capacity.

The first street lighting by electricity was in Buchanan Street and Sauchiehall Street, in 1894.

The first electric tramcars were run between Mitchell Street and Springburn in 1898.

(Haddow, *My 70 Years*)

Scotland's geography made the country ideal for the development of hydro-electric power. In 1937, C. A. Oakley noted:

Source 5.57

Since the end of the War much attention has been given to the water resources of Scotland. The Grampian Hydro Electric Power Scheme was begun in 1928. Two power stations have been built at Loch Rannoch and River Tummel. [Such] developments are of great importance to the people of the Highlands, there are now few villages which are not supplied with electric power.

The government helped the growth of electric power. In 1926 it created the Central Electricity Board. The Board closed small power stations, developed new ones and connected up the system through a national grid of high tension cables transmitting power at a standard voltage. In 1938 the *Scotsman* reported:

Source 5.58

The grid confined itself to selected generating stations and the Central Scottish scheme was the first to be completed in Great Britain. The grid came into operation in Scotland in 1933. The number of electricity consumers served is about 700 000, rather more than 40% of the population is still without a supply of electricity. The construction of 1000s of new houses, the improvement of public services combined with the conversion of industrial consumers to supplies have all contributed to a rapid upward movement . . . Electrical engineering factories in Scotland have been operating at approaching full capacity for several years. The heavy industries are well provided for and a range of apparatus is available to suit the domestic user.

(The Scotsman Trade Review, 1938)

However, the growing industries of the 1920s and 30s came to Scotland all too rarely. Where they emerged, people could prosper. The growing industries tended to settle in southern Britain. A Ministry of Labour report in 1937 commented:

Source 5.59

New enterprise has tended to look favourably upon the south when determining its location and a higher proportion of the local population has been attracted into insurable employment.

The greater prosperity of the south is reflected also in the relative incidence of unemployment. In December the rate of unemployment among insured persons aged 16–64 in the country as a whole was a little below 12 per cent. On the other hand, all the northern groups were less fortunate than the national average. . . . Broadly speaking, the incidence of unemployment was twice as severe in the north, excepting the north eastern division and three times as severe in Wales as in the south.

(Ministry of Labour, Report for the year 1937)

Industries making goods for the home market tended to prefer to settle in prosperous places not in communities with high unemployment. Behind their success lay one of the most important reasons for economic growth – a fall in the cost of living. Between 1920 and 1939 the cost of living dropped by a third. But Scotland failed to attract enough growing industries to offset the problems created by the difficulties being endured by the older industries of coal, iron and steel, and shipbuilding. Too many suffered the fate of Scotland's car industry. In 1935 Scotland supplied just 1½% of British car production. The Argyll Company's attempt to produce cars on a big scale failed in 1912. Small-scale specialist manufacturers remained in operation, but neither British nor American mass-producers chose to come to Scotland.

Source 5.60
A Dundee mill in the early 1900s

Case Study (v) – Travel

During the 1880s, according to this Black Isle resident:

Source 5.61

It was mostly walking everywhere in the 1880s . . . a few carts and pony traps or hurlie barrows. A lot of people walked barefoot, too, maybe to Inverness, then when they came to the outskirts of the town they'd put on their shoes to be a perfect swell in the town.

I remember market day here with folk down from the glens, and their cattle, horses and flocks of sheep milling around in the square.

(Anna Blair, *Croft and Creel*, 1987)

To people living at this time horse-drawn traffic was a common sight. The men who drove these vehicles worked long hours. A Royal Commission of the 1890s found carters in Glasgow worked 98-hour weeks, getting up at 4.30 am and returning home at 9.30 pm on at least five of their six working days. But other ways of travelling were starting to challenge the importance of horse-traffic. Bicycles developed until, by the 1900s, they had all the features of modern cycles. By 1932 a cycle could be bought for £5 and keen cyclists could join organisations like the Cyclists Touring Club. In the 1890s electric power began to replace horse power on the tramways of Scotland's cities.

Source 5.63
Passengers on a tram

The trams connected up the different parts of cities and spread into the suburbs. They provided a way of travelling that ordinary

Source 5.62

Source 5.64
Women cyclists

people could afford. In Glasgow an underground railway opened in 1896. The *Glasgow Herald* reported:

Source 5.65

The Glasgow District Subway was opened for public traffic yesterday. The early cars were taken advantage of by workmen. Unfortunately there was a complete breakdown on the outer circle between 3.0 and 4.0 o'clock in the afternoon. Passengers had to get out and walk along the line to the nearest station. About 11.0 at night a car was waiting for the signal to advance to the platform at St Enoch. This car was run into with considerable violence by another one which came up behind. The passengers were all greatly agitated.

(*Glasgow Herald* 15 Dec. 1896)

Steam-powered cables pulled the carriages until 1935. Then electric power was introduced.

In the 1880s and 1890s long journeys were made by train. Around 130 private companies ran Britain's separate railway companies. Scottish Companies like the Caledonian and North British were keen rivals with each other. The railways employed a great many people and expected them to work hard. A Royal Commission of the 1890s collected evidence like this:

Source 5.67

On a train in the Dunfermline district an engine driver and fireman were on duty 18½ hours on 16th July 1892; 17¾ hours on the 18th; 22 hours 55 minutes on the 19th; 23 hours on the 21st and 18 hours on the 25th beginning at midnight on Sunday 24th.

(Smout, *A Century of the Scottish People*)

Source 5.68

Arrival of 1.15pm at Corstorphine station, Edinburgh 1906

Source 5.66

Coal wagons at Burntisland, 1879. With the coming of the railways this sleepy town became a major port for the handling of coal

Source 5.69

St Enoch station, Glasgow, 1887

The railways spread across the country, reaching most towns and many villages. Their importance, and the work they did, can be seen from the illustrations. During the First World War the railways were so important the government took control of them. In 1921 it handed them back to private ownership – though to four large companies formed by mergers of the former far more numerous ones. During the following years (1921–38) railway freight traffic fell by 17% and passenger traffic by 40%. The reason for this decline can be found in the emergence of a new form of transport.

Below An early motor car at Kerriehill House, Falkirk
Right A fleet of buses at Donibristle, 1925

In 1883 the German inventor, Daimler, produced a workable motor car. J. H. Macdonald was one of those Scots who soon realised they were seeing a transport revolution. He wrote:

Source 5.70 ——————————

The advent of the power vehicle has once more brought the road into a position of prominence in the interest of the public. When the railroad absorbed the mass of the traffic, the construction and upkeep of the road received little attention. Men without skill in road-making were appointed surveyors, and the workers on the road were too often physically unfit, being given wages in order to keep them off the rates for relief of the poor. With the introduction of power traction, the necessity of skill in the making and management of roads became at once apparent, and the consequent increased burden upon the rates caused the government to perceive that some aid must be given to encourage the local road authorities to improve the condition of the highways.

(Macdonald, *Life Jottings*)

On average cars in the 1900s cost £390. Only the wealthy could afford them. At first their speed was limited (by a law that had been designed to control farm machinery) to 4 mph (6.5 kph). In 1896 this limit was raised to 12 mph (19 kph) and in 1903 to 20 mph (32 kph). In 1896 a Scottish magazine reported:

Source 5.71 ——————————

The motor-car era may be said to have [begun] on Saturday last. On that day came into force the Locomotives on Highways Act. Before there were many restrictions on the use of any other than horse power. In passing a law whereby the autocar may be driven at 12 mph [19 kph] quite a revolution has taken place. Up to now the steam-propelled machine, whether for road rolling or for threshing mills, had to be preceded by a man carrying a red flag to announce the coming dangers. Some of the advocates of motor-cars are complaining that 12 mph [19 kph] is far too slow. But it is better to err on the safe side . . . There have long been complaints against some of the railway companies . . . in this day of the automobile they had better put their house in order.

(Quoted in the *Dundee Courier*, 7 May 1977)

The first sight of a car usually remained vividly in the minds of the observer:

Source 5.72 ——————————

The first motor that I can remember . . . I was standing at a wee shop in New Street in Musselburgh and this motor came along from the Races. It had solid tyres and it wasna steered by a wheel but a straight handle that you turned whatever way you wanted to go . . . like a rudder . . . Well I don't know what happened but we heard some awfie bangs and th' was lumps of solid tyre flying up in the air and then he swung right round and straight into a shop.

(Blair, *Croft and Creel*)

Even in the 1920s car driving was hard work. Lavinia Derwent lived in the Borders then. Her father bought his first car:

Source 5.73 ——————————

It had to be cranked up with a starting-handle before it showed any signs of life. Then suddenly it would begin to shiver and shake as if struck by the ague. It coughed and spluttered, sparks began to fly, and my father leapt into the driving-seat and fiddled with the gears. There was no driving test. He just took the motor into a field and went round and round until he got the hang of it. But he never quite mastered its mysteries, and even in later years when he bought bigger and better cars he was more at home with horse-flesh than with horse-power.

Though it widened our horizons in so many ways it was a long time before we lost our fear of the motor.

'Pomp the horn!' my mother would cry when we emerged into the main road or came near a corner. Even though we were travelling at a snail's pace there was always a sense of danger. Father knew nothing of the inner workings of the engine, and when we stuck, he used to get out, open the bonnet and fiddle away at the 'internals', with a perplexed expression on his face.

We never went on an expedition without having some mishap. We ran short of petrol, water, oil; we had frequent punctures; the horn would start blowing and refuse to stop.

(L. Derwent, *A Breath of Border Air*, 1975)

Mass-produced cars from Ford, Morris and Austin gradually brought car-ownership within the reach of more people. In 1922 an Austin 7 cost £205 – which was still 80 times an average weekly wage. In 1935 there was a car to every 36 people in Scotland, and some vehicles cost as little as £100. However, motor-bus services developed, too.

James Dawson began work in 1925 driving buses in Fife. He recalled:

Source 5.74 ――――――――――――

The vehicles were chain driven, had solid tyres, were lit by carbide gas, had no windscreen wipers and were cranked by a starting handle. He actually lost all his front teeth when he was struck by a starting handle after the engine back-fired.

(*Central Fife Times*, 1970)

The growing number of motor vehicles cut into the business of railways, trams, and horse-drawn vehicles. They led to the spread of garages (often developed from smithies) and filling stations. In 1919 the Ministry of Transport was created. Traffic began to be organised by road signs, roundabouts and traffic lights.

Road accidents, too, increased. In 1934 there were more than 7300 deaths in Britain. These developments in transport meant that, by 1938:

Source 5.75 ――――――――――――

Travel in Scotland is an easy and luxurious affair. Motor buses run through almost every parish. Swift trains, with luxurious dining cars take you over all the railway systems. New and larger steamers have been built. By means of advertising the railway and steamship companies have greatly increased the number of visitors to the Highlands.

(*The Scotsman Trade Review*, 1938)

Certainly the organisers of the Glasgow Festival of 1938 believed that there was plenty to celebrate, in the Scottish economy, despite the troubles suffered in some industries. Twelve and a half million people visited the Exhibition, wandering round its 200 palaces and pavilions.

Source 5.76 ――――――――――――――――――――――――――――――
Bairds Garage in the Springburn Road, Glasgow, 1931

Source 5.77
Part of the Glasgow Exhibition of 1938

1 List as many instances as possible, from the sources of Scottish industries that were in trouble in the 1920s and 30s. (K.U)

2 What reasons for their difficulties did these industries have in common? (E.2)

3 In what ways did the government try to help these industries? (K.U)

4 Choose one of these troubled industries. As a foreign visitor from one of Britain's competitors write and report for your government explaining the opportunities that await your country. (E.2)

5 What evidence can you find in this chapter that shows there were signs of hope for the Scottish economy? (K.U)

6 Why weren't these industries more successful in replacing the industries that were in trouble? (E.2)

7 'A time of changing technology'. What evidence of this can you find in the sources? (K.U)

8 Which source in this section seems to you to be the most biased? Explain why you have chosen this source and give examples of bias. (E.l)

9 Design an advertisement to explain the merits and advantages of motor-car travel over other forms of travel. (E.2)

10 In what ways do the pictures in sources 5.65, 5.67 & 5.68 show the value of travel by rail? (K.U)

11 What problems did early motorists face? (K.U)

12 What sort of jobs do you think suffered a decline because of the coming of motor travel? (E.2)

13 'Interview your Grandfather – 1938' A school class of 1938, about to visit the Glasgow Exhibition, are required to interview their grandfathers about the changes they have seen since the 1888 Exhibition. Choose a suitable job that 'your' grandfather would have done. Would he have regretted any of the changes he has seen? Plan and write an interview with 'your' grandfather. (E.2)

6 Living and Working Conditions

Between the 1880s and the 1930s there were many changes in the working and living conditions of the Scottish people. For quite a number of people there were times when finding work was itself a very great problem. Being out of work inevitably affected the living conditions of those who suffered this misfortune. The sources in this chapter provide evidence of what it was like to live and work in Scotland during these years.

Working Conditions

A hard life

During this period, for most people, working life began at the age of fourteen. Many boys found their first jobs as delivery boys. In 1907 half the boys, on leaving Glasgow schools, became van boys and milk boys. One of them was Thomas Bell:

Source 6.1 _____

My first job on leaving school was with one of these dairymen. My hours were from 6.30 am to 6 pm and sometimes 7 pm. For duty I had to assist in getting the horse harnessed and loading the van; go round the streets (two rounds a day) ringing a bell for customers, and run up stairs with special deliveries. I had to scrub the milk barrels and cans, clean the horse's harness and the brasses of the cart, and wash out the yard. After numerous other odd jobs, I walked two miles [3 km] home; and earned a wage of 3s 6d [17p] per week of seven days.

There was no set time for meals. Going out so early in the morning, often without any breakfast, I was ravenously hungry by eight o'clock. More than once, when I had had no chance to eat up to nine or ten o'clock, I picked up a crust of bread from the road to keep me going.

(Thomas Bell, *Pioneering Days*, 1941)

Some started work at an even earlier age. A child able to show he or she had reached a suitable level in reading, writing and arithmetic could either leave school at the age of ten or work half time. (This age was later raised to twelve.) The system of allowing half-time work and half-time schooling went on till 1936. Dundee especially looked favourably on pleas from poor parents that their children be allowed to start half-time working. In 1900, for example, there were 5000 girls in Dundee, aged twelve and thirteen, on half-time working.

The hours that people worked varied greatly. By the 1890s some Fife miners worked a 44-hour week: Glasgow carters, at the other extreme, worked a 98-hour week. In general working hours fell during this period and a half-day holiday on Saturday became increasingly common. By the 1920s a working week of 48 hours was usual in many trades. Occasionally Parliamentary intervention helped this trend. In 1909 a new law limited miners' daily work underground to 8 hours. In 1913 another law gave shop assistants a maximum 64-hour working week. But in the many small workshops that still survived far longer hours were worked. Harry McShane saw such places in Glasgow. He wrote:

Source 6.2 _____

Here and there in some of the back courts were little workshops. They were often owned by blacksmiths. All the shoes were nailed in those days. One of my relatives worked as a baker in a back court and did well out of making rolls. You can still see the remains of these little buildings in some of the back courts.

Other men, like Thomas Bell, found work in the heavy industries that still flourished in Scotland. He described his early working life as follows:

Source 6.3 _____

Foundry work is made up of hard physical

labour. Up till the end of the Great War, the working week was one of fifty-four hours, of nine and a half hours a day, from 6 am to 5.30 pm.

The foundry was then the Cinderella of the engineering trade. The conditions under which the moulder worked were vile, filthy and insanitary. The approach to the foundry resembled that of a rag and bone shop, or marine store. The entrance was usually strewn with all kinds of scrap iron and rubbish. The inside was in keeping with the outside. Smoke would make the eyes water. The nose and throat would clog with dust. Drinking water came from the same tap as was used by the hosepipe to water the sand. An iron tumbler or tin can served as drinking vessel until it was filthy or broken, before being replaced by a new one. The lavatory was usually placed near a drying stove, and consisted of open cans that were emptied once a week – a veritable hotbed of disease.

Every night pandemonium reigned while the moulds were being cast. The yelling and cursing of foremen; the rattle of overhead cranes; the smoke and dust illuminated by sparks and flames from the molten metal made the place a perfect inferno. Glad we were, when it was all over, to creep into some corner alive with vermin of all kinds, to close our eyes for a few minutes.

(Bell, *Pioneering Days*)

Slowly improving conditions were partly due to the better organised and more numerous unions of the time. In the early twentieth century many small unions combined to join bigger unions and what had once been Scottish unions sometimes merged with their English counterparts. Out of these changes came unions like the Amalgamated Engineering Union (1920), the Transport and General Workers Union (1922) and the National Union of General and Municipal Workers (1924).

QUESTIONS

1 What reasons do the sources provide to explain why children started work so early? (K.U)

2 Why do you think so many boys began their working life on delivery services? (E.2)

3 The author of source 6.3 was a socialist very keen to transform society. Do you think this might have coloured the way he describes his workplace? (E.1)

Down the mine

Source 6.4

Miners at Gardrum Pit, Slamannen, c. 1910

Coal mining at Newton Grange Pit

Working conditions in mines improved a little during this period. The eight-hour working day of 1909 was, in 1917, cut by an hour as a result of an act of Parliament. More machinery was introduced during the period from 1900 to 1930. Some collieries began to provide pithead baths for miners. Abe Moffat, however, noted that welfare improvements were slow in coming, especially in smaller pits:

Source 6.6

. . . a Coal Mines Bill was passed in 1911 to provide pit-head baths, but there had to be a majority of two-thirds by ballot vote of the miners before an employer was compelled to erect baths, providing the miners paid half the cost, and the owner was not bound to provide such accommodation if the estimated cost of maintenance exceeded 3d [1.2p] per week for each workman. Another part of the Act exempted the coal-owners from erecting baths if the mine employed less than 100 workmen.

(A. Moffat, *My Life with the Miners*, 1965)

Yet mining remained a very hard and dangerous life. The scenes described by David Bremner in 1869 (source 2.23) could still be seen in later years. The next two sources are the reminiscences of miners who worked at this time. Geoffrey Barclay wrote:

Source 6.7

I started work at the age of 14 at the Randolph Colliery, Dysart, in 1910 at the wage of a shilling [5p] for an 8-hour shift. The adult wage was less than 8 shillings [40p] per shift. We had no pithead baths, no guaranteed wage, no holidays with pay, no free tools, not even an ambulance. I can remember dead and maimed miners being transported to their homes in the colliery dust cart.

(*Dundee Courier*, 23 Dec. 1974)

Another miner of the time recalled:

Source 6.8

I left school on the Wednesday afternoon and started down the pit, with my father on the Monday morning, Shieldmains pit at Drongan Station. I started working there on 7 December, 1914. I went right down the pit with my father. I'm none the worse. I'd half a crown [12p] a day and my father 6/6d [32p]. You started at 7 in the morning till 3. You worked 5 days one week and 6 days the next, you'd work a Saturday every fortnight, it was constant day shift. In the winter time you never saw daylight, by the time you got up the pit in the afternoon it was dark. I've seen me comin' up the pit from the coal face and down the road on a bike, and if it happened to be a frosty night, when you went in and dropped your trousers they stood frozen on the floor, because you'd been working in water away up your knees that was freezing around your legs.

(Drongan, The Story of a Mining Village, 1978)

QUESTIONS

1 What evidence can you find in the sources that boys worked underground? (K.U)

2 Find and list all the problems and difficulties miners faced. (K.U)

Working on the land

Farmwork was still a very important activity in Scotland. These were years in which farmworkers had to make increasing use of machinery. However, these were years of struggle, too. Foreign competition made life hard for Scottish farmers. During the First World War the government encouraged farming and supported it. By the 1920s it had returned to allowing farmers to fend for themselves against cheap food imports. Only in the thirties did this begin to change.

For nearly all this period people seeking work on the land had to go to one of the 'feeing markets' held in Scotland's country towns twice a year.

Jim Ogg recalled how he and his fellow workers gathered in Perth for these events:

Source 6.10

Aa the High Street wis all laid wi sweetie stalls. Ye ay kent a ploughman when ye seen him. It wis aa corduroy breeks or moleskin trousers that were worn and tacketty boots. The High Street in Perth wis crowdit; tram cars used tae run down the middle o' the High Street. The stalls wis jist on the wan side o' the street . . . candy an sugar pigs an aathing like that they sellt in thae days. Prentice the Saddlers wis a great place for folk gaun an pittin their names in fir a job. An the fairmers wid come in an hae look at the names . . . Ye had to strike yir ain bargain.

(Tocher, School of Scottish Studies, No. 41)

Source 6.9

A feeing market in Arbroath, 1900

A family moving from one farm to another in North Uist, 1900

Workers often changed their jobs, shifting to different farms in search of a better place.

A doctor working the Borders reported sights like this, as families shifted from one farm to another:

Source 6.12
Tonight, driving home very late from a country visit, we passed several carts loaded with families, 'flitting' from one outlying farm to another. Among the furniture and bundles which crowded the farm-wagons, children of all ages were huddled together, sleeping or waking by turns; the infants, wrapped in shawls, lay cradled in their mothers' arms

(C. B. Gunn, *Leaves from the Life of a Country Doctor*, 1955)

Until 1875 if they left their place before their agreement ran out they could be prosecuted as criminals and sent to prison (whereas a farmer who broke his side of the agreement had only committed a civil offence and might be fined). The Employers and Workmen Act (1875) put the worker on the same footing as the farmer. In 1937 the Agricultural Wages Act began to bring in some standardisation of wages. The old system of individual bargains struck at the feeing fairs faded away. Even so this change came 13 years after a similar reform in England. Scottish farmworkers were not covered by any sort of unemployment insurance until 1937, yet the 1920s especially were a time of unemployment on the land. Even when insurance did finally come in it was at rates of payment lower than those in industry. David Fyfe remembered his first job on the land:

Source 6.13
Being the oldest of a family of 12 I was able to leave school at 13½ in 1921. My father sent me to a dairy farm 3 miles [5 km] away. My first wage was £8 for a 6 month period. I remember my first morning at work being wakened at 5.0 o'clock with a sweaty sock across my face. I leapt out of my chaff bed and put on my long breeks, boots and was about to tie my laces when my senior bed-mate shouted 'Come on lad, ye hinna time for that noo.' I had to run to keep up with him. When we came to the byre he said 'In there.'

I saw the byre lanterns burning over 20 cows and the milkers all sitting. On seeing me the boss rose, fetched a spare pail, and pointed to a large beast.

'Milk that one' he said.

(D. Kerr Cameron, *Cornkister Days*, 1984)

David Thomson saw one of the most common features of harvest time throughout this period:

Source 6.14
At thrashing time, while the traction engine puffed smoke and steam and the thrashing

machine rumbled all day, I would ride, bare-back and sweaty, one of the carthorses inside the barn round and round as the men threw the straw underneath me. The thrashing machine poured the grain into hundred-weight [50 kg] bags, spilled out the straw from one end, and the chaff from the other. The chaff in a huge heap was kept separate in one corner of the barn.

(D. Thomson, *Nairn in Darkness and Light*, 1987)

Source 6.15

Farmers at the Royal Highland Show, Perth, 1924

It was not easy for farmworkers to organise to improve their conditions. They had so little free time, were so scattered and often depended on their employers for the home in which they lived. In the 1870s and 80s Joseph Arch was busy organising an Agricultural Labourers' Union in England. A similar organisation – the Scottish Farm Servants Union – developed between 1886 and 1887 in Aberdeenshire.

Source 6.16

1887 The Aims of Scottish Farm Servants, Carters, and General Labourers Union

- The establishment of branches throughout Scotland.
- To strengthen the power of Farm Servants, Carters and Labourers.
- To obtain monthly payments with indefinite engagements (i.e. long-term employment).

- Weekly half holidays, except during six weeks of harvest.
- The abolition of the bothy systems.
- The improvement of our kitchen dietary scale (i.e. meals) and of our house and sleeping accommodation.
- To protect the interests of members against oppression.
- To establish a sick, benefit and superannuation fund.

(I. Macdougall, *Essays in Scottish Labour History*, 1978)

By 1901 this union had failed. In 1912, at a time of general unrest and union activity, the Scottish Farm Servants Union was set up. It became a section of the Transport and General Workers Union in 1932. Many men found another answer to the long hours of farm work. They left for other jobs.

QUESTIONS

1 Source 6.11 gives the farmworkers' point of view. How might a farmer have described going to a feeing market? What sort of people might he prefer? What questions might he ask? Write 'A farmer's recollections of a feeing market.' (E.2)

2 Go through all the sources to find and note down all the complaints of farmworkers. Use these notes to write a speech that might have been given by a worker to explain to a visitor why he'd left the land to work in the brewery. (E.2)

Women's work

Source 1.8 shows the kinds of jobs carried out by women in 1881. In 1931 the Registrar General for Scotland reported:

Source 6.17

The leading Occupation in the case of females is Personal Service Occupations to which 194 999 are classified, and this is followed by Commercial Occupations (95 915), Textile

Workers (81 668), Clerks and Typists (77 451), Professional Occupations (48 876), and Makers of Textile Goods (39 102).

Personal services – 29.6% of the total number of females (in work). The largest group is that of Domestic Servants (138 679), Charwomen and cleaners (19 808) and laundry workers (12 154). Commercial Occupations – saleswomen and shop assistants have increased – 75 147. The largest number are in Drapery (17 705), Bread etc. (8032), Groceries (8026). Professional Occupations are mostly found in Teaching and Nursing (24 218 and 17 000).

Source 6.18

Herring gutters at work, Oban, 1928

Women were expected to work hard. Some followed the herring fleets round the coast, gutting and packing the fish, as this woman recalled:

Source 6.19

I was just past 13 when I went to start at the herrin'. Ye learnt yesel'. Ye'd just start the job and go along at it and then ye'd come into the speed. If you'd no speed, it was nae use – you couldna make much. When I was a girl in Peterhead, in the old days before the First War, a man would come round tae the house and tell ye that the herrin' would be in the yard at nine o'clock, and sometimes we didna stop till three or four o'clock the next morning. Gutting all the time. Ye got nothing tae eat unless someone brought it. We used tae send somebody across to the coffee shop for a flask o' tea and some pieces. And that was all ye got till ye went home next morning. Oh, I've seen me ganging home at three or four o'clock in the morning and mother would have bowls o' soup on for me, and the left-over dinner was always kept.

(D. Butcher, *Following the Fishing*, 1987)

Women continued to work in the coal industry. An elderly miner remembered how women used to work on the surface, by the pit, picking over the coal to remove rocks:

Source 6.20

It was hard work. The girls used to work two shifts. There was 6.0 am to 2.0 pm and then the back shift.

(*Dundee Courier* 5 April 1977)

Source 6.21

Women surface workers at Blantyre Ferme Colliery, 1898

Women workers were especially popular with the owners of textile factories. In the Dundee jute industry the result was that women workers outnumbered men by about three to one. One of these women described the results:

Source 6.22

The men in Dundee were called 'kettle boilers' meaning that they had the kettle boiling for tea when the wife came home from work because it was an impossibility for men to get a job. They were taken on at 14 and paid off at 19. Men were just not employed. It was a woman's town.

(A. Holdsworth, *Out of the Dolls' House*, 1988)

To such employers women offered a special advantage – they could be paid less than men. Women's wages were commonly half to two thirds those of their male colleagues. In the countryside many farmers liked to recruit men who had wives and daughters who could help out on the land. An enquiry of 1905 commented:

Source 6.23

In all parts of Scotland women are frequently employed at farm work. In the Borders and the Lothians the number of women workers is almost equal to the number of men and on some farms where potatoes are largely grown there are sometimes more women than men. It is a great advantage for the employer to secure the service of strong young women for field work at about half the wages of the men.

(Agricultural Labourers Wages, Earnings and Conditions, 1905 in *Human Documents of the Age of Lloyd George*, 1972)

The female relatives of male workers who provided a labour force at times of especial need were called 'bondagers'. The system suited farmers for it meant they'd extra workers available, but only had to pay the female workers for the days they actually worked.

Source 6.24
Farmworkers in Tayside

Farmers also hired women to cook and clean, etc. in the farmhouse. One woman who did this work remembered:

I was hired out to work with a farmer when I was barely 14. I had to rise at 5.0 sharp. One of my many jobs was to scrub a big concrete square at the back door. My hands often stuck to the icy stone. I had the porridge to make, cows to milk and often the byre to clean out all before breakfast.

(*Dundee Courier* 17 Dec. 1975)

Women were used especially to weed crops and to gather them at harvest time. However, by 1900 the other sorts of opportunities of finding work were changing women's views of work on the land. A reporter to the 1893 Royal Commission on labour noted:

Source 6.26

A young woman will hand over her 'kist' [chest of clothes] to the porter, get her ticket for Glasgow, pull on her gloves, laugh and talk with her parents and comrades, jump onto the train, wave her handkerchief, sit down and thank her stars that she is at last leaving the unwomanly job for domestic service and town society.

(In Smout, *A Century of the Scottish People*)

From the 1880s the spread of inventions like telephones and typewriters provided office work for girls. The expansion of schooling after 1872 both improved their education and offered some of them work as teachers. By the 1900s the growth of big department stores and other sorts of shops meant that here too there was work that was seen as respectable.

Betty Stivens started work in 1932 in a big department store in Edinburgh. She recalled:

Source 6.27

We thought we were frightfully posh yet we got a lot less pay than in a factory. There was the 1st Sales [Assistant], the 2nd Sales, the 3rd Sales, and when you started you would be the 4th Sales. If a woman came in and the 1st Sales wasn't busy, she got the sale. Sometimes you never got a sale because by the time it came round to the 4th there wasn't enough customers. I was promoted just before I was

married up to 1st Sales and we had a different canteen. It was just that one lot sat on benches and another lot sat on chairs, but that was real distinction. I think I got ten shillings [50p] and a penny [0.4p] in the pound commission. You weren't allowed to stop for a second. You had to clean out or dust tops of cupboards or fold all the stuff in the drawers whether or not they'd been done the day before. If you were allowed back to work [after marriage] they would have said 'What a shame. She's got to go and work.' So even if you were hard up the last thing was to go back to work. It was not the done thing.

(WEA *Friday Nght was Brasso Night*, 1987)

The jobs most women found were in domestic service, but even here attitudes were changing.

Source 6.28

Major Playfair's servants in St Andrews

In the early 1900s John Kerr, who was sufficiently well-off to afford servants, wrote:

Source 6.29

It is probably to a large extent true that domestic servants are less satisfactory on the whole than they were fifty years ago, and take less personal interest in the families they serve. Many maintain that this is due to the generally wider spread of education, the ability to read with tolerable ease, and the abundance of trashy literature to which they have ready and cheap access. It is said that from this they get false notions about their true position, begin to ape the manners of their employers in dress, become impatient of being found fault with.

(Kerr, *Leaves from an Inspector's Logbook*)

Servants cost so little to hire that even quite ordinary families might afford one, as this reminiscence shows:

Source 6.30

It was a two-room-and-kitchen tenement we lived in. There were my parents and us three children. I think my mother had big ideas because we had a maid even in that wee house. She wore a white cap and apron in the morning and maybe a pinny for the dirty work. Then she was all done-up in the afternoons in her black and whites . . . very trim, wi' long streamers dangling from her cap and pinny. That was for opening the door and serving up the tea. She took the baby out too, but here, the joke was that she'd him in a shawl instead of a pram and that took the tone down a peg or two. She slept in the kitchen bed recess.

(Blair, *Croft and Creel*)

Women who actually were domestic servants provide a different view of their lives. As one of them recalled:

Source 6.31

It was a big house and I was the kitchen-maid. The housemaids did the rest of the house, and the parlour-maid attended to the family. I helped the cook, swep' the kitchen, washed the black pots wi' scourers, and the copper ones wi' vinegar and salt. I done the dishes wi' washin' sody. Oh and my hands got that raw! I was just a skivvy.

(Blair, *Croft and Creel*)

The First World War brought a change to the way women saw the jobs they could do. Women were needed not only to replace men who had left their jobs to join the forces, but also to work in the new munitions factories that sprang up.

To women who had hitherto been badly-paid domestic servants, the factory work brought better pay and more free time. Margaret Morrison went to work in a West of Scotland shell factory.

Source 6.32

Recruiting officer in Cupar waiting to enrol recruits during the First World War

Source 6.33

Until then I had worked as a laundry maid on a big estate. Most of us had never worked on machines before. We were given a week's instruction by one of the foremen. After a while they said we could do as well as any of the skilled workmen. Of course we didn't get the same pay. Working in the explosives section could be dangerous. We worked a 12-hour shift, but the pay was good.

(A. Marwick, *Women at War*, 1977)

The government provided hostels for many of these women to live in. The biggest gathering of women munition workers was at Gretna. Of the 11 000 living here 36% had formerly been in domestic service and 20% had lived at home without working. The authorities worried about the behaviour of women moved to these hostels and set up a women's police force to keep an eye on them. It brought in rules like this:

Source 6.34

With the object of keeping the workers within the factory area and away from temptation elsewhere, no late ordinary trains were run between Gretna and Carlisle except on Saturday when the latest train left at 9.30.

(Marwick, *Women at War*)

Source 6.35
Women making munitions

Source 6.36
Woman driver and conductress on a tram

Munitions work may have been dangerous but its weekly wages of £2 per woman were in contrast to their pre-war average wage of 11/7 [58p]. As this Edinburgh lady explained in her account of munitions work:

Source 6.37
Ye worked frae six till six unless there was a big push on, then ye worked very late. We had a canteen. That wis the first time I had seen one. You got better money. Twice I had nearly £5, that wis big wages. The war finished and we finished with it. But we had got a taste for working yae and we would nae settle.

(*5/11 a week*, n.d.)

Source 6.38
Women war workers in the canteen

As a factory inspectory noted, women could cope:

Source 6.39
. . . even in fairly heavy work, in rubber manufacture, paper mills, oil-cake and seed-crushing mills, shale oil works, shipyards, iron and tube works, chemical works, gas works and stacking of coal, tan yards, coarse ware and brick making, flour milling and other trades.

(Miss Anderson, HM Principal Lady Inspector of Factories, *Factories and Workshops Report for 1916*)

It was not surprising that, after 1918, women were less prepared to go back to life as it had been. W. S. Speed was a servant himself, working for a family in Fife. He commented:

Source 6.40
Servant girls, especially the younger ones, began to rebel against the long hours and low wages, and although assured of a roof over their heads, began to look for more lucrative employment in factories. The same applied

with the male staff and grooms and even some chauffeurs contemplated other forms of employment in the outside world.

(W. Speed, Very Good Sir, n.d.)

The War may have helped change attitudes, but once it was over women had to leave their wartime work to make way for men. And women in jobs like office work and in teaching were still expected to resign once they got married. Moreover, women's wages continued to be significantly below mens.

QUESTIONS

1 How have women's jobs changed? List the main changes you can find by comparing these sources.   (K.U)

2 Look at sources 6.28 to 6.31.
   a) What sort of duties did servants carry out?   (K.U)
   b) How do the views expressed in these sources differ as to whether servants were content with their circumstances?   (E.1)
   c) Why do you think they differ?   (E.1)

3 Explain briefly why the First World War changed views on women's work, using the sources and any ideas of your own.   (E.2)

4 The author of source 6.27 could have earned more in a factory. Why do you think she chose shop work instead?   (E.2)

5 How does the appearance of the people in source 6.28 show the different sorts of jobs they did?   (K.U)

6 'You don't know how lucky you are'. Use this heading to write the words an elderly working-class woman might speak to her grand-daughter who is about to start her first job in the 1930s.   (E.2)

Living Conditions

The need for improved housing

Between 1912 and 1917 the members of a Royal Commission looked carefully at the sort of homes in which the people of Scotland lived. They reported finding:

Source 6.41 ————————————
Unsatisfactory sites of houses and villages, insufficient supplies of water, unsatisfactory provision for drainage, grossly inadequate provision for the removal of refuse, widespread absence of decent sanitary conveniences, unspeakably filthy privy-middens in many of the mining areas, badly-constructed damp labourers' cottages on farms, whole townships unfit for human occupation in the crofting counties and islands, occupation of one-room houses by large families, groups of lightless and unventilated houses in the older burghs, masses of slums in the cities . . . ill-planned houses that must become slums in a few years, old houses converted without necessary sanitary appliances into tenements for many families. Merely to relieve existing overcrowding and replace houses that should be demolished, 121 000 new houses are required.

(Report by the Royal Commission on Housing, 1918)

Source 6.42 ————————————
Tenements in Dundee

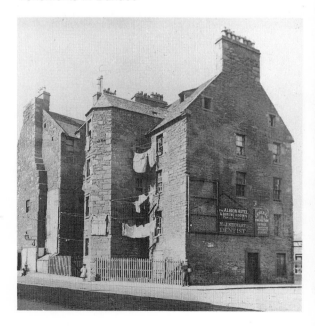

In the countryside many men still lived in the bothies and chaumers described in sources 2.27 and 2.28. The Royal Commission contrasted Scottish housing with almost half of the population living in homes of one or two rooms, with the English situation where only 7% were so housed.

Source 6.43
Inside a bothy at Wellbank near Dundee

Source 6.44
Overcrowding in Scottish homes:- the percentage of the population per room

	More than 4 to a room	3 to 4 to a room	2 to 3 to a room	Not more than 2 to a room
1881	13.2%	14.5%	23.1%	49.2%
1901	9.6%	13.3%	22.8%	54.3%
1911	8.6%	13.3%	23.2%	54.9%

(Census of Scotland, 1931)

Source 6.45
Overcrowding in the four main cities, 1901

Accommodation	Aberdeen families %	Dundee families %	Edinburgh families %	Glasgow families %
1 room	13.1	19.7	17.0	26.1
2 rooms	37.3	52.1	31.4	43.6
3 rooms	26.2	16.5	19.2	16.5
Totals	76.6	88.3	67.6	86.2

(Census, 1901)

As the above source shows, Glasgow especially suffered from overcrowding. In the 1880s Dr Russell, the city's Medical Officer of Health, tried to explain to audiences of well-to-do people what life was like for thousands of their fellow citizens. The figures he quotes are from 1881.

Source 6.46
It is those small houses which produce the high death-rate of Glasgow. Their exhausted air and poor and perverse feeding fill our streets with bandy-legged children. Of all the children who die in Glasgow before they complete their fifth year, 32 per cent die in houses of one apartment; and not 2 per cent in houses of five apartments and upwards. There they die, and their little bodies are laid on a table or on the dresser, so as to be some-what out of the way of their brothers and sisters, who play and sleep and eat in their ghastly company. You mistresses of houses, with bedrooms and parlours, dining-rooms and drawing-rooms, kitchens and washing-houses, pantries and sculleries, how could you put one room to the uses of all? You mothers, with your cooks and housemaids, your nurses and general servants, how would you in your own persons act all those parts in one room, where, too, you must eat and sleep and find your lying-in-room and make your sick-bed?

(J.B. Russell, *Life in One Room*, 1888)

QUESTIONS

1 In which Scottish city were people living in the most overcrowded conditions? (K.U)

2 What sorts of results for people's health, way of life and behaviour do you think might follow from living in the conditions described in 6.41? (E.2)

3 How has the author of source 6.47 tried to persuade his audience of the importance of his argument? (E.1)

4 Can you find any evidence of hardship in sources 6.42 and 6.43? (K.U)

Tackling the problem

Most people in Scotland lived in rented homes. Between 1880 and 1918 too few had been built to house the ever-increasing population. The rising costs involved in building houses led to a sharp decrease in activity after 1905 especially. During the First World War building almost ceased.

Yet some attempts to tackle the housing problem had been made before 1918.

Source 6.47

Attempts at improvement before 1918

a) Local government had been improved (see source 2.54). In 1889 elected County Councils were created. In 1894 a government department, the Local Government Board, was set up. The burghs already had many powers: in 1892 the old burgh councils were merged with the elected police commissioners who had been dealing, in each burgh, with social problems.

b) A number of places had Acts of Parliament passed to allow them to tear down poor housing and even build new properties. Glasgow took this power in 1866, Edinburgh in 1867, Dundee in 1871, Greenock in 1877, Leith in 1880 and Aberdeen in 1884. In Glasgow, especially, the council provided housing – enough for about 1% of the city's population by 1914.

c) Acts of Parliament increased local authority powers. In 1909 a Housing Act gave burghs power to demolish and re-build, they no longer needed to apply for permission before acting.

d) Because a naval dockyard was built at Rosyth, a carefully planned community was laid out to house the workers. The homes and their gardens showed the influence of planners who favoured developing 'garden cities' in which houses were well spaced out.

e) In 1915 a Rent Act froze rents for nearly all working-class people at 1914 levels. Rising rents, especially in wartime, stirred a revolt by families in Clydeside who refused to pay

and organised ways of stopping families from being evicted. At one time 25 000 people were refusing to pay rents.

Source 6.48

Rent strike demonstration in Glasgow, 1915

Source 6.49

Housing in Rosyth, the Garden Village

The rules and regulations that local authorities introduced showed the sort of problems they faced in trying to improve living conditions.

Source 6.50
Bye laws in Inverness 1894

The dung, and other filth shall be conveyed to the streets in buckets, placed on the side of the street, and it shall be emptied by the scavengers.

- No soot shall be thrown out or chaff beds emptied upon the streets.
- Complaints are frequently made of injuries caused by leaving orange skins on the pavements, no person shall drop upon the pavement any orange skin.
- Without the consent of the Police Commissioners no person shall keep any pig nearer to a dwelling house than 100 yards [91 m].
- Every driver of any cart or carriage who may be found sleeping or in a state of intoxication while driving shall be liable to a penalty.

The observations of a Glasgow citizen in 1903 show how much the city was doing. A Glaswegian, he wrote:

Source 6.51

. . . may live in a municipal house, he may walk along a municipal street, or ride in the municipal tramcar and watch the municipal dustcart collecting the refuse. Then he may turn into the municipal market, buy a steak from an animal killed in the municipal slaughterhouse and cook it by the municipal gas stove. He can choose among municipal libraries, art galleries and music in municipal parks.

(Smout, *A Century of the Scottish People*)

Yet these efforts were not enough. The rents many people could afford to pay meant private builders did not find it worth their while constructing homes for them. In 1920 the problem of rising rents once more led to trouble in Glasgow.

A new Rent Act (1920) allowed rents to rise no more than 15%. Further rises up to 25% were allowed in later years provided that necessary repairs were carried out.

Nor did local authorities usually subsidise the rents they charged for the few properties they provided. The Royal Commission stated that the government must intervene to help local authorities.

Between 1919 and 1939, therefore, the government helped local authorities with the cost of council house-building and, in this way, housing that more people could afford began to be built. The government also encouraged private house-builders. Private housing developed and, especially in the 1930s, people began to buy their own homes. This was made possible by the low cost of borrowing money, the expansion of building societies, the reasonable cost of housing, and the fact that people who had jobs were increasingly well off in the 1930s.

Source 6.52

The main reforms, 1919–39

a) *1919 The Housing and Town Planning Act (Scotland).*

At the end of the First World War Lloyd George's Government promised voters that it would provide 'homes fit for heroes'. The Minister of Health, Christopher Addison, was responsible for this reform. Local authorities were required to report on their housing needs and draw up plans to tackle them. The money produced from a 4/5 [1.5/2p] penny rate (in England it was a whole penny!) was to be spent on council house-building. Since this would not produce enough money, the rest of the cost of the house-building would be met by the government. High-quality homes were built under this scheme. In 1921 the government ended it. The high cost of housing at the time meant the bill was very large. But it provided Scotland with 25 540 homes.

b) *1923 Housing Act*

This was the work of the Conservative Minister of Health, Neville Chamberlain. Council house-building was to be subsidised by the government at a level of £6 a year per house for 20 years. Only 4022 homes were built in Scotland under this scheme.

Chamberlain also offered private house-builders a subsidy of £75 a house on houses costing up to £1200. This led to nearly 30 000 houses being built.

c) *1924 Housing Act*

In the first ever Labour Government the

Minister of Health was the Clydeside MP, John Wheatley. He improved the council house-building programme, offering councils £9 a house for 40 years. (In 1926 the Conservatives cut the subsidy to £7.10.0 [£7.50].)

Rural housing got an even bigger subsidy – £12.10.0 a house. This plan led to the building of 75 000 homes in Scotland.

d) 1930 Housing Act
The second Labour Government tried to tackle the problem of clearing slum housing by offering a subsidy of £2.10.0 [£2.50] to councils for every person they re-housed.

e) 1933 Housing Act
The subsidy for council house-building was cut to £3. The numbers built rapidly fell. This change was the work of the Conservative dominated National Government.

f) 1935 Housing Act (Scotland)
The subsidy for council house-building was raised to £6.15.0 [£6.75] a house. The subsidy to private house-building continued, but was to be for homes up to the value of £800. It led to a great boom in the building of bungalows priced at under £800. By 1939 337 173 houses had been built in Scotland over a 20-year period, 230 137 by local authorities, though 1937 had seen the emergence of a new house-building authority – the Scottish Special Areas Housing Association. Much had been done – yet many were still far from well-housed when the outbreak of the Second World War put an end to new house-building. Overcrowding in Scotland was still far worse than in England.

Source 6.53 —————
Post-war housing development in Dunlop Street, Greenock, 1924

Source 6.54 —————
Number of advances made by Scottish building societies in Scotland, 1919-43

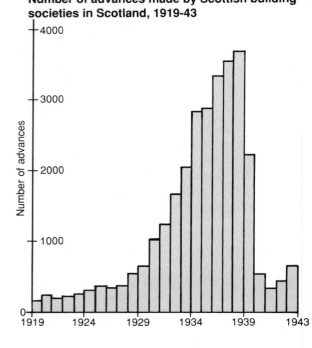

Source 6.55 —————
Bungalow development at Duddingston in Edinburgh in the 1930s

Ralph Glasser saw the spread of private house-building around Glasgow:

Source 6.56

Fields and hedgerows were being eaten away. The mysterious race of country folk was in retreat. Villas had sprung up, others were building, red and raw, in discord with the gentle greys and browns and greens of the old settlements. Prosperous Glasgow people moved out to live in the Mearns, in the country but not of it, proud of this step up in life.

In the villa settlements, lanes and landmarks kept their rural names – Rick Lane, Smiddy Crossing – but the ways of life they signalled were gone, leaving only echoes and symbols, a few oases of greenery, glimpses of distant fields. But a decade or so later most of these residues would disappear under a further wave of building and transformation – shops, garages, workshops, offices. The true 'country' gone for ever.

(R. Glasser, *Growing up in the Gorbals*, 1986)

Nellie Edgar's family moved into one of the new council houses in Glasgow. She explained:

Source 6.57

My mother didnae let any of us see the new Corporation house at the Wellmeadow until the day of the flitting. It was her big *thing*, so's that when we came home that night from the mill or the school, it was to the new place . . . seeing it for the first time. Well see! I walked in that door and there on the floor were beautiful Congoleum squares . . . pink in the girls' room . . . the *girls'* room! And kind of blue for the boys' room. Printed waxcloth it would be without a border, just a square laid in the middle, the way you'd a carpet later-on.

And of all wonderful things, a *wooden* bed. There was a dressing-table, and a wardrobe wi' a mirror and a *lovely* new bedspread. My parents' room was the parlour too, so they had their bed in it and a three-piece-suite. Forbye *that* we'd a real living-room, separate from the kitchen, and a bathroom. No more tin tubs. And there was the garden.

(Anna Blair, *Tea at Miss Cranston's*, 1985)

New housing schemes began to spring up.

However, not all people of the time were impressed by the huge new estates that spread round the cities. In 1937 an English visitor to Glasgow wrote:

Source 6.58

To re-visit Glasgow after several years absence is to realise how swiftly the city has expanded. [But] in the new and sanitary estate shops will be few. In all likelihood there will be small choice with regard to entertainment. Women must suffer more than men from the tedium of life on new suburban estates. A woman doctor told me of women moved from that slummiest of Glasgow districts, Anderston, into sub-sidised dwellings fitted with modern conveniences who were bent on deserting their clean and spacious quarters and returning to Anderston's familiar squalor.

(In Whyte & Berry, *Glasgow Observed*)

QUESTIONS

1 Use source 6.50 to write an account of a walk through the streets of Inverness in the 1890s. (K.U)

2 What were the main reasons for the 1918 housing shortage? (K.U)

3 In what ways is the evidence in source 6.48 trying to persuade the authorities that rent rises are wrong? (E.1)

4 Explain why the figures in source 6.55 rise and fall. (E.2)

5 Use the evidence in the chapter to design an advertisement of a house for sale in the 1930s. (K.U)

6 In what ways did Labour housing reforms differ from Conservative reforms? (K.U)

7 Do you think the author of source 6.58 was in favour of housing schemes? Explain your answer. (E.1)

Daily life

QUESTIONS

You have been asked to research and write a series of short articles explaining what life was like between the 1900s and 1930s entitled 'Life in our great-grandparents' and grandparents' childhoods'.

— In order to do this you will need to carefully examine the evidence in the following sources.
— Decide on the topics of different articles (for example one could be 'washday', another could be 'going shopping').
— Make notes
— Find good quotations to use.
— Compare the past with today.
— Notice how life differed and changed during the period 1900–30.
— Explain why some people have such happy memories.
— Discuss whether you believe all you have read. Why might an elderly person's memories of childhood differ from adult memories of the same time?
— See if you can add to your notes by interviewing an elderly neighbour or relative.

In the country

Source 6.59

Interior of Orkney cottage, Netherby, Deerness, 1900

In 1893 Royal Commission investigators reported that the standard of living in the countryside had improved in the past 20 or 30 years.

Source 6.60

Porridge is the chief breakfast food, but I heard of many houses where tea, bread, cheese, butter and jam had supplanted porridge. For dinner, either broth and meat or meat and pudding [are eaten]. Eggs are purchased. Coffee and tea are drunk. Some housewives buy flour and bake scones. The barley and peasemeal scone seems to have disappeared. Formerly the crockery consisted of a porridge bowl for every member of the family, a few cups and saucers, a teapot and half a dozen soup plates. Go into a labourer's cottage now and the dresser will be seen filled with plates. The cupboard holds its pretty flowered breakfast and tea set, its tumblers and wine glasses, its jugs and mugs, but no horny spoons.

(T. E. Devine, *Farm Servants and Farm Labour*, 1984)

Source 6.61

Washday in Arbroath. Why do you think the washing is being done outside?

Source 6.62 ━━━━━━━━━━
Fetching water from the village well in Longformacus

However, conditions in many areas had changed little. In Caithness, as in other more remote parts of early twentieth-century Scotland:

Source 6.63 ━━━━━━━━━━
There was no piped water supply. Rain or well water was used. There was no indoor sanitation, nor outdoor either. Winter and summer resort to some favourite corner on the hill or in the quarry was the custom for both sexes. Nor was there a bath. A big wooden tub ordinarily sacred to the annual washing of blankets could be used for that purpose. As one of those old stalwarts told me, 'I dinna gang in for them modern innovations. There are two things I have never been in, a bath or a theayter.'

(J. Dundas, in *Scotland's Magazine*, September 1958)

Jean Whittle grew up in a country craftsman's home near Jedburgh:

Source 6.64 ━━━━━━━━━━
Being one of a large family (6 brothers and 3 sisters), it was just expected that I'd stay at home and help mother when I left school in 1923. So there I stayed until I married and left home. We lived in part of a house – with my father's parents who had a joiner's business. There was always an apprentice and a journeyman lived with us. Quite often there would

be 15 of us. I well remember how the grownups were served first, if there wasn't room at the table for us all at once. Just think of all the cooking, baking and washing up!

There was white and brown flour and oatmeal stored in a big chest in the kitchen. Cooking was done on an open grate till Valor Perfection stoves came on the market, and we had a big one of those, which was a great help. The water had to be carried from a tap a few yards away until it was brought into the house. There was a separate building called the wash house where the washing was done, in a big iron boiler lit with sticks, and big tubs and a mangle. It was all 'whites' in those days and quite a lot of things were starched. Ironing was done with a flat iron and bolts heated in the fire. That took hours, especially all those shirts for the men and boys. Oh my!

The usual job first thing every morning was to get the paraffin lamps cleaned and filled and the candles and candlesticks ready for night. There was a 'telling off' if they weren't done when darkness fell. We got electric light later, worked with a generator.

There was so much to do, but it was a happy life. Hens, pigs, cats and dog to feed, cow to milk, butter to make and sell. We had Jenny the horse, who was a great favourite and was used to drive the trap.

(R. H. Campbell, *Changed Days*, 1985)

Andrew Law was one of the many farmworkers whose daily life was spent in bothies. He explained:

Source 6.65 ━━━━━━━━━━
Ye bought yer bread and tea from the baker. There was always plenty o' meal about a bothy. They nivver paid none o' the women tae clean out the bothy. Every man had a week 'on the pan', as they called it. On Saturday afternoon he cut his sticks, carried them in. The foreman sat on his kist [chest] and there was a form for 3 or 4 of ye. And there was a table. There was the orra loon, he made the porridge and the tea in the morning. Dinner time – porridge. They used to slice it up and eat it cold, or fry it. If they didna take that they took brose. Mostly it was bread, butter, syrup, cheese for tea.

(Billy Kay, *Odyssey*, 1980)

Tenement life

Source 6.66
Tenement interiors

Source 6.67
Butchers, Bakers, Milkmen, all made deliveries in horse-drawn carts and floats. A novelty used to be the Milkman's cart with his large multi-gallon cans mounted at the rear and, at the blast of his shrill whistle, the customers would converge on him with jugs . . . Food was simple but staple – fresh vegetables for full-bodied soup made in a large pot and sufficient to last an average-size family for two days; plenty potatoes with a good middle course (on lean days often a liberal helping of stovies), finishing off with a good plate of rice pudding with raisins; all variations of the good old milk puddings with, on special occasions, a clootie dumpling with small silver threepenny [1.2p] pieces wrapped in paper secreted in the middle, and what cries of delight when the lucky person uncovered one.

(N. Moir, *A Motherwell Childhood*, 1985)

Jimmie MacGregor's childhood was spent in a Glasgow tenement:

Source 6.68
Its fashionable now to sigh over the lost warmth and community of the tenement, but it is noticeable that the sighers are usually of an age to have spent only their childhood there. An older generation remembers also dirt, poverty and inconvenience as well as the continual struggle to protect their children from those realities. The success of that struggle is what allows people like me to look back through rose-tinted glasses. There was, nevertheless, a real sense of belonging. Neighbours were always at hand. Doors remained unlocked and few secrets survived for long.

(*Sunday Mail*)

Flora MacDonald was one of ten children, living with their parents in an Edinburgh tenement. She remembered:

Source 6.69
My mother had dark long clothes, always washing, always cleaning and always in black. She was always working and never got out anywhere. Monday was her washing day in the middle of the floor with her tub and a bath in front of the fire. Then ironing and knitting. If my mother came back and saw how we are now she'd get the shock of her life – carpets and that! My brothers were treated like gentlemen. That was general. Well, it was the done thing for the girls to do all the work.

(WEA Edinburgh, *Friday Night was Brasso Night*)

The period saw the setting up of public wash houses – the 'Steamies'. Ralph Glasser visited a Glasgow steamy:

Source 6.70
One dimly saw figures in long skirts, dark blouses, sleeves rolled up, hauling and lifting, scrubbing and banging and carrying. In a clangour of boiler doors, iron buckets and chains, clatter of scrubbing boards and shrill voices calling, they heaved bundles of clothing and blankets about, banged irons, turned the wheel of a mangle. In the streets their leaning outlines were familiar as they trudged to the steamy, backs bent under sagging bundles of washing.

(Glasser, *Growing up in the Gorbals*)

Molly Weir lived in a Glasgow tenement in the inter-war years. By then many homes had solid iron kitchen ranges where the fire also heated an oven. She explained:

Source 6.71 _____
Every bit of our range was used for cooking. The kettle was always on the side of the hob, the big soup pot stood on the other side. The stew pot wasn't far away. Although we only had a-room and kitchen for the 5 of us we never felt over-crowded. One family had 14 children and they all lived in one room.

(Weir, *Shoes were for Sunday*)

Improvements in everyday life

Developments in this period from 1880 to 1939 improved life for families where wages came in regularly. The making of footwear and clothing by factories meant it was more readily and cheaply available. Trams provided cheap travel. By 1900 it was possible to buy a bicycle for £4. The living standards of many families rose as wages went up. Between

Source 6.72 _____
Vacuum cleaner in 1910

1920 and 1939 the cost of living fell by nearly a third. These developments meant many families could buy more meat and fruit.

Upper working-class and middle-class families had an increasing number of electrical gadgets to buy. In the 1930s, with the setting up of the National Grid, these gadgets became widely available. Rene Cutforth noticed that, for better-off housewives:

Source 6.73 _____
The huge kitchen range had to go to be replaced by a gas or electric cooker, hundreds of thousands of people were employed as door to door salesmen demonstrating vacuum cleaners and stainless steel knives came into use along with electric fires. Only the copper and the great iron mangle stayed on for years. Americans had washing machines, but only a few were hardy enough to transplant them to these shores.

(R. Cutforth, *Later Than We Thought*, 1976)

The arrival of a washing machine in a home in a district of Glasgow caused great excitement:

Source 6.74 _____
My husband decided to install a washing machine. It was the wonder of Clarkston for it must've been one of the very first in the neighbourhood. It had a rotary action and friends used to come in and watch the things birling round, and even bring wee bundles of their clothes to get them done for them . . . very sociable really.

(Blair, *Tea at Miss Cranstons*)

In Glasgow in 1932 Thomas Jones noted:

Source 6.75 _____
Food is more varied. Fresh fruit is available all the year round. The milk supply is cleaner and the byres have been driven beyond the city bounds. Drunkenness has diminished. Barefooted women and children were common in the eighties. No one sees them today. The shawl has gone and the hat has taken its place . . . working girls who then tidied themselves only for special occasions, are now always neatly dressed and are careful of hair and teeth and finger-nails – a great change.

(In J. Stevenson, *British Society 1914–45*, 1984)

Women and the changing law

1880 Married Women's Policies of Assurance Act (Scotland).

A wife could take out an insurance policy on her own, or her husband's life, for her own separate use.

1881 Married Women's Property Act (Scotland).

Married women's property was now to be regarded as their own, not their husband's (though husbands could administer wives' property and their consent was needed when disposing of it).

1886 Guardianship of Infants Act.

When couples split fathers would not necessarily get custody of children. The children's welfare would be the prime consideration.

1919 The Sex Disqualification Removal Act.

Women must be allowed access to legal positions and public offices.

1920 Married Women's Property Act (Scotland).

A husband's consent was no longer essential when a wife disposed of her own property.

1923 Matrimonial Causes Act.

The reasons for divorce were made the same for men and women.

1930 Welfare Centres could give birth control advice to married women.

1939 Marriage Act (Scotland).

Civil marriages were now legal.

Source 6.77

Dining-room in the Mackintosh house, Glasgow

The wives of men who prospered did not usually go out to work. A magazine of the thirties suggested:

Source 6.78

As women, even in these levelling times, are at leisure much oftener than men, we give a separate list of pastimes essentially feminine:

Sewing, embroidering, crochet work, and knitting in all their branches.

Macrame (string work useful for bags, belts, coarse laces, etc.)

Fancy cooking (toffee, sweets, etc.)

The making of artificial flowers and floral ornaments

or

Perfumes, pot pourri, and scented sachets

or

Cold cream and cosmetics

or

Babies' toys in felt, plush and velvet.

(June and Doris Langley Moore, *The Pleasure of Your Company*, 1936)

Shopping

Source 6.79

Street market in Dundee

Shop interior in Perth

Woolworths in St Andrews

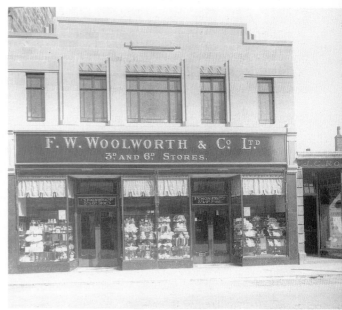

Source 6.82

Street-sellers were to be seen throughout this period.

Though shops grew in size and number in these years, one type of shop continued to matter – the pawnshop. Ralph Glasser, went to a pawnshop where:

Source 6.83 _____

The three golden balls hung from a wrought iron bracket that jutted out, a life saving beacon. In the window a notice said 'Unredeemed Pledges for Sale', adding, with unconscious irony, 'Good Quality!' Eternity rings, wedding rings, gold watches engraved with twenty-first birthday wishes, used blankets and bedlinen, carefully laundered shirts, china teapots, dinner plates, soup tureens, cutlery, a linen tablecloth embroidered with the words: 'To our beloved daughter Bunty on her wedding day. May The Good Lord bless and keep her.'

(Glasser, *Growing up in the Gorbals*)

Another witness from these years, who grew up in Larbert, recalled:

Source 6.84 _____

These were the days when the grocer's shop was a real grocer's shop. The personal attention, the smell of spices, the wide hardwood counter, the polished brass scales and the ham machine which allowed the customer to get what he wanted and in the correct quantities to suit his needs. Butter came in barrels and had to be cut and packed by using butter pats which neatly stood in a glass jar of water when not in use. Large cheeses were rolled into the shop to be deposited in the cool of the cellar to mature when, at a later date, the cheese cloth was unravelled and with deft hand and skilful manipulation of the cheese wire, the required quantity was cut to size.

Sugar, barley, lentils and rice all came in hundredweight [50 kg] sacks requiring to be made up and weighed into manageable amounts for daily use by the housewife. Large wooden drawers beneath the counter were filled with dried fruit, broad shelves were laden with tins and packets contrasting with the hams depending by strings from the rafters in the back shop.

(J. Jenkinson, *Glass Doors and Jeelie Pieces*, 1984)

Among the shops were growing numbers of branches of Liptons the grocers and Boots the chemists. Large department stores selling a wide range of goods were built. Stella Stewart's family went to a Co-op in Edinburgh:

Source 6.85 _____

The Co-op grocers had sawdust on the floor and you sat on a form and moved up as the people were served. Lots of mothers had a red book in which the assistant would list the messages and it would be paid every week or when they could manage it. Mum was a great Co-op fan. She would not buy anything anywhere else if she could help it, even a box of matches.

Every member received a dividend each half-year. I can remember when it was three shillings and sixpence [17p] in the pound, which meant you received that amount for each pound you spent in the store. It was quite a ritual every six months, going for the divvy. It was a day out . . .

That divvy was a real life-saver for many families. The children were clothed with it and many a bill would not have been paid, but for the divvy. I am sorry they have stopped paying it out because it really was the poor man's bank. Not everything changes for the better.

(Campbell, *Changed Days*)

One shop assistant recalled

Source 6.86 _____

These porridge oats came in packets, and people didn't like it at all. We'd been used to weighing it out for them. They had to buy a packet, and they wouldn't buy a packet. They didn't want so much. They only wanted enough for perhaps two breakfasts, small portions.

(R. Overy and P. Pagnamenta, *All our Working Lives*, 1984)

Another expressed his fears about this change.

Source 6.87 _____

We thought that packaging was going to take our jobs away. We had it that we were selling loose things, weighing them out, and that was our labour you see. We used to weigh everything out that there was, currants, raisins, pepper, salt, tea, coffee, cocoa. We used to make these cups, tuck it in, turn it up and present it. We thought if it came in packets there wouldn't be any jobs.

(Overy & Pagnamenta, *All our Working Lives*)

Rene Cutforth shopped in the new stores.

Source 6.88
There was a Woolworths in every High Street where everything cost sixpence or less. A kettle for instance cost sixpence – and its lid sixpence. You could buy a pair of spectacles, the frame cost sixpence and each lens cost sixpence and you tested your own eyes with a card on the counter.

Montague Burton, the Tailor of Taste, lived in the High Street too. He could fit you out with a suit for fifty shillings [£2.50]. It would have a waistcoat, trousers were kept up by a pair of braces. Shirts were white in the thirties.

Welfare

The problem of poverty

Scotland in the late nineteenth century contained many people who could not support themselves. They included orphans, widows with young families, people who were ill or handicapped, people injured at work, and those who were too old to work. People who were unable to find work made up a further group. They were especially numerous in winter when many outdoor workers were unable to find employment.

The system of helping the poor (see sources 2.62 to 2.66) was run by locally elected parochial boards. In 1894 they were replaced by parish councils. These bodies had money, raised from local rates, they used to assist the poor in their homes. They also co-operated to build poorhouses as permanent homes for poor people with nowhere else to go. But they were not obliged to do anything for those able to work – but unemployed.

Able-bodied unemployed people depended on charity, and on help from local councils as in schemes like these mentioned by Harry McShane:

Source 6.89
In those days the unemployed could starve to death. There was no social security, and the parish council wouldn't give money to able-bodied men unless they went into the work-house. Even then, their wives and children would only get a few shillings relief. In 1908 the scale of the unemployment was so terrible that the Corporation of Glasgow started work schemes, something they had always tried to avoid, and on a few occasions they gave out food tickets worth ten shillings [50p] each. My uncle worked on one of the schemes; though he was a skilled blacksmith, he built roads in the park for fifteen shillings [75p] a week. My father was also unemployed, and for a while he and my uncle went round making sunshades for shops.

It wasn't the first period of bad trade during the 1900s. I lived in Govan, near the shipyards which were always hardest hit during a slump, and I remembered seeing soup kitchens being set up before.

(H. McShane, *No Mean Fighter*, 1978)

The numbers of unemployed needing help could be vast. Between 1878 and 1879, for example, nearly 38 000 people turned to the Glasgow Unemployed Relief Fund for help. In 1905 the Unemployed Workers' Act required burghs with populations of over 50 000 to form 'distress committees' from their councils. These committees were to help the unemployed move elsewhere, or organise work for them. The scheme applied to the whole of Britain and had some government money to back it. From 1909 to 1910, for example, Scotland received £42 000.

Elderly people desperate to stay out of their local poorhouse found life especially hard. Old folk in Dundee in 1905, for example, had to manage on help totalling 3 shillings [15p] a week each.

The parochial boards – and the parishes that took over from them – employed inspectors to check that people claiming help were really poor. (From 1901 women could be appointed to these posts.)

The health problem

The country also contained a further problem – that of ill-health. Poor housing, poor diet and poor clothing all played a part. In the 1870s the average age to which people lived was in the early forties. By 1901 it had risen to the later forties. But the country contained diseases that flourished in dirty living conditions, such as typhus and diphtheria. Sources on living conditions in the earlier part of this chapter help explain why such diseases flourished like these, described by a Glasgow resident:

Source 6.90

Scarlet fever and Typhoid and the Measles were very, very common and you got the colly-wobbles when you saw the Van coming down your street to take away whoever had the fever to Hospital. It was mysterious because the Van windows were smokey blue and you couldn't see through. If Scarlet or Typhoid or even the Measles was in your house you were kept off the school for so-many weeks till the infection was gone. They burned your school books as well. Everyone dreaded those fevers and the Diphtheria too of course.

(Blair, *Tea at Miss Cranston's*)

Source 6.91

Scavenger in Inverurie

Cities had been attacking the problems of dirt-removal and supplying pure water more vigorously than smaller towns and villages. In Fife, for example, a late nineteenth-century report recorded that villages took their drinking water from shallow wells dug close to cesspools, with this result:

Source 6.92

The contents of the filth hole [or cesspool] gradually soak away through the surrounding soil and mingle with the water. As the contents of the well are pumped out they are immediately [replaced] from the surrounding disgusting mixture. This is consumed until the cesspool and well receive infected sewage and then an outbreak of disease compels attention to the polluted water.

(In T. Ferguson, *Scottish Social Welfare*, 1958)

Health care

People who were ill did not find it easy to get proper treatment. Doctors and dentists had to be paid. There were far too few hospitals. Some of these were paid for by raising money from charities, others developed out of the wards for the sick that poorhouses provided. The 1909 Royal Commission praised Glasgow's poorhouse hospitals. But, of the rest, it complained they did not have sufficient trained staff.

Source 6.93

There is the use of pauper inmates for nursing. There is a deficiency of night nurses, the extent to which doctors are overworked sometimes passes all belief. In one of them there were about 800 inmates, the numbers rising 25–30% in winter [but] only a single resident medical officer. In many of the large wards there was no trained nurse in attendance.

Outside the larger burghs there are a few county infirmaries supported by voluntary contributions. There are also a number of cottage hospitals – many of them built and endowed by private donors. There is great need for better provision of hospitals in rural areas.

(*Royal Commission*, 1909)

Only around half Scotland's poorhouses had properly trained nurses (yet England had banned the use of poor people as nurses in 1897).

Source 6.94
Doctor on his rounds in Glen Coe, 1900s

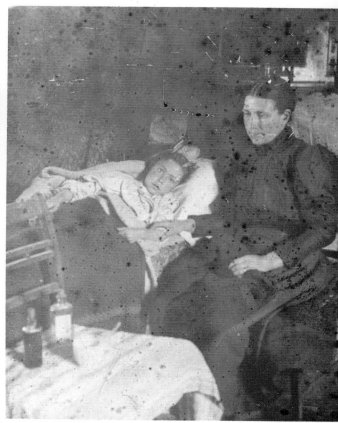

Source 6.96
Sick child in Glen Coe, 1900

Source 6.95
Hospital ward in the early 1900s

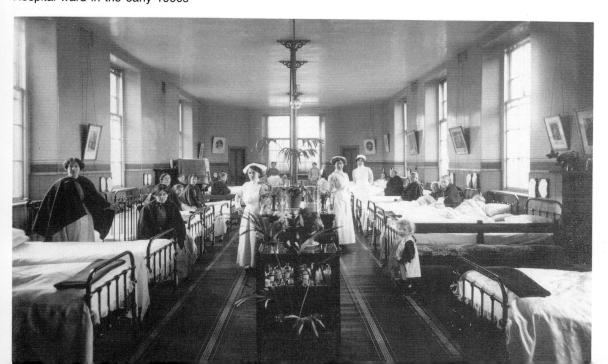

By the twentieth century more was being done. In 1894 the Local Government Board took over national control of local authorities. It forced towns that had hitherto done little, to introduce proper water supplies. A Public Health (Scotland) Act in 1897 increased the powers of local authorities. In particular they began to check food and milk supplies far more thoroughly to see if they were infected.

More local authorities began to build hospitals, especially isolation 'fever' hospitals. Such was the scale of tuberculosis (it accounted for 13% of deaths in Scotland around 1900) that the government agreed to provide half the money local authorities spent on tackling this terrible infection.

The memories of people recalling the early years of the century show what the health of the time was like. The following sources all come from inhabitants of Leith:

Sources 6.97 _____
In all the wards [in Leith Hospital] there used to be brass plates above the beds, 'donated by Gibsons', 'by MacGregors' . . . all the shipowners. And that's how the Leith Hospital was built. Businessmen and the ordinary people with their pennies and halfpennies.

Source 6.98 _____
When you went to visit people there was a box and you put money in. You were provided with a certain amount of feeding but you had to supply a certain amount of your own [mainly] in the shape of eggs. In the morning you got porridge and toast and your own egg boiled. The eggs that you brought in, you used to write your name on them.

Source 6.99 _____
The great majority of doctors had up to 50% bad debts. They tended to charge more to those who could afford to pay and little or nothing to those who couldn't pay. Some unscrupulous doctors were not above eyeing a nice grandfather clock and saying, 'You haven't paid me anything for 5 years for all the medical care, but I do like your grandfather clock.'

Source 6.100 _____
You used to be paying 2/6 [15p] for a visit. I remember my father was ill for a year and the doctor used to come in . . . that was 3/6 [17p] for a visit. My mother was presented with a bill for nearly £100!

Source 6.101 _____
Oh my teeth! She [mother] had to get a neighbour to take me, this was to get your teeth pulled. It was just long forms [at the dentists], no backs or anything. And when we went in – oh the roars! That's what frightened me. And I says 'What are they doing?' She says 'I don't know'. She knew fine. I was going to get my teeth pulled.

(All the above from *The Struggle for Health*, Edinburgh Health Council)

QUESTIONS

1 Briefly list the main causes of poverty. (K.U)

2 Why were there, at times, so many unemployed people? (Source 6.89)(K.U)

3 In what ways does source 6.89 suggest help was provided for the unemployed? (K.U)

4 How might a voluntary hospital have made known its need for help? Design a poster (using the evidence in the sources) that stresses the reasons for needing help. (E.2)

5 Why do you think official help to poor people was so limited in these years? (E.2)

6 The authors of sources 6.97 to 6.101 are elderly ordinary people remembering childhood. Do you think their views accurately show how people felt at the time? (E.1)

Liberal welfare reforms

Health and welfare problems were present in many parts of Britain. The Liberal Government that took power in 1905 was determined to do something about them. The government contained men who were horrified by the circumstances in which the poor lived. The most vigorous of these reformers was David

Lloyd George, a Welsh solicitor who became President of the Board of Trade and then (in 1908) Chancellor of the Exchequer

The government had much evidence of the need for reforms. Surveys by men like Seebohm Rowntree and Charles Booth showed around a third of the British people lived in poverty. Moreover, the recent Boer War had led to alarm about the poor physical condition of many of the men who volunteered for military service. Between 1906 and 1911, therefore, a number of reforms were carried out. Lloyd George was ably supported in his work by other Liberals, especially by Winston Churchill.

Source 6.102 _____

Liberal Reforms

Education (Provision of Meals) Act

1906 Local authorities were allowed to provide school meals. For very poor children these could be provided free. (Not all authorities took the chance to introduce these meals.)

1907 School children to be regularly *medically inspected*.

1908 The *Children's Charter*. Children were forbidden to beg, were to be tried for offences in special Juvenile Courts and were to serve prison sentences in special homes away from adult criminals. A probation service was introduced. Children under 16 were not to go into public houses or buy cigarettes.

1908 *Old Age Pensions*
Pensions were introduced for people over 70 years old whose incomes were small. The highest level of pension – five shillings (25p) a week – was paid to people whose yearly income was no more than £21 a year. Those with higher incomes received less.

Where yearly income no more than
£23.12.6 (£23.62p) – 4/- (20p) a week
£26.5.0 (£26.25p) – 3/- (15p) a week
£28.17.6 (£28.87p) – 2/- (10p) a week
£31.10.0 (£31.50) – 1/- (5p) a week

1909 *Labour exchanges* established. Employers did not have to send in a list of vacant positions. The unemployed did not have to register there.

1911 *Insurance against sickness*
Payments to workers who were off work from illness were to come from a fund built up by:
4d (1.5p) a week from workers earning under £160 p.a
3d (1.2p) from employers
2d (1p) from the state
Benefits. An insured worker could draw 10/- (50p) a week for up to 26 weeks, get free medical treatment by a doctor paid by the Insurance Commission. Doctors got 9/- (45p) for each patient on their 'panel'. Patients had to pay the full cost of prescriptions.
30/- (£1.50) maternity benefit for the birth of each child.

1911 *Insurance against unemployment*
Covered 2¼ million workers in building, shipyards, labouring and engineering. Paid for by

2½d [1p] a week from employer
2½d [1p] a week from employee
1⅔d [0.5p] from the state

Benefits 7/- (35p) a week for up to 15 weeks on the basis of 1 week's benefit for every five weeks contributions. Liberal reforms provided welfare payments that were just enough to keep total disaster at bay and were limited to certain sections of the population. Most people still faced doctors' fees, many occupations were not included in the unemployment insurance scheme, and those workers who were covered only received payments for a limited period.

Source 6.103

Pension day at the post office in Auchtermuchty

Source 6.104

Medical inspection at Dumferline public baths, 1926

THE PHILANTHROPIC HIGHWAYMAN.

The Liberal reforms had their critics. *The Times* complained:

Source 6.106

We have already made a serious inroad upon personal responsibility and personal independence by relieving parents of the duty of educating their children. That is now used as an argument for relieving them of the duty of feeding their children [i.e. school meals]. When we have done that, the argument will be stronger than ever for relieving them of the duty of clothing their children. It will be said that we pay vast sums for teaching and feeding, but that the money is wasted if the children are not properly clad. From that it is an easy step to paying for their proper housing; for what, it will be asked, is the use of feeding, clothing, and teaching children, if they come to school from close and insanitary bed-rooms? . . . The proposed measure would go far to sap the remaining independence of the existing parents; but what are we to expect from the present children when they in turn become parents? The habit of looking to the State for their maintenance would be ingrained in them; everything we now give would be to them a matter of course; and they would infallibly make new demands of their own.

(*The Times* 2 June 1905)

Welfare reforms between the Wars

The Liberal reforms were meant to provide help to the most needy. They did not cover the whole population and, within a few years, further changes in Britain's welfare system were carried out.

Source 6.107

Important welfare changes, 1918–39

1919 The Ministry of Health was established.

1920 The 1911 insurance scheme was widened to include all unemployed formerly earning up to £5 a week except farm workers, domestic servants and civil servants. The rate of benefit was fixed at 15/- (75p) a week.

1921 The Scottish Poor Law was altered to bring it into line with the English Poor Law by allowing able-bodied unemployed people to be given help.

1925 People who had paid at least 5 years worth of health insurance contributions were entitled to pensions at 65 years of age. The pensions were paid regardless of other sources of income.

1929 The old Poor Law system was abolished throughout Britain. County councils and large burghs took over the work of the parish councils boards. They set up Public Assistance Committees to deal with poverty in their areas. The amounts they paid varied from place to place.

1931 The level of benefits paid the unemployed were cut by 10%. Those with no insurance, or who'd used up their 26 week entitlement had to submit to a 'means test'.

1934 The Unemployment Assistance Board took over the work of the P.A.Cs. It obtained its money from the State and paid the unemployed through the labour exchanges. The level of benefits it paid – 17/- (85p) a week for a single man; 26/- (£1.30) for a couple; 3/- (15p) for each child – were national levels. Families could now have savings up to £200 without losing the dole. Previously savings had to be spent first.

The changes made in the 1920s had a number of causes. The First World War showed up the poor state of the nation's health even more forcefully than the Boer War. Between 1917 and 1918 around 2½ million men were examined for military service. Only 36% were passed as fully fit for all military duties. Lloyd George, Prime Minister from 1916 to 1922, put one of his supporters – Christopher Addison – in charge of planning reforms to improve life in Britain. Addison became the country's first Minister of Health. He explained the need for changes:

Sources 6.108

For years attention has been drawn to the fact that we have in our children, [those] who are physically defective or have defective vision, etc. Every year they go and lose themselves in the mass of the population. We forget them until suddenly some great national event occurs which brings it up to us in its reality. That was the case in the War. Then we saw those generations of children we had heard of so often who were represented in the military age by hundreds of thousands of men who were physically unfit and could not pass the very moderate standard of physical fitness which the army required. Then it was revealed as a source of national weakness, which is very great in time of emergency, but it is just as much a source of national weakness in time of peace.

(In A. Marwick, *The Deluge*, 1973)

Improvements in the Scottish Poor Law were explained by the system's chief administrator in a lecture in 1927:

Source 6.109

The Emergency Act of 1921 revolutionised the administration of Scottish Poor Law in that it authorised relief to the able-bodied poor and many are now finding their way to Poorhouses. Relief to the able-bodied has always been legal in England.

Perhaps there is no branch of Poorhouse administration that has made such progress as that of the treatment of the sick. A number of Parish Councils, of which Glasgow is an outstanding example, adopted a high standard many years ago and have established hospitals for the destitute [poor] sick. There are few Institutions now where the Matron at least is not a trained nurse or a person of considerable nursing experience. In Poorhouse Hospitals no doubt a large proportion of the cases are senile.

The tendency is to admit fewer children to Poorhouses except as a temporary measure. The Board of Health prefer that children should be boarded out. Several Parish Councils have provided excellent Children's Homes.

('Scottish Poorhouses', 1927 lecture by the General Superintendent of Poor, Scottish Board of Health)

Source 6.110
Royal Infirmary, Edinburgh, 1919

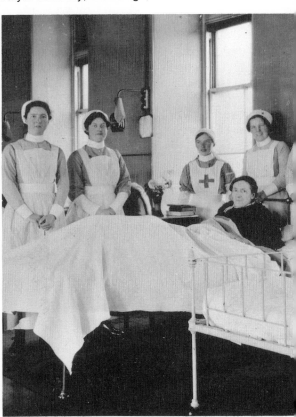

Certainly there do seem to be signs that people's lives did improve.

Source 6.111
a) Expectation of life in Britain

    1871 – 42 years
    1901 – 48 years
    1911 – 53 years
    1931 – 61 years

b) Numbers dying, per 100 000 alive, from major diseases in Scotland

	1861–70	1901–10	1931–9
Tuberculosis	361	209	77
Respiratory diseases	308	277	172
Typhus	106	10	0.6
Scarlet fever	66	9	4
Whooping cough	66	44	11
Diphtheria and croup	64	17	9
Measles	40	34	9
Smallpox	17	1	0

(Flinn, *Scottish Population History*)

The writer George Orwell commented in the 1930s:

Source 6.112 ———————————

The post-war development of cheap luxuries has been a very fortunate thing for our rulers. It is quite likely that fish and chips, art-silk stockings, tinned salmon, cut price chocolate, the movies, the radio, strong tea and the football pools have, between them, averted revolution.

(G. Orwell, *The Road to Wigan Pier*, 1962)

The growth in population was slowing down so that a family's income might well be shared among fewer people. The average number of children born to British couples marrying between 1900 and 1909 was 3.4: but for those marrying in 1920 that number fell to 2.5. The average number of children born to couples marrying in 1930 was down further – to 2.1. Behind these figures lay a revolution in knowledge of and attitudes to birth control.

Until the 1920s women had nowhere to go for help. Printed information on contraception was banned as obscene.

In 1921 Marie Stopes opened the first birth control clinic in London. In 1939 the various birth control clinics that had opened by then united to form the Family Planning Association.

Though health improved, the fact that most people still had to pay to see the doctor meant that all sorts of other 'cures' were tried first. Molly Weir recalled those days:

Sources 6.113 ———————————

One neighbour brought her wee boy, who had bad rickets. My mother had told me that this was because Wee Eck's mother had been too poor to give him real milk when he was an infant and had given him weak tea in his bottle, and his bones hadn't developed. I gazed with interest at his wizened little face and at his poor bent legs . . .

We all shared the nightmare of toothache. Apart from the fact that it cost 2/6 [12p] to have a tooth extracted we were all terrified of the dentist. Adults swore to the relief afforded by a tiny drop of whisky dropped into the throbbing cavity . . . Doctors were only called when all else failed. Apart from the cost we had great faith in the folk medicine. For whooping cough the favourite cure was to suspend the victim over a tar boiler . . . One horrible scourge in our tenements was ringworms. Another head invasion almost impossible to avoid was nits and lice. Worms was another affliction of our infants.

(M. Weir, *Best Foot Forward*, 1972)

Even though people's diet was improving, the work of Sir John Boyd Orr of Aberdeen's Rowett Institute showed that half the country's population could not afford 'a diet completely adequate for health.'

QUESTIONS

1 What reasons in favour of welfare reforms can you find in sections on Liberal Welfare reform (p. 134) and Welfare reform between the Wars (p. 137)? (K.U)

2 What reasons can you find against such reforms? (K.U)

3 What do you think is the point of view of the artist in source 6.105? Was he in favour of Liberal reforms? (E.1)

4 What further reforms do you think might still have been needed by 1939? (E.2)

5 What do you think the author of source 6.112 meant by claiming that cheap luxuries 'averted revolution'? (E.1)

6 Do you think this is a sensible idea? (E.2)

139

The unemployment issue

The evidence in Chapter 5 showed the economic difficulties faced by Britain. As a result between 1920 and 1939 the numbers out of work were high. Between 1930 and 1932 they were particularly severe. Scotland shared this problem. In 1927 over 10% of Scottish workers had no job and by 1932 the figure had risen to over 27%. By 1939 it had fallen to 13.5%. Unemployment did not affect the country evenly but was concentrated in certain places. In 1934, for example, over 36% of Greenock workers had no job, nor had over 37% of those in Motherwell. In other parts of Britain the figures were even worse, with South Wales, Northern Ireland and north-east England especially hard hit. In 1934 in the north-east English shipbuilding town of Jarrow 67.8% of workers were unemployed! Yet in much of south-east and midland England the problem was far less serious. The unemployed workers of Oxford in 1934, for example, totalled 5% of the workforce.

Some unemployed people attempted to protest. In 1921 the National Unemployed Workers Movement was established, its leader was a young Communist, Wal Hannington. By 1929 the NUWM had 10 000 members. It helped organise protest marches in Glasgow. It organised other marches too – the Jarrow March was especially successful in winning publicity. But the Conservative Prime Minister from 1924 to 1929 (and 1935 to 1937), Stanley Baldwin, declared:

Source 6.115

In the opinion of HM Government such marches can do no good to the causes for which they are represented to be undertaken, are liable to cause unnecessary hardship to those taking part in them and are altogether undesirable in this country governed by a Parliamentary system where every area has its representative in the House of Commons to put forward grievance and suggest remedies, processions to London cannot claim to have any constitutional influence on policy . . . Ministers cannot consent to receive any deputation of Marchers.

(*The Times*, 15 Oct. 1936)

Source 6.114

Queueing outside the labour exchange in Clydebank

The numbers of unemployed threatened to swamp the old Poor Law System. Parishes could not afford to keep all those asking for help in areas where unemployment was high. The government tried to meet the problem with 'transitional benefit' – payments from the state to people who had used up all their claim to unemployment insurance. In 1929 Neville Chamberlain, Minister of Health, scrapped the old system throughout Britain. Large-scale local authorities took over the problem. Each set up a 'Public Assistance Committee'. Where possible the PACs – like the parishes before them – tried to find useful work for the unemployed to do. Marion Watt of Aberdeen remembered how her father found work from the council:

Source 6.116

They started giving them six weeks at a time on the streets and roads, tarring. Six weeks, then you was paid off and others got their turn. And then one time he was lucky and he got a year and a half on the roads and he thought he was in for good. But right at our own door he got laid off. He was paving Abbey Road and I was waving to him from the window when the foreman came to him and said 'This is you finished.' They found that he'd been there too long. They'd overlooked him. We thought we was fine, although the wages weren't much, 30/- [£1.50].

Still it was better, and it gave him some self-respect because he was miserable when he was unemployed. He was a proud man and he hated going asking for jobs and them hardly listening to him. He went to the gasworks at 6 o'clock every morning, because they sometimes took on extra hands, and the foreman said one morning, 'I'm fed up seeing your face.' He came home like a sheet – just miserable. That went on, off and on, for 17 years, till 1937.

There was so many unemployed in the town. The Broo was only giving 21/- [£1.5p] for the four of us. The Board of Health said it wasn't enough to keep you alive and that the Councils would have to help the unemployed themselves. They started a scheme to build the golf course at Hazlehead and you would get seven and six [37p] more on your dole for working three days a week. So of course they

all did that. The Hazlehead golf course was built with sweat and tears. They were soaking up to their oxters with the peaty boggy ground. His feet was frozen. He used to come home exhausted. My brother gave him an old bike. We used it for years.

(Marion Watt's father-in-law in N. Gray, *The Worst of Times*, 1986)

The money the unemployed received was commonly known as the 'dole'. The dole had critics, like this newspaper correspondent of 1931, who thought:

Source 6.117

The dole system which makes it easy to exist when increased effort is required tends to encourage laziness in those of weak moral fibre, and increases the number of parasites at the bottom end of the scale. It depreciates character when character is already weak and already under temptation to give in to circumstances, and at the same time it diverts huge sums of money from productive industry, which provides the nation's sustenance and finds work for the people, to the maintenance of an army of unemployed who are required to render no service whatever in return for what is given them.

(In Stevenson, *British Society 1914–45*)

In 1931 the government cut the dole by 10% as part of its efforts to deal with an economic crisis by reducing government spending. It also introduced 'the means test'. Harry McShane who saw it in action in Glasgow explained:

Source 6.118

The Means Test was specially feared and hated by every unemployed worker. The regulations insisted that *any* member of a household who was working was responsible for the household income – that is, he or she had to support the rest of the family. If any one in a house was working – including uncles, aunts, cousins and even lodgers sometimes – then unemployment benefit wasn't paid to the other people in that house.

It broke up families. Sons and daughters went to live away from home; fathers in work became bitter towards their children. Cases were reported in the newspaper where worry over the Means Test had actually led to suicide.

Source 6.119
Means Test March

It produced despair – and also the most massive demonstrations by the unemployed all over the country.

(McShane, *No Mean Fighter*)

Mr and Mrs Freel of Leith recalled these times:

Source 6.120
We were married on the dole, 1937. It was a hand-to-mouth existence. Fifteen bob [75p] a week, that was all we got between the two of us. Well, a family, if you had a brother or a sister or a father working you were put on the means test: you got nothing. That was the reason why my husband came to live with us really. His father was working, his brother was working and he got no dole money. We decided then to get married and we would get the dole money between us and we got 15 shillings a week.

Many o' the other people in the street were idle so we all helped each other. A marrow bone went over 16 tenants. A big marrow bone and we all borrowed it to make soup. This was the sort o' community spirit there was they days. If anyone died in the street it didnae matter if they were Catholic or Protestant, a collection was taken to cover the cost of the funeral.

(*Leith Lives*)

In 1934 the government restored the 10% cut and re-organised the dole on a national basis. But the problem did not disappear until recruitment for the Second World War removed it.

QUESTIONS

1 Explain why you think the old Poor Law was abolished in 1929.   (E.2)

2 Do you agree with the argument in source 6.115?   (E.2)

3 Might the author of Source 6.118 have been on the dole? Give reasons for what you think.   (E.1)

4. What was the effect of the means test on family life?   (K.U)

7 Political Change

Between 1880 and 1939 the right to vote in elections for MPs spread from being something only a small minority possessed, to being a right possessed by all over 21-year-olds. This change helped to alter the kind of political parties that fought for power to rule the country. The sources in this chapter deal with how and why people's political rights changed, and with the results of these changes. These were changes that affected the population of Scotland as part of wider changes in Britain.

Extending the Vote, 1884–5

Source 7.1

Banner of Peebles tailors carried in 1884 reform agitation. It depicts William Gladstone, the Liberal Prime Minister

In 1880 most Scots (like most people in Britain) still could not vote in elections to choose MPs. No women were allowed to vote. Those men who could vote were property owners including householders in towns. By the 1880s the Liberal Party, led by W. E. Gladstone, believed it was right to give the vote to ordinary male householders in the countryside too. The Conservative-controlled House of Lords was not very sympathetic to the proposal. In Scotland, and in other parts of Britain, huge numbers turned out to demonstrate in favour of the bill to extend the

THE CONTENDING SWAINS.

Source 7.2

Source 7.3

Demonstration by Aberdeen trade unionists in favour of the reform bill, 1884

vote. In Glasgow in 1884 a procession of 64 000 made its way to Glasgow Green.

Helped by this support, the 1884 Reform Act became law. It increased the number of men who could vote in Britain from around 3 million to about 5 million. In 1885 the Redistribution of Seats Act reorganised constituences throughout Britain so that only towns of 50 000 to 165 000 still had the old system of having two MPs. The rest of the country had a whole series of single-member constituences. As part of these reforms extra seats were given to Scotland, increasing their number by 12 to 72.

Yet still about 40% of men could not vote. The Liberals had given the vote to householders, people they thought of as respectable. But servants, soldiers in barracks, sons living at home, people getting poor relief and people who had not paid their rates could not vote. The franchise (i.e. the right to vote) was still seen as something that had to be earned by respectable behaviour, not as a right all men should have as citizens. Nor could any women vote. This exclusion of half the population was to become the main issue in the following years.

QUESTIONS

1 Who is the person referred to in source 7.1? (K.U)

2 Explain what the cartoonist is trying to show in source 7.2. (E.1)

Votes for Women

The Reform Act of 1884 was a great disappointment to many women. For a number of years some of them had been trying to persuade the government to give the vote to some women at least. Already some of the voters in local elections for councils, and school boards were women. Women were allowed to be members of school boards, and, after 1894, of parish and district councils too. But Parliament remained closed to them, whether as voters or as MPs. By the 1900s this situation seemed, to a considerable number of women, to demand far more vigorous action. By this time more women were better educated, many of the leaders of the new Independent Labour Party supported their cause and so did a number of the more radically minded Liberals. In 1903 Mrs Emmeline Pankhurst set up the Women's Social and Political Union. This organisation spread rapidly across the country – by 1906 it was established in Scotland. Its first branch was in Glasgow. Mrs Pankhurst and her daughters Sylvia and Christabel gathered around them a number of women with the ability to speak to large meetings, organise processions and gatherings, and write effectively.

Their followers included Scots like Flora Drummond, a telegraphist from Arran who went to London. There she organised huge

Source 7.4
Pro-suffragette demonstration in Edinburgh, 1900

suffragette demonstrations which she led, dressed in uniform, and on horseback. In 1905 a Liberal Government took office. Mrs Pankhurst and her followers (known as suffragettes) waited to see if the Liberals would give them the vote. Mrs Pankhurst wrote of this time:

Source 7.5

We did not begin to fight until we had given the new [Liberal] Government every chance to give us the pledge we wanted. This was the beginning of a campaign. We kept up the work of questioning Cabinet Ministers all over England and Scotland. Now the newspapers were full of us.

(Mrs E. Pankhurst, *My Own Story*, 1914)

When nothing happened the WSPU turned to more noisy and forceful methods. They particularly tried to spoil the campaigns and meetings of the Prime Minister (from 1908), Herbert Asquith, and one of his ministers, Winston Churchill. In 1908 their efforts helped cut the Liberal majority for the Dundee seat Churchill was fighting for in a by-election. The suffragettes not only disrupted meetings, they smashed windows, and set fire to the contents of letter boxes. In 1910, Emily Davison threw herself at the King's horse as it raced in the Derby and died as a result of her fall.

Some suffragettes opposed these activities. They preferred peaceful methods — like refusing to pay taxes. They formed the Women's Freedom League, an organisation with considerable support in Scotland.

Source 7.6
Anna Munro

Source 7.7
Suffragettes chalking slogans on the pavement

The more violent WSPU methods spread to Scotland. In 1908 the Scottish suffragette, Dr Marion Gilchrist, said in her speech at the opening of a new WSPU headquarters in Glasgow:

Source 7.8

[She] at one time thought it a great pity that the militant suffragists should create rows at Westminster, but she had been brought round to another view. She saw clearly now that nobody had done more for the cause than those militant suffragists. They had brought the question to the public notice and that was what the advocates of women suffrage who had carried on the work quietly for 60 years had failed to do.

(S. King, *The Scottish Women's Suffrage Movement*, 1978)

Source 7.9

Examples of militant suffragette activities in Scotland 1913–14:

Glasgow pillar boxes had their contents destroyed by bottles of acid being poured into them;

Telephone wires were cut.

Two elderly sisters, ex-missionaries, tried to set fire to a new stand at Kelso Racecourse;

Ayr Race Course stand was burnt;

Leuchars Station was burnt;

Farrington Hall, Dundee was burnt;

Kelly House, Wemyss Bay, was burnt;

The Royal Observatory, Edinburgh, was damaged by explosion;

The Getty Marine Laboratory, St Andrews, was damaged by fire;

The Prime Minister was physically attacked on Lossiemouth Golf Course by two suffragettes.

The attack on pillar boxes began the campaign. It was carried out by members of the Domestic Workers Union. One of them explained:

Source 7.10

I was able to drop acid into the pillar boxes without being suspected because I walked down from where I was employed in my cap, muslin apron, and black frock – nobody would suspect me of dropping acid through the box.

(King, *The Scottish Women's Suffrage Movement*)

The suffragettes and their opponents used cartoons, posters, banners, indeed anything to argue their cause. Mrs Duncan who lived in Portobello at this time described events:

Source 7.11

I really saw these women in Portobello. They tied themselves to railings and were also trailed along the streets by their arms and legs by the police, who got their big hats knocked off. The police were there with horses too. I thought it was terrible, though I really didn't understand what it was all about. There were perhaps four ladies there, all toffs from the big mansion houses. I'm sure you've heard of Lady Pankhurst who was the leader, but I don't think she was at Portobello. They also went on hunger strike and had to be force fed. They suffered so that women could get the vote, and because they won we have the vote today.

(Campbell, *Changed Days*)

Source 7.12

Do you think the artist supported the suffragettes?

Alastair Philips heard the reminiscences of:

Source 7.13

. . . my Aunt Caroline [who] revelled in being

one of the more vigorous and inventive of her generation of suffragettes in Aberdeen.

She was a concert pianist whose sensitive hands had been known more than once to pour noxious substances into pillar boxes. And on one occasion she had chained herself to railings, to the embarrassment of her brother who, as a journalist in the same town, had occasion to report what he could not avoid seeing. . .

The ploy of which Aunt Carrie was proudest – not for its non-violence but for its insolence and organisation – was the one when she and a raiding party of like-minded feminists, intruded under cover of darkness into the policies of Balmoral Castle when the Monarch was in residence, and replaced all the flags in the holes in the putting green with others bearing the legend 'Votes for Women'.

(A. Philips, *My Uncle George*, 1984)

Parliamentary reform did take place at this time but it dealt with Liberal determination to reduce the power of the Conservative-dominated House of Lords.

Source 7.15
The Parliament Act 1911
(i) The House of Lords lost the right to alter or reject a money bill.
(ii) If the Lords rejected a bill in three successive Parliamentary sessions, yet the Commons approved it, it would still become law.
(iii) The maximum life of Parliament was cut from seven years to five.

1911 Parliament agreed that MPs should in future be paid. MPs were to receive £400 a year. (This was one of the Chartists' demands. It meant that working men could become MPs.)

Suffragette activities in Scotland were very much a part of their overall British campaign. Leaders often came to Scotland to speak. In March 1914 Mrs Pankhurst came to speak in Glasgow even though she knew that the police would try and arrest her since she was breaking the terms of the 'Cat and Mouse' Act.

Source 7.14

A hunger striker being force fed

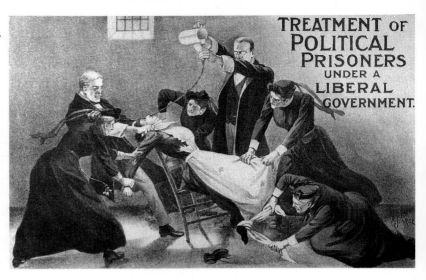

TREATMENT OF
POLITICAL
PRISONERS
UNDER A
LIBERAL
GOVERNMENT.

She was smuggled into the meeting in a laundry basket. When she appeared trouble broke out. The following sources both describe this event. The first is from a policeman, the second from a member of the audience.

Source 7.17

a) *Inspector Walker*

About 8.5 pm I . . . rushed up the stair followed by sergeants and constables . . . I was the first to enter the Hall in uniform in front of the platform . . . we were immediately assailed with chairs, flower pots, water bottles, and other missiles thrown from the platform by men and women who fought like tigers. The platform was well fortified with strands of barbed wire run along in front of it, covered with flags and tissue paper which prevented the progress of the police . . . I drew my baton for the purpose of protecting myself, but I did not strike anyone with it. A number of constables drew their batons but I could not say I saw any person struck by a constable. The ladies were all well armed with clubs.

b) *Mr Leonard Gow*

I had an uninterrupted view of the scene, a scene which must have made the blood of every true man present boil with indignation and shame. I went to the meeting a non-militant, and not being conversant with Suffragette politics was unaware that Mrs Pankhurst was liable to arrest, my object being to learn the Suffragists standpoint from one of their Leaders . . . The audience consisted of over three, probably four thousand people, men and women, and among these present were representatives of our most respected families in the City . . . After Mrs Pankhurst had been speaking for a very few minutes, the platform, which please mark, was occupied solely by women, old and young, was rushed by detectives and policemen with drawn batons who laid out in all directions, hitting and felling women whose only offence was that they crowded around their leader evidently trying to protect her from violence.

(Scottish Record Office, File HH 55/336, 'The Arrest of Mrs Pankhurst in Glasgow', in Berry & Whyte, *Glasgow Observed*)

The outbreak of the First World War ended suffragette activity. A minority of them opposed the War. The majority followed Mrs Pankhurst and did all they could for the War effort. The results of the wartime work of women can be seen in this 1917 speech by their former opponent, Herbert Asquith. (He was putting forward a bill to give women the vote, a bill that became law in 1918.)

Source 7.18

How could we have carried on the War without them? Short of actually bearing arms in the field there is hardly a service which has contributed to our cause in which women have not been at least as active and as efficient as men. What moves me still more is the problem of reconstruction when the War is over. The questions which will then arise in regard to women's labour and women's functions in the new order of things are questions in regard to which I find it impossible to withhold from women the power and the right of making their voices directly heard.

(*Parliament Debates*, vol. XCII, 1917)

Source 7.19
1918 Representation of the People Act
(i) The vote was given to all men, over 21.
(ii) Women over 30 who were householders, or were married to householders or University graduates obtained the vote.
(iii) The Act added 2 million women and 6 million men to the British electorate. 17 women stood as candidates in the 1918 UK election. The one success, Constance Markiewicz (Sinn Fein), refused to take her seat.

Scottish cities where large numbers of men lived who hadn't had the vote, especially felt the difference. In 1911, for example, about 52% of men in Dundee had not had the vote. In Glasgow the figure was over 47% — whereas in Edinburgh it was only 31%.

By 1928 the question of 'votes for women' had so ceased to upset politicians that a new law was passed by a Conservative Government. All political parties agreed that women should have the vote on exactly the same terms as men.

Source 7.20

SHADE OF OLD MILITANT : " So this is what I fought for ! "   *April 29th*, 1927.

Source 7.21
Women in Parliament

Year	Number of candidates	Number elected
1918	17	1
1922	33	2
1923	34	8
1924	41	4
1929	69	14
1931	62	15
1935	67	9

QUESTIONS

1 What 'pledge' did Mrs Pankhurst expect to be given? (source 7.5) (K.U)

2 Find and list the methods of protest used by suffragettes. (K.U)

3 What arguments do you think members of the Women's Freedom League might have used against the Women's Social & Political Union? (E.2)

4 What argument does Marion Gilchrist use in favour of forceful protests? (source 7.8) (K.U)

5 Which do you think is the stronger argument? Give reasons for your answer. (E.2)

6 Look at the 7.14 sources. Which is the most persuasive? (E.1)

7 Explain how the author of your chosen source has tried to convince people looking at it. (E.1)

8 Explain what the scene shown in 7.16 refers to. (K.U)

9 Look at sources 7.17a and b. How do these two accounts differ? Why do you think they differ? Which would you believe? What other evidence might you look for? (E.1)

10 What point is the cartoonist who drew source 7.20 trying to make? (E.1) Can you see any link between that source and source 7.21?

Changing Political Parties

In the 1880s Britain's voters usually chose between two main political parties – the Conservatives and the Liberals. Between 1880 and 1935 the fortunes of these parties changed greatly.

The way that most Scots voted can be seen from the following table showing the percentage of voters choosing each of the main parties, and the number of seats they captured.

Source 7.22

Election results for the United Kingdom

	Conservative	Liberal	Labour	Irish Nationalist	Sinn Fein	Communist
1900	402	184	2	82		
1906	151	400	30	83		
1910	273	275	40	82		
1910	272	272	42	84		
1918	358	161+	60×	7	73	
1922	345	116+	142			
1923	258	159	191			
1924	419	40	151			1
1929	260	59	288			
1931	473	72	65×			
1935	432	20	158×			1

(+ = During these elections the Liberals were split between followers of Lloyd George and followers of Asquith.

× = the Labour result for 1918 includes 10 who followed Lloyd George's leadership in a coalition government. Labour in 1931 was split; 13 supported a Coalition Government. In 1935 four of the Labour MPs, ILP members, formed a separate group.

(D. Butler and J. Freeman, *British Political Facts*, 1964)

Source 7.23

Scottish results – the percentage of people choosing each party and the number of seats won

Year	Labour	Conservative	Liberal	SNP
1880		29.9% 6 seats	70.1% 52	
1885		34.3% 8 "	53.3% 51	
1886		46.4% 27 "	53.6% 43	
1892		44.4% 19 "	53.9% 51	
1895		47.4% 31 "	51.7% 39	
1900		49.0% 36 "	50.2% 34	
1906	2.3% 2 seats	38.2% 10 "	56.4% 58	
1910 Jan	5.1% 2 "	39.6% 9 "	54.2% 58	
1910 Dec	3.6%	49.6% 9 "	53.6% 58	
1918	22.9% 6 "	32.8% 30 "	19.1% 25×	
			15.0% 8	
1922	32.2% 29 "	25.1% 13 "	17.7% 12×	
			21.5% 15	
1923	35.9% 34 "	31.6% 14 "	28.4% 22	
1924	41.1% 26 "	40.7% 36 "	16.6% 8	
1929	42.3% 36 "	35.9% 20 "	18.1% 13	0.2%
1931	32.6% 7 "	49.5% 48 "	8.6% 7	1.0%
			4.8% 8+	
1935	36.8% 20 "	42.0% 35 "	6.7% 3	1.1%
	(5.0% 4 seats)		6.7% 7+	
	(ILP)			

+ = National Liberal   × = Coalition Liberal

(R. Parry, *Scottish Political Facts*, 1987)

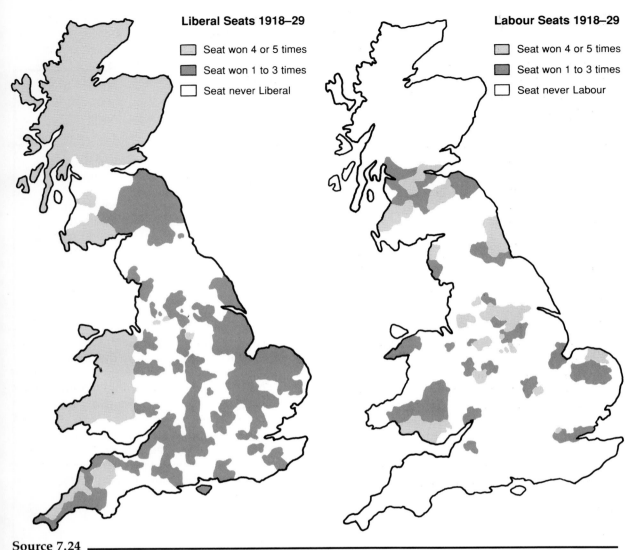

Liberal Seats 1918–29

☐ Seat won 4 or 5 times
■ Seat won 1 to 3 times
☐ Seat never Liberal

Labour Seats 1918–29

☐ Seat won 4 or 5 times
■ Seat won 1 to 3 times
☐ Seat never Labour

Source 7.24

Notice the kinds of areas in Britain and Scotland that were involved in one of the great changes of this period – the decline of the Liberal Party and the rise of the Labour Party.

The extension of the vote, together with the secret ballot, made a big difference to what politicians had to do to win support. During this period politicians had to organise themselves better and make far more effort to win people's support. Leading politicians travelled around the country, making speeches to huge gatherings of supporters. (The growth of the railways had made this sort of campaigning much easier.) By the 1930s party leaders were using the recent development of the radio (or 'wireless') to broadcast to the nation. The Conservative, Neville Chamberlain, was especially skilful at using cinefilm to put himself forward as a man people could trust.

QUESTIONS

1 Do sources 7.22 and 7.23 show that Scots voters followed the preferences of United Kingdom voters? (K.U)

2 Which MPs might welcome the changes described in the above source? (E.2)

The Rise of the Labour Party

As a journalist you have been asked to investigate and report on the rise of the Labour Party between the 1880s and 1930

a) What sort of questions might you be looking for answers to?

Perhaps they might include:

- What sort of people supported Labour?
- What did it offer them?
- Did the weaknesses of opponents help it?
- Did the changes in the franchise help it?

Can you suggest other questions a journalist might be looking for answers to? (N.B.: these questions might make useful topics for paragraphs in your final article.)

b) In order to answer these questions you will need to look for evidence. You might interview people, read useful articles, look at pictures and posters, collect facts and figures. The following sources all deal with the growth of the Labour Party. Read through them all to obtain an overall picture of what was happening.

- Make notes on any information that will help, grouping your notes under the different questions you have decided to ask. (K.U)

- Copy out any short quotes that might make your article more interesting. (K.U)

- Think about the point of view of the authors of the different sources. You may feel that it is worth mentioning someone's evidence, but adding why you don't wholly support this because of the bias of the evidence. (E.1)

- You will need to make clear what *you* think really brought about the rise of Labour. (E.2)

The problem – what should workers in Britain do to improve their position?

The possibilities

a) join one of the many Socialist societies that developed from the 1880s. These included: –

The Social Democratic Federation, set up in 1884 by H. M. Hyndman, a wealthy public-school educated man. It usually favoured very forceful socialist policies.

- The Socialist League, 1884, set up by William Morris and Eleanor Marx, daughter of the famous Socialist thinker, Karl Marx.
- The Independent Labour Party, established 1893, led by the Scot Keir Hardie.
- The Socialist Labour Party, a 1903 Scottish group that broke away from the SDF.
- The Fabian Society, established 1884, it favoured very cautious peaceful reform. It attracted well-to-do intellectuals like the playwright George Bernard Shaw.

b) Join a trade union. Trade unions were growing in size and organisation. In the late 1880s they spread among the less skilled workers as mass organisations. Workers were inspired by the success of strikes by girls working at Bryant and Mays Match Factory and by the dockers in London. But unions were still not strong enough to withstand a counter-attack by employers.

c) Take 'direct action'. By the 1900s some leaders, like Tom Mann, thought that large unions, each dominating a particular industry, and working together could alter society by taking 'direct action' (probably a general strike) to bring about the overthrow of the existing government.

VOTE FOR

...ne Rule.

...nocratic ...ernment.

...e to Labour

...Monopoly.

...andlordism

Temperance Reform.

Healthy Homes.

Fair Rents.

Eight-Hour Day.

Work for the Unemployed.

...EIR HARDIE.

Source 7.26

The Scottish Farm Servant.   DECEMBER, 1915.

Don't Throw Yourself Away Too Cheap!

Big Money Can Be Got For The Asking.

Here are some of the bargains made at the October Hirings. They are no exceptional bargains, but have been got by many men who had the pluck to ask for the money they were worth.

DUNFERMLINE.	30/- per week, 1 ton potatoes, harvest £1.
	25/- per week, 1 pint milk daily, 40 stones meal, 1 ton potatoes, ½ lb. butter weekly, insurance paid.
CUPAR.	£54 per year, 6½ bolls meal, 1 pint milk daily, 2 tons potatoes.
	Single Men—£25 per six months, all found.
DUNDEE.	£56 per year, 6½ bolls meal, 1 pint milk daily, 2 tons potatoes.
	28/- a week, meal, potatoes, harvest £1.
	Single Men in Bothy—£35 per six months, meal, milk potatoes, coal and light.
	Single Men Boarded—£30 per six months, all found.
CRIEFF.	24/- a week, 8d. milk daily, 5 stones meal per month, and potatoes.
STIRLING.	28/- per week, 2 tons potatoes, harvest £1.
	30/- per week, 1 ton potatoes.

House included in each case.

Many men got less, because they asked for less. — Don't you be put off with anything less. —

THESE WERE UNION MEN.

Are You in the Union, and trying to get other men into the Union?

Printed and Published for the Scottish Farm Servants' Union by JOHN BELL & CO., 97 Mitchell Street, Glasgow.

Scottish socialists and trade unionists were very much to the fore in the developments of these years. Keir Hardie was especially prominent. In 1888 he tried, unsuccessfully, to win a by-election in Mid Lanark. Afterwards, he wrote:

Source 7.27

The result of the Mid-Lanark election showed the need for an organisation in Scotland which would enable the workers to exercise their voting power to their own advantage. A number of bodies have been at work in this direction but [their] hold on the working classes has been slight [because] they were content to sink their identity when the interests of the Liberal Party were concerned. Since April Mr Keir Hardie has been devoting most of his spare time to organising a distinct Labour party and on 25 August a conference in Glasgow, gave birth to the new movement. The programme adopted included nationalisation of the land, minerals, railways and banking; an eight-hour (working day) bill; payment of MPs; home rule – N.B.: 'Home rule for each separate nationality or country in the British Empire'; abolition of the House of Lords; free education; adult suffrage (i.e. votes for all men and women).

A monster demonstration was held on the Green, . . . the Scottish Parliamentary Labour Party should be a power in the land.

(R. H. Campbell, J. B. A. Dow, *Scottish Economic and Social History Source Book*, 1968)

The Party also voted for 'Abolition of the present Poor Law System and the substitution of State Insurance to provide for Sickness, Accident, Death or Old Age.'

William Haddow was one of those drawn to the Independent Labour Party into which Hardie merged his Scottish Labour Party. He wrote of Hardie:

Source 7.28

I can see him at one of his great meetings with arms outstretched and in a clear, warm voice making his passionate appeal to the audience – 'Come now, men and women, I plead with you, for your sake and that of your children, for the sakes of the down-trodden poor, the weary, the sore-hearted mothers, the unemployed fathers, for their sakes, and for the sake of our beloved Socialism, the hope of Peace and humanity throughout the world – Men and women, I appeal to you, come and join us and fight with us in the fight where justice and all righteous causes shall prevail.'

There is no doubt that Keir Hardie influenced my whole life and I vowed that I would devote as much of my time as I could to the service of the Labour Movement.

(Haddow, *My 70 Years*)

In 1892 Hardie was elected to Parliament. It was an amazing achievement for the son of a poor Scots servant girl. Moreover, he refused to simply follow the Liberal party line. Yet Hardie, like most leading Scots socialists of the 1880s and 90s, was not a keen follower of the ideas of Karl Marx. Like MacDonald, he hated war (he was a pacifist during the Boer War) and the idea of using violence to over-turn the existing government.

Source 7.29 ———————————
Scottish Labour Party card

In 1880 the three working-class men who were MPs were all Liberals. Ramsay MacDonald who was the illegitimate son of a farm labourer, brought up in Lossiemouth and Elgin by his mother and grandmother, was keenly interested in improving society.

Source 7.30 ———————————
I ceased to trust in the Liberal Party when I was convinced that they were not prepared to courageously face the bread and butter prob-lems of the time, the problems of poverty, stunted lives and cruel conditions of work.

(D. Marquand, *Ramsay MacDonald*, 1977)

Men like Hardie and MacDonald saw that the socialist societies were too divided and too small to win power. Labour MPs would only be

elected if the trade unions brought their strength and money to the cause. In 1899 Hardie's effort helped persuade the Trade Union Congress to agree that:

Source 7.31 ———————————
With a view to securing a better representation of the interests of Labour in the House of Commons it hereby instructs the Parliamentary Committee to invite the co-operation of all the co-operative, socialist, trade union and other organisations to jointly co-operate in convening a special congress to devise ways and means for securing the return of an increased number of Labour members to the next Parliament.

After this a committee of trade unionists and Socialists agreed to work for:

Source 7.32 ———————————
. . . a distinct Labour group in Parliament who shall have their own whips and agree upon their policy which must embrace a readiness to co-operate with any party which may be promoting legislation in the direct interests of Labour.

A number of newspapers tried to spread Socialist ideas. One of the earliest in Scotland was the *Workers Herald*, founded in 1891 in Aberdeen. It promised its readers:

Source 7.33 ———————————
A large portion of the *Workers Herald* will not be taken up with flunkeyish stories in which working men are taught to admire and imitate the follies and snobberies of their 'betters', stories in which the boy hero is introduced in humble circumstances, is one day discovered to be the son of an earl and is able henceforth to live upon other folks labour.

(*Worker's Herald* prospectus, 1891)

The most famous of these newspapers, the *Daily Herald*, was founded in 1911 by George Lansbury. In the 1906 election, Labour candidates, organised by the Labour Representation Committee (whose Secretary was MacDonald) benefited from a deal struck between Labour and the Liberals. In a number of seats they co-operated to defeat the Conservatives. The Labour men who entered Parliament belonged to what was now officially called 'The Labour Party'. It included Labour MPs for Dundee and Glasgow. In their first year they were led by Hardie, a fierce teetotaller who refused to let his fellow Labour MPs go into the House of Commons bar. In the following years the Liberals undid the harm done by the Taff Vale case, agreed to pay MPs, and carried out their own social reforms. However, according to Beatrice Webb, a wealthy member of the Fabian Society:

	Union membership		Numbers affiliated to the Labour Party	Percentage of workforce
1900	2 023 000	1900	353 000	
1913	4 135 000	1912	1 858 000	23.1
1918	6 533 000		2 960 000	35.7
1926	5 219 000		3 352 000	28.3
1932	4 444 000		1 960 000	23.0
1939	6 298 000		2 214 000	

Source 7.34

Labour Members have utterly failed to impress the House of Commons and the constituencies as a live force and have lost confidence. The unions are swelling in membership and funds, but the faith of politically active members is becoming confused. There is little leadership.

(P. Adelman, *The Rise of the Labour Party*, 1972)

People interested in social reform were, on the eve of the First World War, as likely to be Liberals following Lloyd George as members of the Labour Party.

Source 7.35

Labour and the First World War

(i) Before 1914 Labour never put up more than 78 candidates, after it, in 1918, it ran 361 candidates and polled 2¼ million votes.

(ii) In 1914 there was no proper Labour organisation, just that provided by unions and socialist societies: in 1918 Labour had proper separate constituency branches. This work was led by Arthur Henderson, formerly one of Lloyd George's Cabinet.

(iii) By 1918 Labour, who had split over whether to support the War, were re-united. But the Liberal party was very badly split between those who supported Lloyd George and those who followed Asquith.

(iv) By 1918 Labour had developed its own ideas for policies especially the ideas of a minimum wage and democratic control of industry to promote people's welfare.

(v) Trade union membership increased greatly in the War years.

Source 7.36

The 1918 Labour Party Constitution. (This was mainly the work of the Fabian, Sidney Webb.)

1. Name – the Labour Party.
2. Membership – all affiliated organisations together with individual members of a local Labour Party.
3. Party objects (aims).
   a) To organise a Labour Party and ensure the establishment of a local Labour Party in every constituency.
   b) To co-operate with the Parliamentary Committee of the Trades Union Congress.
   c) To give effect, as far as may be practicable, to the principles approved by the Party Conference.
   d) To secure for the producers by hand or by brain the full fruits of their industry and the most equitable distribution thereof that may be possible upon the basis of the common ownership of the means of production and the best obtainable system of popular administration and control of each industry or service.
   (This is the famous 'Clause 4' of the Party constitution that committed Labour to Socialism.)

The years from 1915 to 1921, and 1926, were very restless years in the Labour movement, especially in Scotland.

The government persuaded union leaders that, during the War, they should set aside some of their rules about who could do certain sorts of work. Among some Clyde workers there was considerable opposition to this. Harry McShane explained his point of view on these events. He was a very enthusiastic

Source 7.37
Tanks brought in to supress discontent in Glasgow, 1919

socialist who was soon to become a member of the Communist Party. He noted how a strike for more pay among members of the Amalgamated Society of Engineers played an important part:

Source 7.38
The 'tuppence or nothing' strike brought the shop stewards movement into prominence for the first time. Most of the old shop stewards, whose only job had been to check the ASE cards, disappeared. Many of the younger ones were socialists.

The engineers' victory helped other struggles, particularly the one over rents. John Maclean had great hopes the Glasgow rent strike heralded the development of political strikes in Britain.

The Clyde engineers refusal to accept dilution meant that Lloyd George, the Minister of Munitions, decided to visit Glasgow. Lloyd George got a terrible reception. The government began to arrest key individuals. Maclean was arrested on the charge of making speeches to rouse the workers against the War itself. (He was later released.) Maclean made a speech in defence of the Russian Revolution. He was answering Ramsay MacDonald who said the Bolsheviks were honest men though he didn't agree with them (1918). Despite great hopes, the only Clydesider to be elected was Neil Maclean. In 1918 the atmosphere in the whole Labour movement was one of change. Above all there was the influence of the Russian Revolution.

(McShane, *No Mean Fighter*)

Men like McShane and the Govan ex-teacher John Maclean did not believe the Labour Party was sufficiently bold. In 1919 the Clyde Workers Committee tried to hold a general strike of Glasgow workers in support of a shorter working week. Police, and troops with tanks and machine guns were sent to Glasgow. Strike leaders were imprisoned. But, by 1922, the protests, strikes and demonstrations that troubled parts of Britain, and especially Clydeside, faded. Instead the fear of rising unemployment seemed the most important fact. The Labour Party steadily increased its number of MPs. By 1922 42% of Glasgow's electors were voting Labour. Labour councillors on Glasgow City Council included men of the considerable ability of John Wheatley and 10 of Glasgow's 15 constituencies returned Labour MPs. Labour's success was partly due to the work of men like Wheatley who led Catholic voters into accepting his party, convincing many that its principles did not conflict with Catholic beliefs and agreeing to Catholic demands for their own separate system of schooling. By 1933 Labour had captured control of Glasgow City Council. By 1924, the Labour Party leader, Ramsay MacDonald, was asked to form a government.

A writer working in 1923 noted:

Source 7.39
When a distinct Labour Party was organised it was content for a number of years to act as a wing of the Liberal Party. The Great War brought to an end this alignment. Labour, having never faced the task of government, was not handicapped by any record of imperfect achievement. It had obtained control, for political purposes, of the powerful organisation of trade unions and co-operative societies. It drew into its ranks younger and more progressive Liberals who had lost patience with the shattered Liberal Party. It could appeal to all that vague yearning for a new heaven and a new earth which inspired many men after the horrors of the War.

(R. Muir, *Politics and Progress*, 1923)

Source 7.40
Ramsay, Macdonald addressing a rally at Kilsyth, 1924

The Labour Government did not last long. It depended on Liberal support to keep it there and when it lost that support a new election was held in which the Conservatives triumphed. MacDonald was now a leading politician.

The General Strike

In the mid 1920s the Labour Party once more seemed to take a back seat. The centre of the stage was occupied by the unions, especially the miners. In 1926 a general strike took place in Britain. MacDonald worried that his view of peaceful progress achieved through a Parliamentary Labour Party was under threat. He wrote:

Source 7.41
The General Strike is a weapon that cannot be wielded for industrial purposes. It is clumsy and ineffectual. I hope that the result will be a thorough re-consideration of trade union tactics. If the wonderful unity in the strike would be shown in politics, Labour could solve the mining and similar difficulties through the ballot box.

(In Adelman, *The Rise of the Labour Party*)

The miners had the support of the TUC in their determination to resist wage cuts. But the government was only willing to meet the bill for avoiding the wage cuts employers wanted to make for a short period. Thus, two quite different views as to why the strike took place were held. A Conservative MP explained one view.

Source 7.42
In the coal industry the situation had become critical. Pits were closing down on every hand, and something like 300 000 miners were already out of work. Discussions between mine owners and miners led nowhere. The owners, not prepared to work their mines at a loss, could see no remedy except in reducing costs by lowering wages or returning to the eight-hours' day. The miners, who had been led by the fantastic rise in coal prices at the end of the War and during the occupation of the Ruhr to regard the advances gained as a mere instalment of more to come, were indignant.

(L. S. Amery, *My Political Life*, vol. 2)

The miners' president, Herbert Smith, took a different view of why a crisis had developed. He blamed governments of the past for turning down a plan to nationalise coal mines.

Source 7.43
You are responsible for the position we are in – your Government. Our inquiry was held in 1919 and certain findings were the result of that inquiry. A Coalition Government was in power at that time, and both pledged themselves. Yet you have refused to accept it. Or, in other words, you believe in private enterprise, although private enterprise had failed to function. It is your baby, which you must supply with milk . . . We were not prepared to meet the owners to discuss their proposals because we could accept no reduction – not a cent – nor work a minute's extension of time.

(In M. Morris, *The General Strike*, 1976)

Moreover Baldwin's Conservatives had other worries. One of the Prime Minister's close friends, J. C. Davidson, explained:

Source 7.44
We were at this time particularly worried about revolutionary activities in this country . . . The

Communist Party in this country was small
. . . but we thought it was gaining in strength
and we knew that by consistently taking the
lead in industrial disputes it could gain a
secure hold on certain parts of the trade union
movement. We were particularly worried by
the attempts to organise the unemployed.
Committees of Action had been set up in many
factories and trade unions, factory newspapers
were used to influence workers, and demands
were made for more nationalisation and
increased unemployment pay. MacDonald's
failure to act, and the mounting unemployment figures while the Labour Party had been
in office, made for a growing disillusion in the
Labour movement that was dangerous . . .

(Morris, *The General Strike*)

The fiery revolutionary speeches of A. J. Cook,
the Secretary of the Miners Federation, worried
MacDonald almost as much as the
government.

The government represented the way other
unions came out on strike in support of the
miners as a most serious political action.

Source 7.45 ————————————

UNDER WHICH FLAG?

JOHN BULL. 'ONE OF THESE TWO FLAGS HAS GOT TO COME DOWN—AND IT WON'T
BE MINE.'

Winston Churchill was the driving force in the
government newspaper the *British Gazette*. On
6 May 1926 it argued:

Source 7.46 ————————————
The strike is intended as a direct hold-up of the
nation to ransom. 'This moment,' as the Prime
Minister pointed out in the House of Commons,
'has been chosen to challenge the existing
Constitution of the country and to substitute
the reign of force for that which now exists
. . . I do not believe there has been anything
like a thorough-going consultation with the
rank and file before this despotic power was
put into the hands of a small executive in
London . . . I do not think all the leaders who
assented to order a general strike fully realised
that they were threatening the basis of ordered
government and coming nearer to proclaiming
civil war than we have been for centuries past.

Through its own paper the *British Worker* the
TUC replied to this case on 7 May:

Source 7.47 ————————————
The General Council does not challenge the
Constitution. The sole aim of the Council is to
secure for the miners, a decent standard of life.
The Council is engaged in an Industrial
Dispute. There is no Constitutional crisis . . .

It is . . . fantastic for the Prime Minister to
pretend that the Trade Unions are engaged in
an attack upon the Constitution of the
Country. Every instruction issued by the
General Council is evidence of their determination to maintain the struggle strictly on the
basis of an industrial dispute. They have
ordered every member taking part to be exem-
plary in his conduct and not to give any cause
for police interference. The General Council
struggled hard for peace. They are anxious that
an honourable peace shall be secured as soon
as possible. They are not attacking the Constitution. They are not fighting the community.
They are defending the mine workers against
the mine owners.

The strike failed. Labour politicians, TUC
leaders and many union leaders were not
prepared for a long battle. The government
was. It was well organised, used volunteers to
run essential services and was determined not
to give way. Union leaders grabbed the

chance to end the strike offered by an unofficial scheme for reform put forward by the Liberal politician Herbert Samuel.

The defeat pushed many union leaders to look more carefully at backing MacDonald's cautious Labour Party: perhaps slow progress to eventual political power was the way forward.

The General Strike spread over nine days in May 1926. The miners struggled on alone till poverty forced them back to work by the end of the year.

Source 7.48
Strike money

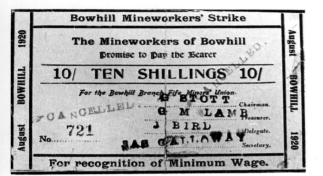

The 1929 election showed the benefits the Labour Party obtained from support for its programme of peaceful reform. Ramsay MacDonald now led the party that had the most MPs in Parliament. Though the following years were to bring many troubles, the rise of the Labour Party to a most important position in politics was an inescapable fact. When in 1932 the ILP broke away, irritated by Labour's caution, it never achieved much success. The Communist candidate, William Gallacher, captured West Fife in 1931; but the Communists could do no better and Labour consistently refused to allow them to affiliate with Labour. The Scottish National Party was established in 1934. But in the following five years it never put up more than six candidates for Parliament. None were successful. It was Labour that had established itself as a formidable force in Britain, and in parts of Scotland in particular.

Source 7.49
The committee rooms of the Communist, William Gallacher

8 Scottish Culture

Between 1880 and 1939 many factors were at work affecting the ideas, attitudes and outlook of people in Scotland. Your work so far will have shown you some of these – such as changing travel and the increase in local authority and state intervention into ordinary lives. The sources in this chapter deal with further factors including education and the kind of influences helping Scots to know more about the outside world. In one part of the country people tried to defend their way of life from changes that had been threatening to destroy it.

Education

Source 8.1
Knoxland School, Dumbarton, 1906

Source8.2
Inside a Dundee classroom

Source 8.3
A drill lesson

By the 1880s all Scottish children had to go to school. Although they were supposed to stay till they were 13, many were able to leave before that age provided they did moderately well at their work (see Section A, Chapter 4). The 'Board' schools to which most children went, charged fees of two (0.4p) or three pence (1.2p) a week. In addition there were 'higher class' schools for those who could afford to keep their children on beyond the age of 13. These offered foreign languages, classical languages, advanced mathematics, and literature. They were usually old burgh schools, now taken over by school boards. In addition there were industrial schools. They took children guilty of minor offences and truancy. Three of these schools were housed in ships. One of these ships, the *Mars*, was anchored in the Tay. It had been built in 1840 and, at times, held as many as 400 boys. Until it was broken up in 1929 the *Mars* was home for many boys. They were strictly disciplined, had to be up by 6.00 am, and had to learn a trade as well as have lessons.

Source 8.4
The *Mars*

However, during the period 1880 to the 1930s there were a number of changes made to schooling.

Source 8.5

Important developments in Scottish schools, 1880–1939

1883 The school leaving age was raised from 13 to 14, but exemptions were allowed.

1885 The Scotch Education Department became a more important organisation with more power to control education. (In 1918 it changed to 'The Scottish Education Department'. In 1939 it officially moved from London to Edinburgh.)

1888 A Leaving Certificate was introduced for pupils in the fee-paying 'higher-class' schools.

1889 Fees in elementary schools were abolished.

1892 £60 000 was provided to develop secondary education in Scotland. Committees in counties and cities used their share of money to help higher grade work in ordinary elementary schools. Pupils from these schools were now allowed to enter for the Leaving Certificate.

1899 'Higher grade' schools were officially recognised. The school boards could draw on rates to help them.

1901 Many of the exemptions letting pupils leave before they were 14 were abolished. A clear separation was made at 11–12 years between higher (or Secondary education) and the two years further work at an elementary school beyond 12 years. The latter had different and less demanding work.

1905 The maximum class size was cut from 70 to 60. The Scotch Education Department took over control of teacher training from the churches. The growth of these colleges had led to teaching becoming a mainly female occupation. On average women teachers were paid salaries half the size of men's.

1918 Elected county authorities replaced school boards. The voluntary religious schools (most of which were Catholic) could accept Local Authority control and support. Most did. They kept their own religious worship and teaching and checked the beliefs of applicants for posts. posts in these schools.

1928 The maximum class size was cut to 50.

1929 County councils and cities took charge of education.

What was it like to go to a 'Board' (or 'elementary') school? Plenty of people who attended one of these schools have vivid memories of them.

Amy Stewart Fraser went to a rural Aberdeenshire school in the late nineteenth century. She remembered:

Source 8.6

Our school was a bare barn of a place. It was cold. In winter we [took turns] to group ourselves round the fire. Girls entered by one porch, boys by a similar one. Scholars sat on narrow benches facing scarred tops scarcely worthy of the name of desks. All grades were taught by a single teacher. Each group stood in turn round the teacher's chair and answered questions. My first teacher used the tawse unkindly, reducing even the biggest boys to tears.

The 3Rs, Reading, 'Riting, 'Rithmetic, were hammered home by repetition. We received instruction in geography and history; these consisted of long feats of memory – names, long strings of dates. Our classwork was done on slates. After learning to write on slates we were promoted to copy books, pen and ink, dipping the pen in the inkwell sunk in the desk. We copied sayings like 'Honesty is the best policy'. No crayons or coloured pencils were used.

Normally only the children who lived near the school went home at mid-day, the rest brought their pieces, bread soaked with jam. Scholars took it in turns to fetch water from a well.

(Amy Stewart Fraser, *The Hills of Home*, 1973)

This is the curriculum offered in a Glasgow school to children of around 12 years old:

Source 8.7

Religious Knowledge (Bible and Catechism), Reading, Recitation, Spelling, Writing, Dictation, Etymology, Arithmetic (Compound Proportion, Vulgar and Decimal Fractions, Interest, Discount, Metric System, etc.), Grammar, Composition (Essay and Letter Writing), British History, Geography of the World, Map Drawing, English Literature, French, German, Mathematics, Drawing, Practical Cookery, Music, Industrial Work, Elementary Science, Physical Drill, Gymnastics, Manual Instruction.

But, for most children; the chance to study in more depth, to study a wider range of subjects and to stay longer at school depended on going to one of the 'Higher Grade' schools that eventually developed into Secondary schools. This is how Beath Higher Grade School (in Cowdenbeath) advertised itself in 1910:

Source 8.8
Beath Higher Grade School

The curriculum is designed to suit pupils who, after completing the elementary course in a primary school, intend to pursue for 3 years or more a course of higher education in preparation for technical, commercial or professional pursuits. A course is provided comprising English, History, Geography, French, German and Latin; Arithmetic, Mathematics, Science and Drawing.

A supplementary course is provided for those who are to leave school at 14, providing Science and Woodwork for boys and Cookery, laundry work and Household Management for Girls.

By 1938 over 150 000 pupils were in Scottish Secondary schools. The majority, however, left school at 14 after following one of the less academic 'supplementary' courses. In Glasgow Molly Weir experienced these practical courses. She wrote:

Source 8.9
A laundry class

For laundry lessons we went down to a dark, damp, steamy basement. Little tubs were filled with soapy water and we were shown how to scrub the garments we'd been asked to bring. Hot stoves were ranged along one wall, and their fierce heat soon dried out washings, while we listened to the teacher tell us how we must scrub some materials gently, and that we must never rub woollens, and how socks and handkerchiefs had to be washed separately. Little flat-irons were neatly ranged against the hot stoves and were heating while we absorbed all this information.

(Weir, *Shoes were for Sunday*)

Source 8.11

A cookery class in Dunfermline

The numbers able to stay on even beyond the secondary school stage in order to go to university were tiny. The majority of these undergraduates had to be able to pay the fees that universities charged. A small number won bursaries that paid for their costs. Others struggled like this man (recalled here by John Boyd Orr):

Source 8.12

. . . life was hard for many of the sons of the poor families. After a dinner I was attending of the Glasgow and Aberdeen University graduates in the north of England about 1930 a doctor came up to me and said, 'I doubt if you will remember me'. Though his face seemed familiar I could not remember his name or even where I had met him. He told me he had been a medical student in Glasgow at the same time as myself. He had worked in the pits on the night shift and attended his classes at the university during the day. It took him an extra two years to get through, but there he was now, in full evening dress, a highly successful medical practitioner.

(J. Boyd Orr, *As I Recall*, 1966)

The universities were considerably changed during the 30 years after 1880.

Source 8.13

Important developments in university education in Scotland after 1880

1887 Queen Margaret College was established in Glasgow. It offered courses to degree level.

1889 The Universities (Scotland) Act. Women were to be allowed into all university faculties. A 4-year honours degree structure was developed to run alongside the 3-year ordinary degree. New subjects began to be added. Fixed salaries developed for lecturers. Students paid fees to the university not individual lecturers.

1892 The entrance examination system for entry to university was established. English, Maths, Latin or Greek and one other subject were required. Glasgow produced the Scottish universities first two women graduates.

1908 The 3-term year was introduced.

(The numbers at universities in Scotland rose from 6000 in 1900 to 10 000 in 1938).

Plans to improve education further, giving all children a proper secondary schooling and raising the school leaving age to 15 were ruined by the outbreak of war in 1939.

QUESTIONS

1 From all that you have studied so far in this book suggest reasons why the governments of the 1880–1930s time thought they ought to try to further change education. (E.2)

2 What do you think was the most important of all the changes mentioned here? Give reasons for your answer. (E.2)

3 Which of the sources describing board school life (both written and visual) do you think gives the clearest and most vivid insight into schooling then? Justify your choice. (E.1)

4 Source 8.8 mentions the possible careers of higher grade pupils. What sort of careers might lie ahead for those taking a supplementary course? (E.2)

Population Movements

Coming to Scotland

The population of Scotland grew in size during this period. It changed in other ways, too. Figures in the census returns show people coming to Scotland from other lands.

Source 8.14 ──────────
a) **Numbers of Irish-born in Scotland**

1881	218 745	The counties in which
1901	205 064	the largest number are
1921	159 020	(found) are Lanark,
1931	124 296	Renfrew and
		Dumbarton. The
		numbers in large
		burghs include
		Glasgow – 52 379,
		Edinburgh 5961.

b) **Number of English and Welsh-born in Scotland**

1881	91 823
1901	134 023
1921	194 276
1931	168 640

(*Census of Scotland*, 1931)

c) People also came to Scotland from foreign lands and during the early twentieth century their numbers increased.

1901	resident foreigners living in Scotland	17 654
1911		24 739

The largest numbers came from Italy. The 1931 census estimated there were around 5000 Italian born people in Scotland. Another sizeable group were Jewish people escaping from persecution in Russia and Poland.

Leaving Scotland

Source 8.15 ──────────
Lochaber No More – a painting of emigrants

In the early twentieth century William Anderson, an Edinburgh coalman, wrote in his diary

Source 8.16 ──────────
This evening I went over and interviewed the Canadian Agent with a view to going to that

great colony. The conditions – 10/weekly [50p] and board – did not suit me. The land may be flowing with milk and honey but it is meal and cold water for the poor labourers. What a crime it is to be poor.

(W. Anderson, *No Ordinary Man*, 1986)

The numbers leaving Scotland fell sharply after 1930. The world slump hit countries to which Scots had been going. The rising unemployment in these countries now meant they were no longer as attractive or as welcoming.

Source 8.17 —————————————

NOTICE

Exceptional Chance for Lewis Girls

FOR

Domestic Service in Canada.

FULL INFORMATION CAN BE OBTAINED FROM

MURDO MACLEAN,

46 Point Street. Stornoway.

30th Nov. 1929.

Source 8.18 —————————————

Emigrants from the Hebrides depart to find a new home, April 1924

Source 8.19 —————————————

Numbers of people of Scottish origin emigrating abroad

Year	Number	
1882	32 242	'Over the period 1895 to 1938
1888	35 873	1 378 219 emigrants (from
1904	37 445	Scotland) were offset by
1912	72 626	531 351 immigrants' – around
1915	10 130	380 00 of these were
1918	1 088	probably returning Scots.
1920	46 523	'Most of the Scottish
1923	86 584	emigrants crossed the
1929	42 911	Atlantic to America . . .
1931	5 866	nearly 170 000 emigrated to
1935	4 056	Canada 1910–14.'
1938	4 474	

(Flinn, *Scottish Population History*)

QUESTIONS

1 Why do you think some Scots who left the country later returned? (E.2)

2 What feelings and points of view is the artist who painted source 8.15 trying to show? Is he in favour of emigration? (E.1)

3 Source 8.15 is a painting. Do you think paintings make useful sources? Might they be less useful than photographs? Give reasons for your answer. (E.1)

4 Why do you think the figures in source 8.19 vary so much? (E.2)

Resisting change – the Crofters' Battle

Source 8.20
Mingulay, 1905

Source 8.22
Skye crofter

Source 8.21
St Kilda

A REAL "SCOTTISH GRIEVANCE."

DUNCAN.—"Oh! but my mother is frail, and can't be sent out of the country in that ship; will you not let Flora and her ———"
FACTOR.— [sternly] "No, no lad—move on with the old woman; she will not be here in the way of his Lordship's sheep and deer."

Source 8.23

Many of the people leaving Scotland during the nineteenth century came from the Highlands and Islands (see Chapter 4 in Section A). But during the 1880s the mood in this region seemed to change. Instead of accepting their fate and leaving their homes, people in this area began to organise and resist some of the things that were happening to them. In 1882, for example, on the Island of Skye, there were events that showed this new determination. In the east of the island crofters organised a rent strike in protest at the loss of traditional grazing land on Ben Lee. When the sheriff came to serve legal notices to crofters about their failure to pay, the crofters seized these 'summonses' and burned them. 50 police had to be drafted in from Glasgow. Despite being pelted with mud and stones they managed to arrest several crofters. The trial of these men led to fines being imposed on them. These fines were paid by a well-to-do sympathiser.

Tension and clashes continued for several years. A newspaper produced in Inverness – the *Highlander* – carried articles strongly attacking landlords. Its editor, John Murdoch, was one of many in the Highlands who were strongly influenced by events in Ireland. There the Irish Land League was demanding 'fair rents, fixity of tenure and freedom to inherit a land holding'. The Irish leaders Michael Davitt and Charles Parnell encouraged their followers to refuse to pay rents and to stand up for themselves. This example encouraged crofters to be more positive.

In 1887 around 100 men on the island of Lewis, armed with guns, invaded a newly-created sporting estate and shot and cooked the deer. To an official of the time it seemed:

Source 8.24

From 1882 down to 1887 the Highlands and Islands were in a state of unrest – in many places there was open lawlessness. Rents were withheld, lands were seized and a reign of terror prevailed. To cope with the situation the Police Force was [increased] in some cases doubled. Troopships with marines cruised about the Hebrides in order to support the Civil Authorities in their endeavour to maintain law and order.'

(In Eric Richards, *A History of the Highland Clearances*, 1985)

The events were widely reported in the newspapers of the time. In 1883 the government agreed to an investigation of the problems that had led to so much trouble. The Royal Commission it set up was led by Lord Napier, a former administrator in British India. During 1883 the Commission travelled around the Highlands and Islands gathering evidence. Since many of those who gave evidence spoke Gaelic, the Commissioners needed an interpreter.

Read through evidence in the following sources and look at sources 8.20–24.

1 Describe the crofters living conditions. (K.U)

2 How did they earn a living? (K.U)

3 What were their main complaints? (K.U)

4 What sort of reforms do you think were needed? (E.2)

The evidence of John Macpherson (the leader of Glendale Crofters on Skye):

Source 8.25

All the money we get is earned by people going south and getting wages, unless we sell a stirk. We are not home scarcely for a week with our earnings when we pay it over to the proprietors, and they are off to London and elsewhere abroad to spend it. Not a penny of it is spent on the place for which the rent is paid. My croft is about three acres [1.214 hectare] of very shallow land. I have no horse. We and our wives do the ploughing and harrowing of our land, turning or tilling it with the cas-chrom, the most primitive mode of tilling, I believe, in existence.

With more families sharing the hill pasture and cutting peats on it, hill grazing is scarce and people suffer badly. Instead of the milk they had formerly, now they have only treacle and tea to wash down the food. Our staple food is meal, potatoes, fish when it is got, our only drink being tea. I don't count the number of hens we have at home, but I don't think it is more than five or six. If we had more, we would have to buy feeding for them.

A single Aberdeenshire cow would outweigh three of ours. The amount of milk they give is very meagre. The food with which we winter our stirks we have to buy in Glasgow.

Our dwelling houses are thatched with straw. As our crofts do not produce enough straw for fodder for the cattle as well as for thatch, and as we are prohibited from cutting rushes or pulling heather, our houses in rainy weather are most deplorable. Above our beds comes pattering down the rain, rendered dirty and black by the soot on the ceiling, and so the inmates of the beds have to look for shelter on the lee side of the house. Of the twenty houses there are only two in which the cattle are not under the same roof as the family.

The evidence of Norman Robertson of Skye:

Source 8.26

Those who have nets go to the Loch fishing but there are not many in our township who have nets. They are not able to buy them.

I have not seen so much destitution [poverty] as this season – such want of food – not since the great potato famine of 1846.

In Sutherland 63-year-old Alexander Ross stated:

Source 8.27

My rent was £8 and I kept two cows and a heifer and a mare and a foal. I gave no offence to the proprietor except that I was not present at the time of the paying of the rent, and was a little behind with it afterwards. As soon as I was able I paid the rent, all except £2, and I would have paid that too, if they had only given me time.

I was removed a year from Whitsunday last. They knocked down the house, and we were two nights obliged to live on the hillside. I then got a house from a tenant of Mr MacKay at Achnahannet. Now there isn't much work to be had.

Sporting estates had been spreading in the Highlands for some years. From the 1870s they increased not only because of the popularity of the sport and the improved travel of the time allowing such sportsman to reach the area, but also because foreign competition made sheep farming less profitable. Many crofter witnesses complained of this development. One of them asked:

Source 8.28

What good can we get out of deer? The sheep are bad enough. They were the cause of the people being expelled from their places, but still they are better than deer. We can get no use of the deer, whereas if we can afford to buy a sheep, it will at all events provide us with clothes. As for the deer, we are not allowed to kill or eat them. The sheep need shepherds and there is some work connected with sheep for us in the way of smearing and shearing. But deer require no herd, and they can leap the fences and eat our crops. I don't know any work in connection with the deer except some gillies, perhaps.

(All the above from the Napier Commission, 1883)

The results of the unrest

Angry crofters organised 'the Highland Land Law Reform Association'. It soon had 15 000 members and began organising rent strikes. When the government sent marines and extra police, crofters did not fight. Instead they continued to refuse to pay rents. The extension of the vote meant that in the 1885 election five MPs who represented crofters were chosen. Gladstone's Liberal Government needed their support. The Napier Commission had suggested a number of reforms; now the government introduced its own plan.

Source 8.29 ——————————
1886 The Crofter's Act
- crofters at last got security of tenure
- crofters could pass on their crofts to their family
- crofters won the right to compensation for any improvements they carried out
- strict controls were placed on the sale of crofts
- a land court – the Crofters' Commission – gave judgements when there was argument about what was a fair rent.

However, the Act did not do anything for the landless, nor did it plan to give back to crofters the lands they claimed and which might have made crofts bigger and more economically secure.

In the 1940s Norman Maclean interviewed an elderly Skye man to see if the battle of the 1880s had really solved the crofters problems:

Source 8.30 ——————————
I asked him if he remembered saying to my father that the golden age would come back again when they got Ben Lee, and that a whole community of skilled craftsmen would spring up; that their sons and daughters would no longer need to search for a living in Glasgow and Greenock.

'Yes, I remember that, and much else,' he replied, 'but things have not turned out as we expected. It is very strange how when you are dead certain of anything in this world it is the very opposite that turns up.'

'There were two shoemakers in the Braes not so long ago,' I said; 'how many are there now?'

'There's none now,' answered Murdo; 'nowadays if you want a boot patched you must walk seven miles to Portree.'

'There was a good tailor,' I went on, 'and I remember the amazement of the folk when he got a sewing-machine. They thought it the greatest miracle of the age.'

'So they did; quite a nine days' wonder; but there is no tailor now.'

'There was a boatbuilder and a joiner.'

'There is neither the one nor the other now.'

'There was a good weaver. I remember watching him at the loom long ago and thinking how quick and steady his hands were.'

'There is no weaver now; the weaver died and the loom was burnt one winter when the peats were wet.'

'There were three or more herring-fishing boats in each township; probably twenty in all. What has become of them?'

'They are rotting on the shores; for there are no men to work them.'

(Norman Maclean, *The Former Days*, 1945)

By 1931 the population of crofter parishes had fallen to 120 000, 60 less than the figure of 1881. Yet later acts of Parliament helped crofts to grow in size and established new crofts. Studies of the population of the crofting areas in the inter-war years show that it was increasingly elderly. Many of the young left the area for a life elsewhere.

Life changed in other ways too. Some witnesses to the Napier Commission in 1883 could only speak Gaelic. The 1931 census figures show the change that took place between these dates. The Crofting reforms had helped preserve a way of life. But the attractions of a wealthier life elsewhere were a magnet to some. Nor was the crofters' way of life helped by the sharp decline in the Scottish fishing industry in the 1920s.

CENSUS	POPULATION AGED 3 YEARS AND OVER	SPEAKERS OF GAELIC	SPEAKERS OF GAELIC AND ENGLISH	SPEAKERS OF GAELIC BUT NOT ENGLISH	PERCENTAGE OF POPULATION AGED 3 YEARS AND OVER		
					Speaking Gaelic	Speaking Gaelic and English	Speaking Gaelic but not English
1881	3 425 151	231 594	—	—	6.76	—	—
1891	3 721 778	254 415	210 677	43 738	6.84	5.66	1.18
1901	4 146 733	230 806	202 700	28 106	5.57	4.89	0.68
1911	4 439 802	202 398	183 998	18 400	4.56	4.14	0.41
1921	4 573 471	158 779	148 950	9 829	3.47	3.26	0.21
1931	4 588 909	136 135	129 419	6 716	2.97	2.82	0.15

Distribution of Gaelic-speaking Population. The Three principal Gaelic-speaking counties so far as numbers are concerned, are Inverness, Ross and Cromarty and Argyll, which together in 1931 account for 90 080 Gaelic speakers or 66.2 per cent of the total – the numbers enumerated in the individual counties being 34 455 in Inverness, 34 391 in Ross and Cromarty and 21 234 in Argyll. In Lanarkshire Gaelic speakers number 17 851, in Sutherland 6794, in Perthshire 4859, and in the rest of Scotland 16 551. (Tables 50 and 51).

(Census of Scotland, 1931)

The Media

Reading

Source 8.32

J. H. MacDonald, writing in his old age, deplored this threat to the appearance of Edinburgh:

Source 8.33

At one time about the end of last century Edinburgh was threatened with a shameful attack on its amenity, more especially at night, but also in the daytime. There were erected on the face of the old town looking towards Princes Street enormous letters constituting advertisements – Bovril opposite the top of the Mound, Vinolia Soap on one side of North Bridge, and Bermaline Bread on the other side, and which if allowed to remain would have been followed by others – Monkey Brand, Oxo, Lemco, etc., etc. These great letters were objectionable in the daytime, but unendurable at night, when they were lined out in electric light, and made to wink and flash in varying colours over the face of the old town, so picturesque with its ordinary window lights after dark. I wrote to Lord Playfair, who was the Chairman of the Bovril Company, and he, as one would have expected, at once took steps to put a stop to the outrage. The others were not so easily dealt with, and it was only by statutory authorisation that the Magistrates were able to put an end to such a disfigurement of the city.

(Macdonald, Life Jottings)

The sights that so offended him were to be seen across Britain's towns and cities, on walls, in shops and on special hoardings. They are a sign of one of the forces that has done much to shape Scottish life since 1880 – the growth of an organised media. Through posters, newspapers, magazines, advertisers and journalists tried to influence people's views, attitudes and shopping habits. John Kerr looked back over his life in the nineteenth century and wrote:

Between 1880 and 1939 it became much easier for people to buy or borrow books. The 30s, Rene Cutforth remembered:

Source 8.36

Libraries in Great Britain

Number of books in stock		*Number issued*
1911	10 874 000	54 256 000
1924	14 784 000	85 668 000
1939	32 549 000	246 335 000

(A. H. Halsey, *Trends in British Society*, 1972)

During the 1890s and 1900s Andrew Carnegie, a Scot who had emigrated and made a fortune, used some of his wealth to provide libraries in many Scottish communities. The firm of J. and P. Coats gave books to all Scottish schools and the 1918 Education Act made school libraries an important part of the county library service.

The public libraries did an increasing amount of business.

During the thirties cheap paperback books became widely available including (from 1935) Penguin Books. Children's comics were numerous.

Above all this was the age in which the popular mass-circulation newspaper was born. The abolition of the stamp tax on newspapers in 1855 made it possible to produce penny papers more people could afford to buy. The educational reform of 1872 greatly increased the numbers who could read, and provided popular papers with a mass readership. In the 1880s numerous newspapers flourished in Scotland, many of them serving quite small localities. In 1896 Alfred Harmsworth founded the *Daily Mail*. His paper aimed to reach a large readership. By 1901 it was selling a million copies a day in Britain. Other newspapers developed to challenge the *Mail* including the *Mirror*, the *Daily Express* and the *Daily Herald*. By 1939 the latter two papers were each selling two million copies a day in Britain. During the inter-war years these newspapers spread into Scotland. In 1928 Lord Beaverbrook, owner of the *Daily Express*, started the Scottish *Daily Express*. His paper, like its rivals, tried to win readers by offering all sorts of free gifts. The popular papers stressed stories about crime, adventure and sport. They developed columns of expert advice on all sorts of subjects.

QUESTIONS

1 What reasons can you suggest to explain the growth of popular national newspapers at this time? (E.2)

2 What is the point of view on advertising of the author of 8.33? Quote words that show his point of view. (E.1)

Going out

The years 1880 to 1939 contained many changes in popular entertainment. At the start of the twentieth century, Abe Moffat wrote:

Source 8.37 _____
We had no radio or television in my childhood, and we had to make our own music and entertainment. It so happened that when I was at school, my father decided to buy me a violin, and my teacher was his younger brother. I do not know why I was selected – it was impossible to supply musical instruments to all the members of the family. However, it brought enjoyment to all of us when I used to sit and play, not only at New Year, but on many other occasions when they would all dance together.

(Moffat, *My Life with the Miners*)

Filling spare time was a problem for the young. A writer of 1901 described Glasgow's Sauchiehall Street:

Source 8.38 _____
Here come every night the young persons who have spent the day cooped in shops or warehouses or offices and who find sitting at home in dreary lodgings an intolerable torture. On Saturday they come in all the greater number. They have no other place in which to spend spare time. The lighted street demands no admission money.

(Cage, *The Working Class in Glasgow*)

But changes were underway that were to greatly increase the opportunities of going to entertainments. The old theatres and music halls (see Chapter 4, Section A) continued: a number of fine new theatres were also built around 1900. In Glasgow, especially, audiences abused entertainers they didn't like.

Source 8.39 _____
The Glasgow Empire was famous for that. If they didn't like them they shouted 'Git off', 'Git away'. Sometimes they would throw orange peel and stuff like that. I once went into the Gods in the Alhambra – there was no back seats or anything. We got up to the Gods and there was all these fat Glasgow women with their shawls on and when one laughed, they all laughed.

(*5/11 a week*, Community Service Volunteers, Edinburgh)

Source 8.40 _____

During the twentieth century the country's towns and cities entertainments gained a further attraction – dance halls. The new dance halls of the twenties owed much to American influence. American music, American dances like the foxtrot (1914) and the Charleston (1925) became popular in Scotland. Flo Gillespie went to most of Edinburgh's dance halls. She recalled:

Source 8.41 _____
The Marine Gardens in Portobello was my favourite place to go dancing. We used to go on a Sunday and there was a band. We'd have afternoon tea and a dance.

I've heard ever so many bands in the Marine Gardens. When one stopped, another would come round on the revolving stage. There would be dancing and roller skating.

We used to meet our clicks at the dancing. You used to get clicks on Princes Street. We used to go to the cafes for a cup of coffee or tea and icecream. It was in the cafes or in Princes Street Gardens where you used to meet people and arrange to see them at the Palais or the Marine Gardens. This was when I was 18 or 19. I liked the Marine Gardens the best. Stewart's Dance Hall was a very select place.

I've been to all the dance halls, at least once. There's a first time for everything. Fairley's in Leith Street used to get raided by the police. That was where women used to walk up and down the pavements. Soldiers and sailors used to go to Fairley's.

There used to be a place in the West End, open on a Saturday. You went up stairs to get to it. We went in the afternoon. It was a great meeting place for the young set. We got tea and a band would be playing.

I only went dancing once a week, at the weekends mostly, because I worked during the week. I looked forward to it all week.

(Campbell, *Changed Days*)

Source 8.42
Fashionable clothes in the 1920s

The First World War had helped to free women from the strict rules of earlier times about going out alone. Nor did women, when dressing up, wear the uncomfortable clothes of earlier times. Make-up became far more fashionable and smoking openly was acceptable, too.

Source 8.43

Public houses in Gorbals shown on a map published by the Scottish Permissive Bill and Temperance Association (1903)

Public houses were, for men especially, even more popular than dance halls. Some men, as this witness recalls:

Source 8.44
. . . did drink a lot in those days and women just didn't go into pubs, they went into the Jug Bar. It was a little room at the side where they could go in and have their glass. They were certainly segregated. They didn't go into the main place, it was very much the sawdust area. The men stood there and got stoned, then came out and went home. It was a matter of course to see a drunk wandering up the street.

(Leith Lives, *It wisn'ae a' work*, 1987)

Temperance societies tried to stop adult drinking. The Band of Hope (the Scottish branch began in 1871) attempted to prevent children from ever starting to drink. Meg Berrington remembered going to Band of Hope meetings in Leith:

Source 8.45 ────────────
When we were very young we used to go to the Band of Hope. We used to see magic lanterns, but they were very sad. They were nearly always about a drunken father who wasn't very nice to his wife or children. Us children used to sit and cry all night.

(Leith Lives, *It wisn'ae a' work*)

The ILP passed measures (planning to ban the sale of alcohol) as late as 1926. After the First World War the Temperance (Scotland) Act of 1913 came into force. In each locality, if 55% of local electors voted for it, then that locality could ban the sale of alcohol. 41 of the 584 localities that held polls in 1920 voted to go 'dry'. They included places such as Wick and Stromness. The rest of Scotland continued drinking much as usual.

The 'wireless'

From the 1900s people could listen to the music they enjoyed on wind-up 'gramophone' records. From the mid-1920s they could also hear it on the radio (or 'wireless' as it was commonly called). Radio broadcasting had developed rapidly in the early twentieth century. Wireless amateurs pressed the Post Office to begin regular broadcasts. The Post Office set up a British Broadcasting Company in 1922, issuing licenses to those who wished to listen to its programmes. Around 36 000 enthusiasts struggled, in the early twenties, with the complex equipment needed. Bert Murray, in Aberdeen, had a wireless. It was.

Source 8.46 ────────────
. . . a small box containing a cylinder wound with thin copper wire and two small terminals at each end. A small pair of earphones connected to two of the terminals, and a wire hanging across the room, aerial, another connected to a water or gas pipe, earth, connected to other terminals.

On top of the box was fitted a small piece of crystal, and a tiny handle with a small piece of wire, 'Catswhisker'. By manoeuvering the point of the 'Catswhisker' on to the crystal, you quickly learned how to get the best reception in your earphones.

These do-it-yourself kits with instructions cost a few shillings. Moving on later to a larger box or cabinet, with a knob for tuning, another for volume. Inside were cylinders, wires, glass valves, powered by a wet battery, which required charging from time to time.

(Bert Murray, *3 Score Years and 10*, 1986)

The development of valved sets with attached speakers meant that groups of people could listen to a wireless. The numbers of sets increased and, in 1926, the Conservative Government decided to set up a public corporation to take charge of broadcasting. The British Broadcasting Corporation was put under the control of Sir John Reith, a Scot of strict principles and stern religious beliefs. Early broadcasts consisted chiefly of plays and classical music. Until 1938 no broadcasting took place before 12.30 pm on Sundays lest it interfere with church services. In the 1930s Leith allowed the development of a 'light programme' of popular music.

The Labour MP Ellen Wilkinson did not like the strict control over broadcasts that was exercised by the Director of the BBC. She said:

Source 8.47 ────────────
We English should have learned by now that it is unsafe to give a Scotsman any opportunity for directing other people for their own good. Sir John Reith has made himself the Judge of What We Ought to Want.

(In R. Blythe, *The Age of Illusion*, 1963)

Though radio sets improved, the early valved sets were still large and awkward objects. During the thirties much neater wooden and bakelite sets with built-in speakers were developed. The number of people with wireless licenses had climbed to 8 million by 1940, even though (at ten shilling (50p)) licenses were not cheap. Nor were wireless sets ever really cheap, though their prices fell from around £15 in 1930 to around £3 by 1939.

A Scottish inventor, John Logie Baird, was busy in the 1920s trying to develop television. In 1925 his work produced the world's first television pictures. In 1936 the BBC began a regular TV service that, by 1939, had persuaded 20 000 people to buy sets at around £22 each. However, the system the BBC finally adopted was not Baird's. Nor did its transmissions reach beyond the London area.

Listening to the wireless had become a genuinely popular activity by 1939. It encouraged the spending of more leisure time at home. It brought news of great events directly to the country's population – as when Neville Chamberlain, Prime Minister in 1939, announced that Britain and Germany were at war. It provided a 'Children's Hour', stories, plays and music. The culture of a wider world reached directly into Scottish homes.

The cinema

Through new technology, the wireless brought news, information and entertainment into the home. During the same period the development of cinema technology led to the creation of an entertainment of enormous popularity that took people out of the home to places other than public houses and music halls.

In the 1880s and 90s the showing of lantern slides was a well established form of entertainment. The first showing of moving pictures took place in December 1895 in Glasgow. Showings of short films soon became a common feature of music hall programmes.

One of the first cinema shows ever held in Edinburgh – in 1896 – was described in the *Scotsman*:

Source 8.48

When the first of the series of pictures appeared on the screen they [the audience] applauded heartily and as one picture after another was exhibited their enthusiasm grew. The movements of the figures were wonderfully natural. Altogether the Cinematographe proved one of the greatest attractions which has been seen at the Empire for some time and the audience were so enthusiastic in their applause that the curtain was raised and a beautiful sea-scape under moonlight – the waves dashing upon the rocks – was shown.

(*Scotsman* 14 April 1896)

Source 8.49

THIS PROGRAMME NOT LATER THAN MAY OF 1897.

DON'T MISS THE
GRAND EXHIBITION OF
CINEMATOGRAPH
MOVING   PHOTOGRAPHS
AND CONCERT

Mr. CALDER has just returned from London with New and Fascinating Pictures and the Most Approved Apparatus.

The Living Pictures
WILL BE ALTERNATED WITH ARTISTIC
Floral Tableaux Vivants
And all the Songs and Readings will be fully Illustrated by REALISTIC DISSOLVING VIEWS.

SKETCH PROGRAMME (Subject to Alteration)
OVERTURE.

Song	"The Better Land"	Miss Calder
Animated Photographs	The Czar in Paris, Boys Bathing in the Surf, Blacksmiths at Work, Street Scene in Paris, Kissing Scene, Feeding the Elephant, Balloon Ascent, &c., &c.	
Song	"Where hath Scotland Found her Fame?"	Mr. G. W. Walker
Animated Photographs	Factory Gates Opened, Fan Artist, Railway Station, Ladies' Toilet, On the Sands at Brighton, Lord Mayor's Show, London, Trafalgar, &c., &c.	
Song	"Daddy"	Miss Calder
Song	"Simon, the Cellarer"	Mr. G. W. Walker
Animated Photographs	Musical Drill, Soldiers Marching, Lightning Artist, Learning the Bicycle, House on Fire, Off to the Rescue, Brigade called out, Return of Troops, Horse Jumping Hurdles, &c.	
Song	"Scotch Medley"	Mr. G. W. Walker
Animated Photographs	Leap Frog, Serpentine Dance, Stick no Bills, Gardener at Work, Dinner Party, Midnight Visitor, Lovers Caught, Runaway Knock (Comic), London Street Fight, &c.	

Doors Open at 7.30.   Commence at 8 prompt.

Reserved Seats, **2**s.; other Seats **1**s.; a few at **6**d. if room

Come and See the Bewildering Beauties of this Latest Scientific Marvel.
Read what the Press says (over).

The early centres of cinema shows were usually in working-class areas. Cinema prices were low enough to let in people who couldn't afford to go to the theatre. In 1908 Glasgow's councillors visited cinemas. One of them reported:

Source 8.50

There is very little to elevate the mind in the whole show and what there is is drowned by the vulgar performances. The admission charge is very low, from 1d [0.4p] to 6d [2.5p]. In many instances, girls aged 8 to 12 years had infants in their arms and other younger children under their charge. They were all the poorer working-class children, many of them barefoot and ragged. There was a small percentage of women and most of them had infants in their arms, beshawled and bareheaded. The remainder were made up of men of the working class and young lads and lassies.

(Cage, *The Working Class in Glasgow*)

175

The quality of silent films rapidly improved from the early shaky brief films run by a projectionist who had to watch the used film tumble down into a basket on the floor. From 1903 film makers moved on from simply trying to amaze the audience with the mere fact of moving pictures. Properly planned films telling stories were made. Travelling cinemas took the new wonder to the remoter parts of Scotland. By 1914 films were being made that lasted as long as 30 minutes. Glasgow alone had 57 picture houses. Many of them were not very comfortable. In one Edinburgh cinema:

Source 8.51
In the 'Salon' they used to come and squirt disinfectant over you! The 'Salon' wasn't a nice picture house. It was a flea pit.

(*Friday Night was Brasso Night*. WEA, 1987).

But purpose-built cinemas were now being constructed. In Aberdeen, for example, the La Scala opened in 1914 and was able to accommodate almost 1000 people. Yet even this cinema had to advertise that:

Source 8.52
Few cinemas in Scotland are better adapted to carry out the recommendations of the medical experts than La Scala. The cinema is lofty, perfect ventilation, sprayed at short intervals with the fragrant but deadly effective germ killer, pine oil and Septol.

(In M. Thomson, *Silver Screen in the Silver City*, 1988)

Source 8.53
Penny Matinee at the Picturedrome, Easter Road, Edinburgh, 1923

During the 1920s the cinema industry continued to grow. Special Saturday afternoon shows for children attracted huge audiences.

Source 8.54
We had pictures out at Dalkeith. It was two-pence [1p] to go in and a jam jar. We used to shout 'Watch Mister! He's got a gun!' in the silent films. You see you got so excited.

(*Friday Night was Brasso Night*)

The many people without work especially enjoyed the warmth and comfort of the cinemas, as Mary Mitchell recalls:

Source 8.55
I used to go to the pictures as often as I could get a penny or a jeely jar. The picture houses sold the jars back to the makers. It was really for people who were not working. A programme would last a good few hours. The silent pictures were good because you were always wondering what they were thinking.

(*As Time Goes By*, n.d. CSV Community Project)

The newer cinemas provided luxury normally beyond the reach of ordinary people. Their style and their names – Granada, Alhambra – were often Spanish. In 1927 'talkies' arrived. At first they suffered from technical difficulties, but by 1929 these had been overcome. Wherever Al Jolson's film of that year appeared in Scotland, people queued to see it. Aberdeen's *Evening Express* reported:

Source 8.56
Occasionally there flashes across the film firmament a particularly bright comet. None has been brighter than 'The Singing Fool'; which is being shown at the picture house all this week. The thousands who queued up yesterday were rewarded by seeing and hearing a talkie that is a triumph of up-to-the-minute motion picture art . . . the man who makes it, is, of course, Al Jolson.

(In Thomson, *Silver Screen in the Silver City*)

Between films audiences were entertained by orchestras or by organs. By the late thirties there were 98 cinemas in Glasgow. In Aberdeen there were 19, and few smaller communities were without their cinema. Going to the cinema was one of the most popular forms of entertainment. Nearly everybody went at least once a week.

Source 8.57 _____

Outstanding among the stars of the period following the First World War was Rudolph Valentino, dancing here with Alice Terry, in Rex Ingram's *The Four Horsemen of the Apocalypse* (1921).

Source 8.58 _____

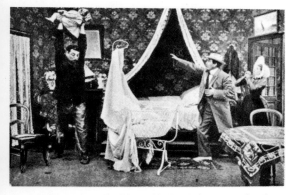

A typical scene from the " horrorific " melodramas, produced on the Continent, which were widely shown in the early days of the cinema.

The period was dominated by American films. The next source refers to a romantic hero of the screen.

Source 8.59 _____

Remember Valentino's funeral with all the women throwing themselves down and weeping over the coffin? Even then the stars did dictate a lot of our lives. It carried us into a different world and our own lives were drab.

(*Friday Night was Brasso Night*, WEA, 1987).

The cinema brought to Scots people all sorts of images of the outside world. During the thirties documentaries began to be made and newsreels were commonly shown as part of the programme. But a Board of Censors exercised stern control over what was permissable in a film. It banned:

Source 8.60 _____

Cruelty to animals.
Cruelty to young infants.
Realistic horrors of warfare
Executions
Gruesome murders
Surgical operations
Women fighting with knives
Animals gnawing men, women and children
Commitment of crime by children
Views of men and women in bed together
Nude figures
Unnecessary exhibitions of women's underclothing
Indecorous dancing
Improper bathing scenes
Excessively passionate love scenes
Advocacy of the doctrine of free love
Scenes tending to disparage public characters and institutions
Scenes in which the king and officers are seen in an odious light
Subjects in which sympathy is enlisted for criminals

(J. Laver, *Between the Wars*, 1961)

QUESTIONS

1 Briefly list the main changes in entertainment between 1890 and 1939. (K.U)

2 Do you think these changes improved people's lives? Explain your answer. (E.2)

3 'The new media threatened the traditional Scottish way of life.' Do you agree? (E.2)

4 What do you think the authors of source 8.60 were worried about in making up this list? How did they think the cinema might affect people? (E.2)

5 Do you think the author of source 8.50 was in favour of cinemas? Give reasons for your answer. (E.1)

The 'great outdoors' and holidays

'Outdoors' for many children meant playing in the street. In Glasgow, Molly Weir's childhood friends were fond of:

Source 8.61

playing peever, which was our name for hop-scotch, and the greatest thing in the world then was to hop skilfully from bed to bed without touching the chalked line, sending the marble disc or peever into the next bed with poised toe; and then, for no apparent reason, we were all hunting out our girds. The gird or hoop season was starting and we didn't want to miss a minute.'

(Weir, *Shoes were for Sunday*)

In Leith working-class girls enjoyed:

Source 8.62

Playing at shops. We made our own. Our butter was earth made up with water and patted down. Broken leaves for cabbages, stones for sugar. Potato – you cut it up thinly for bacon. Occasionally you had 2 ounces [28 g] of dolly mixtures to sell.

(*Friday Night was Brasso Night*)

Source 8.63

Dunfermline swimming baths opened in 1887

Source 8.64

Children play pitch and toss in a Leith Street, 1909

Despite the growth of traffic the working-class streets of the thirties were much safer to play in than modern streets. By the 1900s many towns and cities had swimming pools. They also had parks, usually with bandstands in them. Most possessed that major centre of modern entertainment – a football stadium. Scottish football was already organised by the 1880s (see Chapter 4 of Section A). By the 1890s there were well over 100 clubs in the Scottish Football Association. Glasgow Celtic, 1887, were one of the later clubs to be founded. The club was set up by Brother Walford, the Catholic headmaster of the Sacred Heart School. Its establishment was part of an effort to raise money to provide clothing and food for the poor living in the largely Catholic east end. The idea of having a club that drew mainly on Catholic support was not new. Hibernian (1875) had a clause in its rules declaring its players had to be practising Catholics. (This clause was dropped in 1893.) In Dundee, Harps FC attracted Catholic support, too. Irish immigration into Scotland had done much to bring about these developments. When, in 1887, Harps played an important game a newspaper of the time commented:

Source 8.65

The Irish are nothing if not patriotic and on occasions so momentous as these the vast Celtic population of this city [i.e. Glasgow] and also of Dundee turn out to give their compatriots an encouraging cheer. People who never witness a football match are attracted to the scene by the political aspect of the game and not because they are possessed of any enthusiasm for football.

(In W. J. Murray, *The Scottish Catholic Community and the Celtic FC*, 1983)

Source 8.66
Football

A circular of 1888 announced Celtic's arrival on the football scene:

Source 8.67
Celtic Football and Athletic Club.
His Grace the Archbishop of Glasgow and the Clergy of St Mary's, Sacred Heart and St Michael Missions and the principal Catholic Laymen of the East End.

The above club was formed in November 1887 by a number of the Catholics of the East End of the City. The main object is to supply the St Vincent de Paul Society with funds for the maintenance of the 'Dinner Tables' of our needy children. Many cases of sheer poverty are left unaided through lack of means.

We have already several of the leading Catholic football players of the west of Scotland on our membership list and we know that we can select a team that will do credit to the Catholics of the west of Scotland as the Hibernians have been doing in the east.

Again, there is the desire to have a large recreation ground where our Catholic young men will be able to enjoy the various sports. Any subscriptions may be handed to any of the clergy of the 3 missions.

(Murray, *The Scottish Catholic Community and the Celtic F. C.*)

In the 1890s Celtic built a stadium able to hold 70 000 people. Tension between Celtic and Rangers soon developed, indeed the 1909 cup final between them led to a serious riot. Football was now an enormously popular attraction, especially with working-class men.

Improved working hours, more money to spend and easier travel caused a great growth in day trips and longer holidays. Scotland's seaside resorts benefited from this.

Source 8.68
Paddleboats at Broomielaw, Glasgow

Source 8.69
At the seaside showing bathing machines where the wealthy changed their clothes

The well-to-do enjoyed holidays in hotels and rented properties in the Highlands as well as at the seaside. The Scottish countryside was visited by increasing numbers of ordinary people, too. In the inter-war years a cult of fresh air and exercise developed. Cycling clubs roamed the countryside. The Scottish Youth Hostel Association was set up in 1931, its first hostel being a row of old cottages near Selkirk. The Women's League of Health and Beauty attracted large numbers of recruits. In 1938 it held in Glasgow a vast open air demonstration of its members' disciplined agility. Golf flourished.

Source 8.70 _____
Bobbie Jones, on the old course at St Andrews, 1936

For a working-class family a week away from home, on holiday, was a big event. Molly Weir's mother managed to save enough to take her family to Girvan. They set off, full of excitement.

Source 8.71 _____
The station was seething with Glasgow Fair holiday-makers when we got there on the Saturday forenoon, and my mother was in a ferment of anxiety in case any of us would fall out of the train door. As all the other parents

shared this belief in the murderous possibilities of trains, nobody really enjoyed the journey very much.

We walked from the station. My heart gave a great bound when we found the street we sought – it ran straight down to the sea. And, joy of joys, the holiday house had a red pipe-clay doorstep and the door opened right on to the pavement. After living two storeys up in a Glasgow tenement, this was the very stuff of story-book holidays . . .

Everything about that holiday was unforgettable. The shops were excitingly different from the familiar Glasgow stores. Ice-cream parlours were filled with brightly dressed holiday-makers, eating sugar wafers at 11 o'clock in the forenoon.'

(Weir, *Shoes were for Sunday*)

Most Scots able to afford such a holiday stayed in their own country, though a growing number were drawn to the booming Lancashire resort of Blackpool. The period from 1880 to 1939 was a time when outside influences reached into Scotland as never before. It was also a time when more ordinary Scots began to be able to explore other parts of Britain.

QUESTIONS

1 Explain why Molly Weir was so impressed by her holiday home.   (K.U)

2 List three reasons why leisure activities grew at this time.   (K.U)

3 What evidence in Source 8.64 shows it is not a modern scene?   (K.U)

4 'The evidence in source 8.63 and 8.69 proves it was colder at that time.' Do you agree? Give reasons for your answer.   E.2)

Warfare and Welfare – Scotland since 1939

9 The Changing Economy since 1939

There have been great changes in the Scottish economy since 1939. Some industries have declined, others have developed, and new industries have come to Scotland. The sources in this chapter deal with some of these changes and the reasons why they took place.

A Changing Population

The total size of Scotland's population, and the areas where people chose to live changed during these years.

Source 9.2

The Scottish population

1931	4 842 980
1951	5 096 415
1971	5 228 963
1981	5 130 735
1986	5 121 000

Where people decide to live is strongly shaped by where work is available. The following source shows the kind of work people did in the different regions.

Source 9.1

Population of Scotland's Regions (in thousands)

Year	1871	1891	1911	1931	1951	1961	1971	1981
Borders	119	130	118	112	109	102	98	100
Central	130	165	205	212	233	245	263	273
Dumfries & Galloway	155	150	143	141	148	146	143	145
Fife	161	187	268	276	307	321	327	327
Grampian	381	422	455	433	451	440	439	472
Highland	215	201	188	164	162	164	175	200
Lothian	398	513	615	639	691	710	746	738
Strathclyde	1340	1758	2270	2400	2524	2584	2576	2405
Tayside	358	395	398	384	396	398	398	392
Orkney	31	30	26	22	21	19	17	19
Shetland	32	29	28	21	19	18	17	27
Western Isles	39	45	47	39	36	33	30	32

(Census of Scotland, 1981)

The percentage of people working in different jobs in the different regions – 1984

	Agriculture	Energy and water supply	Manufacturing	Construction	Services
	2%	3%	23%	7%	65%
Borders	8	1	36	6	49
Central	1	5	25	6	62
Dumfries and Galloway	10	3	23	7	57
Fife	2	7	30	8	53
Grampian	3	9	16	8	63
Highland	4	1	13	10	71
Lothian	1	3	17	7	71
Strathclyde	1	2	26	7	64
Tayside	3	2	22	6	67
Orkney	8	1	9	7	75
Shetland	2	10	13	8	67
Western Isles	5	2	16	10	68

The next table gives a more detailed picture of the kinds of jobs available and the numbers working in them in 1984.

Source 9.4

Number of males at work	1 053 000
Number of females at work	851 000
Part-time female workers	346 000
Numbers in different industries	
Agriculture, forestry, fishing	36 700
Fuel extraction, processing	39 500
Other energy and water	25 700
Metal manufacturing, ore, other mineral extraction	32 200
Chemicals, man-made fibres	20 500
Mechanical engineering	69 200
Office machinery, electrical engineering, instruments	62 400
Motor vehicles and parts	6 800
Other transport equipment	34 100
Metal goods	15 100
Food, drink and tobacco	73 100
Textiles, leather, clothing	58 000
Timber, rubber, plastics, etc.	28 100
Paper, printing, publishing	34 300
Construction	138 900
Wholesale distrib., repairs	89 700
Hotels and catering	103 700
Retail distribution	186 300
Transport	85 600
Post, telecommunications	29 500
Banking, finance, insurance	146 200
Public administration, defence	169 600
Education	133 400
Health, veterinary services	143 500
Other services	142 000

(*Scottish Economic Bulletin*, 1987)

Behind these figures lay a number of important changes; they will be explored in the following sections.

QUESTIONS

1 Which regions have grown in population and which have declined since the 1930s? (K.U)

2 Compare these sources with those at the beginning of Section B.
a) Write a sentence commenting on the country's population figures 1931–86 compared to its figures 1881–1931. (K.U)

b) Which were the three most important jobs in 1881, in 1931, and in 1984? (K.U)

c) How do you think this changing pattern of work has affected which regions have grown or shrunk in population size? (E.2)

The Impact of War

Source 9.5

From autumn 1939 the ordinary experiences of existence in Scotland were swept aside by an event that transformed life.

From 1 September 1939 to 14 August 1945 Britain was at war. The fight against Germany, Italy and Japan took British servicemen all over the world. The speedy success of German forces in 1940 drove the British out of mainland Europe: for the army at least there were not to be the huge and costly conflicts of the First World War. But for Britain's airmen and sailors the War was, at times, desperate.

Source 9.6

British losses 1939–45

Armed forces killed	270 000
Merchant seamen killed	35 000
Civilians killed	60 000
Houses destroyed	475 000 approx.
Houses damaged	4 000 000 approx.

They fought to prevent invasion in 1940, to reduce the German air force's raids on Britain and to stop German ships and submarines starving Britain into defeat by sinking shipping. The War hurt ordinary civilians too.

Victory came as a result of the entry into the War of the USSR and the USA. The terrible battles of the First World War were repeated – but on the eastern front and fought by the Red Army. Britain's aircraft bombed Germany; her soldiers helped the far bigger American forces defeat Germany and Japan. The struggle demanded great sacrifices by the British people; by 1945 nearly eight million British people were in one of the branches of the forces or the uniformed groups who supported them.

The War was very expensive, as the table shows.

Source 9.7

Government spending 1937/38–1944/45

	Total	Defence	Percentage on defence
1937/38	£ 919.9 million	£ 197.3 million	21.45
1939/40	£1408.2 million	£ 626.4 million	44.48
1941/42	£4876.3 million	£4085.0 million	83.77
1944/45	£6179.5 million	£5125.0 million	82.94

(*Statistical digest of the War*, HMSO 1951)

In August 1939, through the Emergency Powers Act, the government greatly increased its authority. New ministries were set up such as Food, Supply, Economic Warfare and Information. An expansion of the civil service followed, swelling numbers from 387 700 (1939) to 704 700 by the end of the War. Men between the age of 18 and 41 were (from 1939) conscripted into the forces (unless they were in essential jobs) and into vital occupations like coal mining. From 1940 as Minister of Labour the trade union leader Ernest Bevin took charge of this huge task of organising the British people for the War effort. In 1941 unmarried childless women between the ages of 20 and 30 were conscripted, too, some into the forces, many thousands into jobs where the departure of men had left shortages. They worked especially at producing the weapons of war; the number of British women employed in ordnance factories rose between 1939 and 1944 from 7000 to 260 000. From 1943 women between the ages of 18 and 50 were liable to be conscripted. No people mobilised for war as fully as the British; ordinary people found themselves bombarded with orders and advice.

Source 9.8 _____

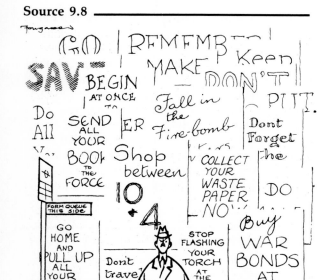

To pay the enormous costs of the War, the government raised income tax to ten shillings (50p) in the pound but this was not enough: by the end of the War it owed a debt of £3500 million, more than seven times the pre-war figure. American goods, supplied without immediate payment being required, helped sustain Britain's struggle, but even so £1000 million worth of investments overseas had to be sold off. Since winning the War took priority, activities like retailing, building, pottery, clothes-making suffered a 50% fall in their labour forces.

Source 9.9 _____

Some economic results of the War for Britain
a) Government spending abroad – £16 million in 1938, £300 million in 1946.
b) Invisible income (shipping, insurance, banking, etc.) – £248 million in 1938; £120 million in 1946.
c) Deficit on visible trade – £300 million in 1938; £650 million in 1946.

d) 1939–43, tenfold increase in small arms and shell production.
e) Aircraft output, 2800 in 1938, over 26 000 in 1944.
f) The total area of tilled land increased 66%: tractors increased (1939–45) from 56 000 to 203 000; combine harvesters increased from 1000 to 2500; government subsidies of £2 an acre were paid for ploughing up land unploughed for 7 years and subsidies provided for certain foods; the yield per acre for wheat – 1938 – 17.7 hundredweights [899 kg], by 1945 – 19.7 hundredweights [1000 kg]; nitrogen applied to land increased from 60 000 to 165 000 tons; phosphates rose from 170 000 to 359 000 and lime from 1 300 000 to 2 000 000 tons.
g) Number of radio valves made: 1940 – 12 million, 1944 – 35 million.
h) Machine tool industry produced 35 000 machine tools in 1939 and 100 000 in 1942.
i) Employment in explosives and chemicals rose from 174 000 to 235 500.

During the War scientific discoveries were rapidly applied in industry. The period saw the coming of jet aircraft, the improvement of radar, electronic computing, antibiotics, artificial rubber and textiles. But some industries became badly strained by wartime. Coal output fell from 231 million tons to 175 million tons, the iron and steel industry and the shipyards struggled to increase output from workplaces that were often out of date and which there was no time to modernise. The need for timber led to the felling of 60% of softwoods and 40% of hardwoods in the forests. A Board of Trade report at the end of the War reviewed the poor state of the railways (even though the government had taken control of them).

Source 9.10 _____
During the War the industry lost a large part of its experienced labour force and for six years the normal process of recruitment and training was interrupted. Many young craftsmen were conscripted for national service. Other men who left the industry during the War had lost much of their skill by the time they returned.

(*Board of Trade report 1947*, in S. Pollard, *The Development of the British Economy*, 1962)

Other older industries suffered from the same problems.

The impact on Scotland

Scotland played its part in this huge national effort. The War brought less direct damage to Scotland than to parts of England. A number of towns and cities suffered minor bombing attacks. A major air attack by the Luftwaffe in March 1941 was recalled by Tom Johnston (Secretary of State for Scotland during the War). He was distressed by:

Source 9.11

. . . the ghastly bombing of Clydebank when only 12 houses escaped damage. In the raids 1500 people were killed and 2000 seriously injured. Of the population of 55 000 only 2000 could find any kind of [home] and poor shivering folk [without] their worldly goods had to be sheltered in widely scattered homes; and the stink of the burning oil from the great containers which had been hit. But . . . one recalls with pride the workers of John Brown & Co. turning up next morning, grim and purposeful, at the work gates. Within 48 hours $\frac{3}{4}$ of the industrial production of the neighbourhood was resumed.

(T. Johnston, *Memories*, 1952)

Source 9.12

Warships under construction on the Clyde

Source 9.13

Clydebank after the blitz

The target was not surprising. The Clyde was the centre of Scottish efforts to supply warships and merchant ships. The Clyde's average yearly output came to 400 000 tons a year; the industry's unemployment problems vanished. Other shipyards – like Robb Caledon in Dundee and Hall Russell in Aberdeen – contributed too. At Ardrossan, a local inhabitant noted:

Source 9.14

During the 1939–1945 War the yard became very busy employing up to 700 men. Over the War years 25 new ships were built:-
11 mine-sweeping trawlers, 5 boom defence ships and 2 cargo ships for the Ministry of War Transport and 7 cargo ships for private owners. A good deal of repair work was also done. 49 submarines, 31 destroyers, 10 frigates and 8 corvettes were repaired apart from 359 Admiralty ships and 288 merchant ships. It was claimed that you could have walked across Ardrossan harbour during the War from one ship to another.

(C. Levy, *Ardrossan Shipyards*, WEA n.d.)

However, in 1942 Tom Johnston believed that Scotland was not getting its fair share of government-supported industries. He explained how he tried to tackle this problem:

Source 9.15
In 1942 we had formed the Scottish Council on Industry. It was to be an independent body; its functions were the safeguarding and the encouragement of Scottish industrial development. We had seen the car industry [and] calico printing go south. We had seen the re-armament factories being started in England; all we got in Scotland was storage capacity. Unless drastic steps had been taken to correct these drifts the outlook for Scottish industry had been bleak indeed.

Between 1942 and 1945 over 700 new industrial enterprises had been authorised in Scotland involving a labour force of 90 000. We got Crown lands in Scotland handed over for administration to the Scottish Office; we got equality rights in the Forestry Commission. What worried us was that the new aircraft industry was passing us by. [By 1949] there were 37 firms in England: in Scotland only 2.

(Johnston, *Memories*)

In 1943 Johnston secured the setting up of the Hydro Board. During the War Scottish shipyards, coal mines, heavy engineering and iron and steel industries were needed to produce as much as possible. Unemployment levels fell to 1.6%. Farmers benefited too. Scotland's arable acreage increased by 15%; yields of cereals and potatoes increased greatly. During the War the number of tractors working Scottish farms rose from 6250 to 19 000. The need to grow food encouraged farmers to invest in tractors. The overall result was that old industries revived. In 1939 16% of Scotland's workers had been employed in heavy industry: by 1945 the figure had grown to 25%. But these industries were not modernised and re-equipped. Nor did Scotland do well in winning new industries – though a Rolls Royce aero-engine plant opened at Hillington. The War ended with the Scottish economy apparently in a far more flourishing condition than it had been pre-war. Whether it was ready for a competitive peacetime world was another matter.

QUESTIONS

1 In what ways did the War lead to the government taking more control over the economy? (K.U)

2 'The War benefited the Scottish economy.'
   a) What evidence supports this view? (K.U)
   b) What evidence conflicts with this view? (K.U)
   c) What do you think is the right view to hold?
   Give reasons for your answer. (E.2)

The Post-War Struggle – 1945–51

Between 1945 and 1951 a Labour Government led by Clement Attlee struggled with the problems of restoring the economy to peacetime conditions. There was little unemployment in these years – indeed the government was soon appealing to women to take up work where possible. British industry worked hard to supply exports. Many of our peacetime rivals had been shattered by the War and could not offer serious competition.

Ronald Towndrow worked for Colville's in Scotland. He commented:

Source 9.16
It was a producers' world. The customers were queueing up for products. The boss rang you up every morning and said, 'You didn't make very much yesterday, could you do a little better today?' It was a trememdous boost to morale, working in those exciting times when there never seemed to be any limit to the demand for steel.

(Pagnamenta and Overy, *All Our Working Lives*)

The War had led the government to play a big part in managing the economy. The Attlee Ministry was determined to maintain this policy in peacetime too. Farmers continued to get government aid. The Minister for Agriculture declared:

Source 9.17

During the War, the farmers and farmworkers of Britain stood between us and starvation. Today they are still fighting the battle for bread. When that battle has been won, they will be able to bring us more of the other foods we want: milk, meat, eggs, vegetables, fruit. But they must not be let down as they were after the 1914–18 War. The Agriculture Bill aims at giving farmers an assured market and guaranteed prices for their principal products, while at the same time ensuring a higher level of efficiency.

(Pagnamenta and Overy, *All Our Working Lives*)

To farmworkers like Len Sharman, on £5 a week, it seemed:

Source 9.18

They gave farmers subsidies on practically every commodity they had, on all the corn, on the milk, the cattle, on the fertilisers, the drainage, the ditching, practically everything. They had subsidies, well, they called them feather-bedded farmers and of course they were in those days. They had it jolly good.

(Pagnamenta and Overy, *All Our Working Lives*)

This prosperity encouraged private firms like Fisons, to spend on research, as the government was already doing. British farming became increasingly efficient and productive.

Source 9.19
Farming output

	1938	1946	1950
Grain crops harvested	4.95 m. tons	7.22 m. tons	7.78 m. tons
Potatoes	5.11 m. tons	10.17 m. tons	9.51 m. tons
Fruit and vegetables	2.33 m. tons	3.67 m. tons	3.85 m. tons
Number of cattle (in millions)	8.76	9.63	10.62
Number of poultry (in millions)	74.25	67.12	96.11

(Pollard, *The Development of the British Economy*)

The government concentrated its efforts on re-building the economy. This meant that there was little to spare for making life more comfortable at home. As an inhabitant of Motherwell noted:

Source 9.20

Britain could hardly pay for more than half the necessary imports, while the export industries – on which the country was now more dependent than ever – had been shattered by the War. On top of this, large forces had to be maintained overseas and in occupied Germany. Britain had won the War – but at a heavy cost in life and materials. Those townspeople, therefore, who had been taking an interest in political and economic affairs were somewhat indignant and bitter when, in August, 1945, America stopped the Lend-lease Scheme before Britain had time to recover its position as a major trading country. Motherwell folk, however, did not fully appreciate then that the next years were going to be years of austerity.

(J. Stirling, *Motherwell Post War*, 1987)

Source 9.21

The economist J. M. Keynes was sent to North America. He negotiated a loan of $3750 million from the USA and further help ($1500 million) came from Canada. Yet more money came in

1948 from 'Marshall Aid' once the USA had decided it must pour money into reviving Western Europe to make it a strong barrier to Soviet Russia. World trade slowly revived too. These factors helped Britain recover from the war. But rationing and wartime controls remained.

Nationalisation

In 1918 the Labour Party had committed itself to 'Clause 4', agreeing that it would work for public ownership of important parts of the economy. This policy was now carried out, directed by Herbert Morrison. But, at first, it only dealt with parts of the economy in great need of help and re-organisation. Emmanuel Shinwell was a key figure in this programme:

Source 9.22

I was asked by Attlee to go to the Ministry of Fuel and Power with a seat in the cabinet and to nationalise the mines, the electricity supply and gas . . . The coal industry was pretty bad at the time because it had been neglected during the War. Thousands of men had left the pits either to go into the Forces or to enter the munitions industries. Meanwhile, industrial production was increasing at a rapid rate and demands were made for more coal. When we had nationalised the industry, of course, all sorts of problems presented themselves (shortage of labour, shortage of equipment) and so there was trouble.

(A. Thompson, *The Day before Yesterday*, 1971)

Source 9.23

The Scottish Communist, Abe Moffat, expressed his view on these events:

Source 9.24

Nationalisation of the mines had been the demand of the Scottish miners for generations. Indeed, it was their representative who submitted the first resolution calling for nationalisation to the British TUC at the end of the last century.

After the Labour Party became the Government in 1945 and proposed to set up the National Coal Board, we supported the idea of nationalisation, even though it was not the type of nationalisation that I and many others would have wanted. Proof of that fact was the composition of the National Coal Board, on which there has always been a majority of people who had never supported nationalisation in their lives, and never even supported Labour. We felt that there should have been more representation from the trade union movement, not a majority of people who held Conservative opinions.

(Moffat, *My Life with the Miners*)

Source 9.25

- The Bank of England was nationalised, and received a charter in 1946.
- The Coal Industry was nationalised by the Coal Industry Nationalisation Act, 1946, which set up the National Coal Board.
- Civil Aviation was nationalised by the Civil Aviation Act, 1946. This covered the British Overseas Airways Corporation (set up in 1939), and two new corporations, British European Airways and British South American Airways.
- Public Transport (and some private transport) was nationalised by the Transport Act, 1947. The British Transport Commission was established, and the Docks and Inland Waterways, Hotels, Railways, London Transport, Road Haulage, and long distance Road Passenger Transport were administered by six executive boards.
- Electricity was nationalised by the Electricity Act, 1947, which set up the British Electricity Authority in place of the Central Electricity Board.
- Gas was nationalised by the Gas Act, 1948, which established the Gas Council and twelve Area Gas Boards.

Owners received compensation. Many Conservatives did not vigorously oppose the policy – until it affected the profitable road haulage and iron and steel industries.

Source 9.26

WHY NATIONALISE TRANSPORT?

• The Government propose to introduce a Bill to nationalise transport.

• The Railways and the Road Hauliers have submitted a plan to the Government which, while securing the co-ordination of freight transport, would leave the traders and the public with complete freedom to use any form of transport including their own.

• As stated by the Lord President of the Council : "LET THE ARGUMENT BE DIRECTED TO THE MERITS AND LET THE TEST BE THE PUBLIC INTEREST."

• The Public are asked to support the demand for an enquiry before being committed to any scheme which might damage irretrievably the country's industrial prosperity.

G W R · L M S · L N E R · S R
ROAD HAULAGE ASSOCIATION

WHY?

The advocates of state monopoly say that nationalisation or semi-nationalisation of road passenger transport is necessary in order to secure a properly integrated system. But co-ordination of services between company and company, between company and municipality, and between road and rail, has long since been established and is constantly being extended.

So **WHY** set up a vast and costly STATE authority or a series of Regional Boards to do something which is already done under the existing organisation?

The British Omnibus Companies Public Relations Committee

There were critics of the policy, however, like the economist, J. Jewkes. He argued:

Source 9.27
The planned economy destroys the independent habits and attitudes through which alone freedom can be preserved. As private property diminishes in importance fewer and fewer people are in the independent position in which they can fearlessly criticise Government policy without risking their livelihood and the security of their family. The number of people grows whose incomes wholly or partly depend upon keeping their mouths shut. The planned economy always involves a great increase in the number of Government officials who can hardly criticise their employer without risking their chances of promotion. Perhaps, however, for the mass of the people the whole atmosphere of independence and freedom is most destroyed by the increase of minor officials, essential for the working of the plan, each of whom is charged with powers over our everyday actions.

(R. N. Breach and R. M. Hartwell, *British Economy and Society 1870–1970*, 1972)

The Scottish situation

The Scottish economy was swept along by events in the wider world. Its 275 mines were nationalised, its railways became part of the nationalised network. But even in 1946 reports were emerging that suggested there were special reasons for concern in Scotland. A government report noted:

Source 9.28
There is a considerable way to go before Scotland's economy is on an entirely sound basis. The evil effects of 20 years lack of planning at a time when many new industries were developing was not [easy to correct]. Effort is needed to overcome shortages of materials and supplies.

(In R. Saville, *The Economic Development of Modern Scotland*, 1985)

In 1946, also, another official report looked especially at the Clyde. It commented on shipbuilding:

Source 9.29
This great industry has been a source of tremendous strength to the Region, but now, to some extent, it is a source of weakness. The need to concentrate on quality rather than quantity and the high degree of specialisation

required, has tended to [develop] a high degree of conservatism into Clydeside industry, making it difficult to adapt to modern mass-production methods. Shipbuilding has, perhaps, too much monopolised the inventive and engineering genius of the people.

(In Saville, *The Economic Development of Modern Scotland*)

For the moment all seemed well. In 1947 Britain provided half the world's shipping and the Clyde built 38% of this British effort. Up to 1951 there were never more than 1% of Scottish miners out of work. A Motherwell inhabitant saw signs of hope in the town:

Source 9.30 ————————————

One new light industry, S. Smith and Son, Carfin Clock Factory, was the only one of its kind in Scotland. It had made the transition from wartime easily, from producing aircraft precision instruments, to manufacturing electric clocks, alarm clocks and watches in every style and colour. On average, 6000 clocks were produced every week – a vast number for export. When in full production, as many as 600 factory workers (mostly women) were in jobs. Exports from the heavy industries, too, were finding their way into the world's markets helping the great national export drive. Prospects were good enough for the steelworks – as long as Clyde Shipbuilding yards were busy – which they were. A big new development scheme at Stewart and Lloyds, Mossend, was under way to be completed by 1947, the huge tube mill would bring work for over 1000.

(Stirling, *Motherwell Post War*)

But the economist Sir Alec Cairncross worried that:

Source 9.31 ————————————

Shipbuilding and marine engineering, constructional engineering, locomotive building, foundry-work, and the making of iron and steel tubes, are all heavily concentrated in Scotland, while the vast new industries that have grown up in England – motor vehicles, radio, aircraft and electrical apparatus, are almost entirely absent.

(C. Harvie, *The People's Story*, 1986)

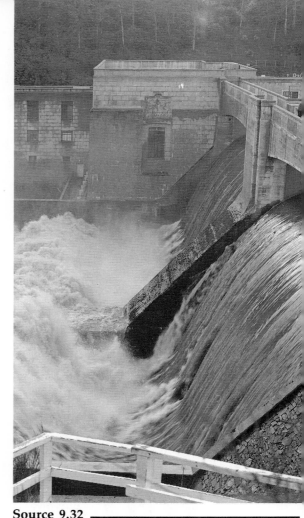

Source 9.32 ————————————
Hydro-electric power station at Pitlochry

At least the Hydro-Electric Board was a success story. Tom Johnston left his post as Secretary of State for Scotland to take charge of the Board. He faced various problems, as he later recalled:

Source 9.33 ————————————
Barely had we started operations 'ere there came upon us great pressure to [set aside] large blocks of power for gigantic electro-metallurgical and chemical corporations at cost price. But we replied that if the corporations were of such importance they should be subsidised, do not expect us to evade our social obligations to the Highland population . . .

Many newspapers opened their columns to letters, fantastic imaginations from beauty lovers, some of whom saw the Highlands

190

being converted into an amalgam of a Black Country, a rubbish tip and a desolation: commercial salmon interests, anglers and hoteliers. There were the ones who knew the Hydro Board was a plot to sell Highland water power cheaply to England . . . It was not the peasant or his wife who gave the hydro-electricity trouble in the late 40s. It was – in the main – people who wanted a solitude for themselves during the summer and autumn months.

(Johnston, *Memories*)

James Hunter lived in one of the areas that benefited from Johnston's work. He wrote:

Source 9.34 ────────────────
One of my earliest memories stems from the evening in the 1950s when I was able to greet my father's return from work by flicking a switch and filling our kitchen with light. Mains electricity had reached our corner of Argyll. We were able to relegate candlesticks and paraffin lamps to the cupboards. A radio that you plugged in, electric cookers, kettles and washing machines, [and] a yellow freezer appeared in our local shop. All this we owed to the Hydro Board. Make no mistake about it, the almost universal availability of mains electricity has been by far the most important element in the survival of rural communities.

(*Press and Journal*, 28 Nov. 1987)

The energetic Johnston also saw the importance of the tourist industry. He obtained the setting up of an independent Scottish Tourist Board. He explained:

Source 9.35 ────────────────
We would publish guide books, registers of accommodation; we would publicise Scotland's scenic and historical attractions; we would assist Scots airports; we would assist in organising annual 'fiestas' like the Edinburgh Festival; we would attract more bus tours to Scotland; we would endeavour to convince local authorities they had an interest in securing decent holiday facilities; we would run information bureaux, encourage improved cookery of our native produce. This tourist industry, in terms of employment, was in 1949 our 6th largest industry.

(Johnston, *Memories*)

In 1951 the Labour Government was defeated. A Conservative Ministry led by Churchill was elected. It promised a more prosperous and freer Britain.

Source 9.36 ────────────────────────

QUESTIONS

1 What were the main problems likely to face the Scottish economy after the immediate post-war years? (K.U)

2 In what ways has the author of source 9.27 tried to persuade his readers that nationalisation was a mistaken policy? (E.1)

3 What is the point of view of the artist of source 9.36? Give reasons for your answer. (E.1)

4 Do you think that sources 9.17, 9.18 and 9.19 prove that the government was right to subsidise peacetime farming? (E.2)

5 How has the author of source 9.33 tried to show his critics in a poor light? (E.1)

Prosperity and Problems

The new Chancellor of the Exchequer in charge of the economy was R. A. Butler. He recalled:

Source 9.37

I had a great opportunity, which you haven't got nowadays, in that everything was war-controlled. My first task, over the first two years, was to liberate some of these controls. I remember, for example, freeing meat from the ration, and making a speech in Gloucester when I said: 'You've been burning most of your books of ration cards . . .' We wanted to free the economy. The other thing is that by encouraging the relief of taxation, I encouraged expansion.

(Thompson, *The Day Before Yesterday*)

The Conservatives de-nationalised the iron and steel industry in 1953. In the same year they greatly reduced the nationalised road haulage industry. However, they had to accept that nuclear power needed state control. In 1954 the United Kingdom Atomic Energy Authority was established. Its programme of building nuclear power stations included Scotland.

During the 1950s British people enjoyed increasing prosperity and in the following decades many people became increasingly wealthy. However, by the 1960s, it was becoming clear that the British economy was not in as flourishing a state as most wished it to be. Rival countries seemed to be doing better.

Source 9.38
Clues to British difficulties

a) Number of man-hours needed to produce a unit of steel, 1959, in the Netherlands – 62, Germany – 100, Sweden – 104, France – 119, Britain – 157.

b) Percentage of a country's wealth used to invest to improve its efficiency and productivity between 1950 and 1960: West Germany – 24%, Italy – 20.8%, France – 19.1%, Sweden – 21.3%, Britain – 15.4%.

c) By 1961 60% of buildings and 38% of plant and machinery in British manufacturing dated from before 1948.

d) Britain's share of the world's export trade in manufactured goods fell from 25.4% in 1950 to 16.2% in 1961.

John Colville served in senior posts in government service. He blamed:

Source 9.39

The structure of industry, the featherbedding of those who owned, managed and worked in it, the out-dated equipment of the factories, and a lack of resources to exploit ingenious inventions and initiatives. As the years passed there were other causes, not least the failure of management and workers to co-operate, and the denial by successive governments of incentives to hard-working managers with imaginative ideas and a modern outlook.

In 1952 both industry and the trade unions were unprofitably fragmented. The Craft Unions were jealously intent on defending their own membership, on ensuring that the jobs of which they believed they should have a monopoly were protected from their rivals. Employers conducted the affairs of thousands of small companies, often family-owned and directed, by methods which their grandparents had found effective. There were, indeed, a handful of well-run giants, like ICI, Shell and Unilever; but even the comparatively large companies in the steel, electrical and engineering industries were too small, and often too conservative, to face the challenges about to be offered.

(J. Colville, *The New Elizabethans*, 1977)

A growing tide of foreign goods poured into Britain. Goods made abroad increasingly threatened Britain's world trade. The British government responded by trying to improve its planning of the economy and by seeking to join the European Economic Community that had been set up in 1957. The first application was blocked by the French leader, General de Gaulle, in 1963. A later application in 1973 succeeded.

Scottish Economic Troubles

Scotland was powerfully affected by the economic troubles that had become clear by the 1960s. The coal and shipbuilding industries suffered especially. Scottish mines were increasingly unprofitable. 70% of Lanark coal was cut from seams under three feet [0.9144 m] thick. Factors like this helped make Scottish coal increasingly costly. It soon became a third dearer than coal mined in the English East Midlands. Pit closures could not be avoided. Between 1951 and 1971 the Lanarkshire mining labour force fell 83%, West Lothian's by 72% and Fife's by 67%.

Source 9.40

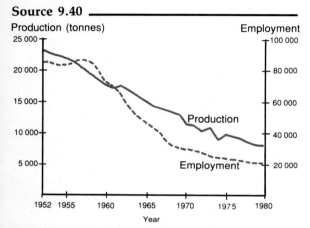

Production and emplyment in the Scottish coal industry, 1952–80

Moreover, coal faced competition from other fuels, including nuclear plants at Dounreay, Hunterston, and Chapelcross.

Source 9.41

Heat supplied to Scotland in millions of therms

	Solid (Coal)	Gas	Electricity	Liquid
1952	4037	232	173	103
1958	4307	208	245	878
1962	2771	195	389	1400
1968	1740	325	602	2448
1972	1102	469	733	2841
1976	945	655	843	2888
1978	812	833	875	2882
1980	709	963	875	2627

(Saville, *The Economic Development of Modern Scotland*)

Shipbuilding

Scottish shipyards suffered along with the rest of Britain's shipbuilding industry. By 1954

Germany had replaced Britain as the major supplier to foreign buyers. In 1956 Japan passed Britain, too. More recently, Korea has moved into a leading position. Until the later seventies the problem was not a lack of demand. British yards increasingly failed to supply even the needs of British shipping firms. Whereas in 1963 they had met 80% of British needs, five years later they were only meeting 20%. British yards suffered from a growing reputation for building over-expensive vessels that took too long to construct and were often late for their delivery dates. Nor did British yards adapt quickly and successfully to the development of a production-line approach, putting together the pre-fabricated sections of huge carrier vessels. This approach helped Japanese yards pull further away from Britain.

Within this gloomy scene Scottish yards did not do well. In 1946 the Clyde had been producing 32.4% of British output. By 1976 it was making only 16.2%.

Source 9.42

Merchant tonnage launched 1950–82 UK and world

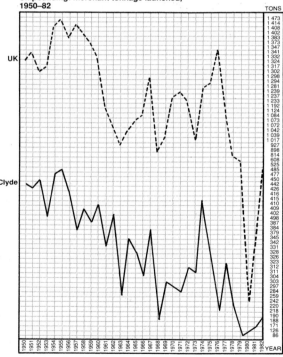

The years between 1961 and 1963 saw the closure of both Denny's of Dumbarton and the Govan yard operated by Harland and Wolff. In

1965 the giant yard, Fairfields, where 3000 men worked and which had just been modernised, went into liquidation. The government rescued it with a million pounds. It then went on to reorganise the industry. Fairfields, Yarrows, Connells, John Browns and Stephen's became the Upper Clyde Shipbuilders. These yards, together with Scott Lithgow on the Lower Clyde, and Robb Caledon at Dundee received nearly £77 millions of state support. It was not enough to avert further crises. In 1972 disaster loomed over UCS. Only Yarrows, with its naval building speciality, made a profit, and Yarrow's broke away from UCS. The work force continued to occupy their threatened yards and the government eventually rescued them once more. Fairfield and Connells became Govan Shipbuilders, Brown's Clydebank yard was sold to Marathon for oil-rig building. In 1977 the government nationalised the industry, but by now world demand for ships was falling. Scott Lithgow had to be rescued by Trafalgar House. Robb Caledon failed. The Govan yard was sold to a Norwegian group. By the late 1980s little remained of the once-great shipbuilding industry. Whisky brought in more profits from exports than Scottish-built ships. An official report of 1987 commented:

Source 9.43

The shipbuilding sector remains depressed in 1987. This is the result of a worldwide surplus of ships. Major redundancies were announced at Scott Lithgow. The yard has no orders other than the Ocean Alliance drilling rig for Britoil. Yarrows is currently building two Type 22 and three Type 23 frigates.

(*Scottish Economic Bulletin*, 1987)

Source 9.45

Launch of the north sea oil rig Penrod 64, from Clydebank, 1973

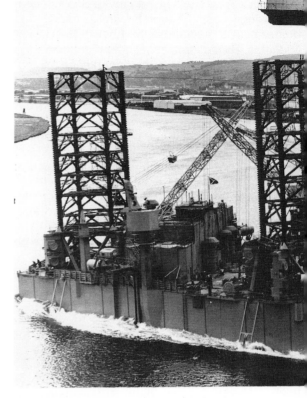

The impact on employment in Clydebank was dramatic.

Table 12.2 Clydebank: The growth in unemployment, 1951–81

	Male	% rate	Female	% rate	Total	% rate
1951	325	2.2	131	2.0	456	2.1
1961	540	3.4	200	2.6	740	3.2
1971	1600	9.5	360	4.4	1960	8.6
1981	3023	20.8	930	9.7	3953	18.2

Source 9.44

Table 12.1 Clydebank: Employment change, 1952–81

	Total employment	Manuf.	Ship + eng.	% in all jobs in ship./eng.	Services	% in all jobs in services
1952	35 020	27 181	23 841	68.1	7 793	22.3
1963	37 120	26 949	24 255	65.3	10 134	27.3
1968	35 028	24 214	19 635	56.1	10 746	30.7
1973	28 919	17 141	12 998	44.9	11 778	40.7
1978	23 023	11 699	8 816	38.3	11 324	49.2
1981	14 881	4 321	3 126	21.0	10 560	68.9

(Department of Employment, Annual Census in J. Hood, *Clydebank*, 1988)

There was no shortage, in the post-war years, of plans and of reports on what was wrong. In 1961 the officially appointed Toothill Committee summarised its findings on Scotland's problems:

Source 9.46

The economy has sustained a run down on two major industries and at the same time increased total employment. This has been partly due to Government measures. Output has not grown as much as it should. Unemployment rates in Scotland have for many years been consistently double those in Britain. Emigration accounted for 44% of the natural increase, 1931–44 and from 1951–60 – for 76%. Emigration generally means the loss of the more skilled workers. Scotland has too many of the older industries and not enough of the new. The tendency is to persist in doing what has long been done well.

Why did new industries not grow to a substantial extent in Scotland? [Because of] the pull of the large markets for industries producing consumer goods. The easiest centre of communications is in the south east [of England].

The need is for a plan which will tackle the problem. The benefits the south offers have to be weighed against the disadvantages of congestion and labour shortage.

(Inquiry into the Scottish Economy 1960–1)

Individuals, too, added their views. In the 1960s Dr Ian Mackintosh returned to his native Scotland. He settled in Glenrothes, intent on helping new industry develop. He later recalled:

Source 9.47

I can remember about 1969, going around trying to raise the reasonably humble sum of half a million pounds going on two million pounds, to start a British independent semi-conductor company. I went to quite a number of senior civil servants and financiers but the result was completely disastrous, nobody wanted to know, nobody really seemed to care.

There was during the sixties an extraordinary lack of awareness on the part of the men in power in Britain, the ministers, people in the city, members of the academic research establishment, managers of electronic companies,

that we were at an industrial watershed, that we were at the beginning of a major new industrial revolution of enormous economic significance.

(Overy and Pagnamenta, All our Working Days)

Improvements in Scotland

The Toothill Committee went on to make positive proposals. They noted:

Source 9.48

We need better communications. This means improved railways, an urgent speeding up of work on roads. Shortages of skilled labour are appearing and industry must be ready to deal with them – for example, by the use of Government training. We have recommendation for closer co-operation between local education authorities and industry and for better opportunities for specialisation in scientific and technical subjects in the schools.

From the mid 1960's governments intervened more and more to try and stimulate the Scottish economy. In 1966 most of Scotland (apart from the Edinburgh area) was labelled a 'development zone'. This entitled incoming industries to all sorts of grants. It led to the setting up of an aluminium smelter in Invergordon and a paper pulp mill in Fort William, for example. Local authorities were encouraged to develop industrial estates along the lines established in new towns like Cumbernauld and Glenrothes. In Cumbernauld:

Source 9.49

Fully serviced sites are available for the building of factories. The corporation will build a factory to the requirements of an industrialist. Among the 200 firms are manufacturers of electronic components, computers, labels, carpets, underwear, parts for the motor industry and light engineering.

(Official Guide, 1978)

Source 9.50

Manufacturing industries qualify for building grants, loans, training subsidies. The Board of Trade is also empowered to make grants for expenditure on new plant and machinery.

(Cumbernauld Development Corporation, 1970)

(Such efforts were not always wholly successful. The Invergordon smelter, for example, closed in 1982.)

The Highlands and Islands Development Board (1965) has poured money into encouraging fishing, industry and tourism. In 1975 the Scottish Development Agency was set up. It has used government money to assist and attract industry to Scotland as in this example:

Source 9.51 ─────────────
The entire oil and gas division of one of Britain's major engineering companies is moving to Aberdeen in a £3 million investment in the city. The relocation stems from talks between British Hydro Mechanics Research Association and the Scottish Development Agency. The SDA has supplied the funds for the building and the site, understood to form £1 million of the £3 million cash injection.

(*Evening Express* 30 Nov. 1988)

Places in parts of Britain that have especially serious economic trouble have been labelled 'enterprise zones'. Clydebank was one of the first of these. Firms coming to these zones enjoyed a ten-year period without paying rates. They can obtain low-interest loans, are exempt from certain taxes, and are free from some of the regulations that control other areas.

Source 9.52 ─────────────

Source 9.53 ─────────────
Timex factory in Dundee

These efforts have produced results like this:

Source 9.54 ─────────────
Electronics, one of Scotland's most important industries which employs 45 000 people, is poised for further expansion. American Electronics companies are expected to invest heavily in Scotland, creating more than 3500 jobs. Much of Scotland's success is attributed to the efforts of the Scottish Development Agency and the efforts of the Scottish new towns.

(*Dundee Courier*, 19 Feb. 1987)

Scotland has also gained from the rapid emergence of a new industry – oil. Dutch exploration successes encouraged oil companies to begin drilling in the North Sea. A world rise in oil prices made it worthwhile to battle with the difficult conditions in the area. In 1975 the first oil flowed ashore – from the Argyll field.

Later in 1975 the *Scotsman* reported:

Source 9.55 ─────────────
The Queen pressed the button which set the whole BP Forties oil system in operation for the first time today. If used properly this flood of energy could, without doubt, much improve Britain's economic well being. Prime Minister Harold Wilson forecast that a new industrial

revolution will follow. He said this as he demanded more orders for equipment to go to Scotland and the North of England.

(*Scotsman*, 3 Nov. 1975)

Source 9.56

Tony Benn participates in the pumping of the first oil from the Argyll field to the BP refinery on the Isle of Grain in the Thames Estuary, 1975

Source 9.57

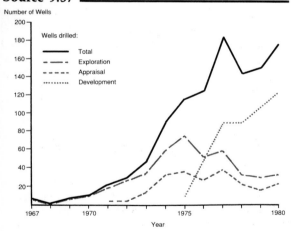

Drilling activity offshore Scotland, 1967–80

The oil industry brought new jobs to the Grampian Region, especially, and also to Orkney and Shetland. By the 1980s it had provided over 30 000 jobs in Grampian. Moreover, oil exploration is closely linked to the discovery of natural gas. The success in finding this fuel has been such that, between 1970 and 1977 the whole of Scotland has

been converted from coal gas to natural gas.

These developments have led to changes in the balance of the Scottish economy.

Source 9.58

Principal oil and gas developments, 1980

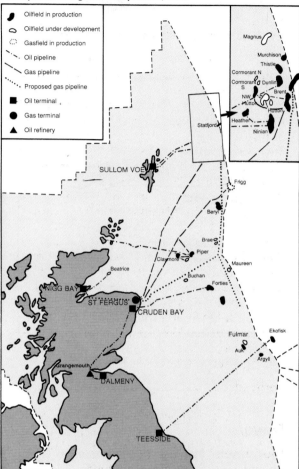

Percentages of people in different jobs

Source 9.59

Industry	1951	1960	1970	1980
Agriculture, Forestry, Fishing	7.3%	4.7%	2.8%	2.2%
Mining and Quarrying	4.4%	4.3%	1.9%	2.1%
Manufacturing	35.9%	35.0%	35.6%	26.7%
Construction	6.2%	7.6%	8.3%	7.7%
Gas, Electricity, Water	1.4%	1.4%	1.4%	1.4%
Services	44.7%	47.0%	49.9%	59.9%

(Saville, *The Economic Development of Modern Scotland*)

Source 9.60

Employees in emplyoment in service industries

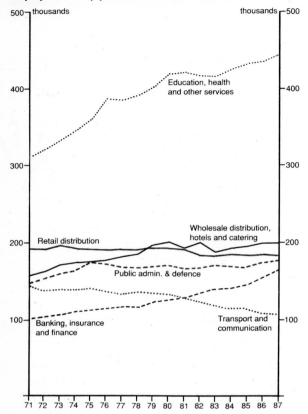

For many people, public transport by road was most important:

Source 9.61

People under 18, many of the elderly, many housewives, tourists, disabled and others, these are all dependent on public transport. Unlike many other rural areas the situation in the Highlands and Islands has improved in recent years, particularly with the introduction of Post Office minibuses on routes not previously served.

(*Highlands and Islands Transport Review*, 1975)

Similar services developed in the Borders and the south-west of scotland.

Source 9.62

Percentage of private households with a car or van

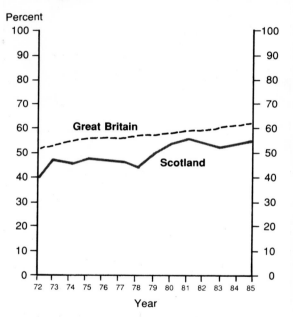

Travel

The 'service' industry includes tourism. This industry, like other older industries, needs good communications. The Toothill Committee had already seen the need for work to be done on this area.

A programme of road improvements began. In the Edinburgh–Glasgow–Perth area motorways were built. Other roads were upgraded. By 1988 there were plans to build a motorway down the western flank of Scotland to connect up to motorways in England. Bridge-building activities increased. In 1964 a road bridge spanned the Forth, north of Edinburgh. In 1966 the Tay Road Bridge opened at Dundee. Later developments included the Kessock Bridge linking Inverness to the Black Isle.

Car ownership in Scotland increased but there were different views on whether the growth of road traffic was really an improvement in life. This inhabitant of a remote Scottish glen observed:

Source 9.63

In the old days everyone had bicycles. It used to mean quite a thing to a person to get a decent bicycle. But you find now that there's few young people without either a motor cycle or a car. And half the time they are people who can't afford it. So that has to cut down their standard of living. People have become lazy. They'll never think about cycling anywhere now. They must have motorised transport. It's regarded as essential. For those who don't own cars, if you live off a main bus route then the difficulties are enormous. Local shops have closed down. We had a railway not far from here at one time. The axe fell on the railway. The small bus company was taken over by the large one, the services worsened.

(R. Grant, *Strathalder*, 1978)

Source 9.64

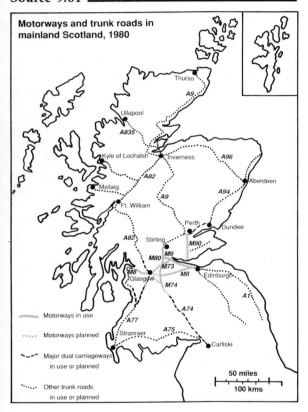

Motorways and trunk roads in mainland Scotland, 1980

Source 9.65

Traffic congestion at Halbeath on A902

An observer of life in the 1960s commented:

Source 9.66

Transport improved daily; methods of moving freight in 'container' lorries and trains revolutionised (to the great suspicion of the workers) the entire pattern of shifting merchandise. The new giant lorries were hailed, rightly, as the way to a better standard of living for all, and the workers who would not operate them for fear of losing their jobs were denounced. But the lorries cracked and ruined the roads, polluted the verges with the filth they exuded, and brought noise-levels, long unbearable, to the point at which they became mentally and physically dangerous. The ownership of cars proliferated; another admirable sign of rising prosperity. But every car added its burden to the impossibly over-crowded roads, contributed its poison to the atmosphere.

(B. Levin, *The Pendulum Years*, 1970)

In 1948 3.8 million motor vehicles travelled Britain's roads. By 1970 the figure was 15.3. million. In 1963 Colin Buchanan, a civil engineer produced a report 'Traffic in Towns'. He suggested ways in which towns and cities could try and stop motor vehicles from ruining their environments. The 'pedestrian precinct' areas developed in recent years are signs of the influence of his thinking.

Source 9.67

Traffic-free shopping in Glasgow

In the rush to improve road travel, smaller places were increasingly by-passed. The people of these places suffered less from traffic noise and pollution, as a result. But there were also ways in which a new by-pass might damage their lives. An official survey of five by-passed towns reported:

Source 9.68 _____

Accommodation and catering and retail businesses suffered the greatest drop in trade after the opening of the by-pass, with half noticing an immediate reduction. In the garage trade less than half the operators noticed an immediate reduction. Half of accommodation and catering businesses never reached pre-by-pass trade levels. There was a higher incidence of recovery in the garage trade. Food shops, newsagents and tobacconists were the most hit retail businesses.

(Highlands and Islands Development Board, 1979)

The people and goods that crowded increasingly onto the roads injured rail travel. From 1963 many minor lines in Scotland were closed as a result of a report drawn up by Dr Beeching. He had been asked to find out how to make the railways more profitable. His proposals meant the end of local rail travel for many smaller towns and villages. The closure of the North British Locomotive Works in 1962 was a further sign of the decline of railways. The works had provided employment for many in the Springburn area of Glasgow. Its steam engines had once been exported throughout the world. Even though it eventually began building diesels, it could not survive.

Nor did Scotland develop a flourishing motor-building industry. British Leyland's heavy vehicle plant at Bathgate opened in 1961; Rootes opened a car factory at Linwood in 1963. Both came to Scotland in response to official pressure. Neither proved a long-term success.

In 1984 the journalist, Ian Jack, visited Glasgow. His comments highlight the changing Scottish economy's main features. He wrote:

Source 9.70 _____

Employment in the old industries has declined spectacularly. Since 1971 more than 40% of jobs in the shipbuilding and marine engineering industries have disappeared. The figure for jobs in metal manufacturing is 80%; for printing and publishing 40%; for mechanical engineering 50%; for electrical engineering 48%; in transport 31%; in vehicle manufacture 31%. The only categories of work that now employ more people are the professions, public administration, general services and banking. More than twice as many people now work in banks, insurance companies and stock-broker's offices as do in shipyards and engine shops. And many more, about 60 000 of them, do not work at all. At first Glasgow tried to resist this destruction which was raining down on it from West Germany and Japan. Sometimes closure threats prompted 'Work-ins' but even the most celebrated of these, at Upper Clyde Shipbuilders, did not much more than postpone the evil Friday of the final pay packet. Today the city advertises itself to the world as a 'centre'; a business centre, an educational centre, a cultural centre, a tourist centre.

(I. Jack, *Before the Oil Ran Out*, 1987)

Source 9.69 _____

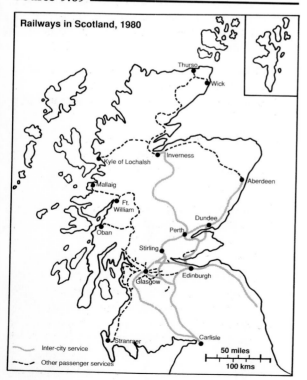

Railways in Scotland, 1980

Thurso

Wick

Kyle of Lochalsh

Inverness

Mallaig

Ft. William

Aberdeen

Oban

Dundee

Perth

Stirling

Glasgow

Edinburgh

Carlisle

Stranraer

Inter-city service

Other passenger services

50 miles

100 kms

Since 1979 the Conservative Government has altered economic circumstances in which Scots live. It has sold off several nationalised industries, including the gas industry and British Petroleum. It has developed a number of training programmes for young people. But it has not managed to remove the unemployment that is such a clear sign of Scotland's economic troubles.

Source 9.71

Percentage of the Scottish working population, unemployed

1978	6.4%
1979	6.2%
1980	8.7%
1981	11.1%
1982	12.1%
1983	12.8%
1984	13.2%
1985	13.5%
1986	14.0%
1987	13.7%

(*Scottish Economic Bulletin*, 1987)

Source 9.72

QUESTIONS

1 Look through the sources to find and list all the reasons that explain Scotland's postwar economic troubles. (K.U)

2 Which do you think are the most important reasons? Explain your answer. (E.2)

3 Which industries suffered sharp decline? (K.U)

4 How have the popularity of different sources of power changed since 1950? (K.U)

5 Look at source 9.44. Explain how the decline in shipbuilding altered the sort of work that people in Clydebank were able to do. (E.2)

6 In what ways did governments try and help the Scottish economy? (K.U)

7 What signs of optimism for the Scottish economy can you find in the sources? (K.U)

8 Between 1952 and 1980 the coal industry became more efficient. How does source 9.40 provide evidence for this? (K.U)

9 Compare source 9.53 with factory pictures in the early part of this book. Does the comparison show conditions had changed? (E.2)

10 How can you tell from source 9.63 the speaker is elderly? Does this affect your view on the value of the source? (E.1)

11 Look at source 9.42. How does it show that 'the years 1967–73 were especially worrying for Clyde shipbuilders'? (K.U)

12 Do you think the author of source 9.70 approved of the changes he described? Give reasons for your answer. (E.1)

13 How might an elderly inhabitant of Scotland in the 1980s have described the changes in travel and transport he had seen? Would such a person have welcomed all the changes? (E.2)

10 Living and Working Conditions

In the years after 1939 there were remarkable changes in the conditions in which people in Scotland lived and worked. At first life was dominated by the Second World War. For several years after the War life continued to be a struggle, but by the 1950s increasing signs of greater wealth and comfort can be seen in the lives of many people. The sources in this chapter deal with these changes.

The Impact of War

Women at work

The outbreak of War transformed daily life. Many men had to join the armed forces, like this Glaswegian:

Source 10.1

I was called up at thirty-eight years old. I was a banker, married with a young baby and at first I went on to the lower deck of a destroyer and slept in a hammock. It was a big change, I can tell you, from the bank and the comfortable home in the suburbs.

(Blair, *Tea at Miss Cranston's*)

Other men were called into the emergency services to deal with the effects of bombing, or to fight any German invaders who managed to land. Women, too, were called into the forces. In Glasgow, Molly Weir noted:

Source 10.2

Men drilled and practised Air Raid Precautions and there was a body of men called the Local Defence Volunteers. I was determined to go down fighting if the Germans parachuted down and I carried a pepper pot to blind them if they got within firing distance.

(M. Weir, *A Toe on the Ladder*, 1978)

Many women were recruited to work at jobs once done by men.

Source 10.3

Women working on the railway outside Cathcart in 1942. By this time most men were in the forces

Source 10.4

Landgirls in Aberdeen

In Aberdeen, Bert Murray saw:

Source 10.5
Women began to take over most of the jobs previously done by men, in the Armed Forces, Civil Defence, Police, Fire Service. They trained in driving various vehicles, and working in heavy and light industry. The Womans Land Army was formed, where they worked on farms and the land.

(Murray, *3 Score Years and 10*)

Mrs J. Grimmond was a landgirl. She recalled:

Source 10.6
My niece and I worked in the gardens of Stracathro Hospital, helping to make the footpaths and tending and gathering vegetables. It was cold working outside in winter but we had a kind boss. On very cold days he sent us to work in the heated conservatory. In the summer it was delightful working outside.

(*Dundee Courier* 19 Nov. 1977)

Many women worked on buses and trams, like this Glasgow lady:

Source 10.7
I was made to be a clippie in the War. If you werenae in the forces you got sent to what they called essential work, munitions or that. Wi' me it was the buses. It was quite cold in the winter and it was difficult at night in the blackout because you'd only a kind of dim blue light inside the bus for takin' fares and countin' your change.

(Blair, *Tea at Miss Cranston's*)

Women worked in all sorts of factories. They were recruited into areas traditionally reserved for men like shipbuilding. The Ministry of Labour stated:

Source 10.8
The average woman takes to welding as readily as she takes to knitting. Indeed the 2 occupations have much in common since they both require a small fairly complex manipulative movement which is repeated many times combined with a kind of subconscious concentration at which women excel.

(Ministry of Labour, in A. Holdsworth, *Out of the Doll's House*, 1988)

All who could work and wanted to work were needed. Between 1939 and 1943 Britain's employed population rose by 2.9 millions.

Coping with the Blitz

Source 10.9

"We'll give her another ten minutes, and then warn her."

When War began people throughout Britain waited fearfully for German bombers to arrive. The government insisted that a 'blackout' be enforced. In Glasgow, Bob Crampsey, wrote:

Source 10.10
We watched, spellbound, as the one man in the street who had a private car fitted his two thicknesses of newspaper inside his side lights, leaving a small aperture for a beam of feeble light. The uneventful nature of those first months was something of a real disappointment and we felt vaguely let down by the Germans. What was the point of a war when nothing was happening? There were signs that we were at war, our windows were crisscrossed with paper strips as a protection against blast and black-out material for curtains was bought in hundreds of thousands of yards.

We carried our gas-masks everywhere and our young sister, Julie, had a Mickey Mouse model which was somehow far more horrific than the orthodox kind.

(Bob Crampsey, *The Young Civilian*, 1987)

Source 10.11
Schoolchildren at Abbeyhill, Edinburgh trying on gas masks

The government organised an 'evacuation' scheme to move children from areas likely to be bombed, to more remote places.

Source 10.12
Government Evacuation Scheme Letter to Parents in Glasgow
1. The Government have decided that parents or guardians of children living in Edinburgh, Glasgow and Dundee should be given a chance to send their children to places where they will be safer from air raids. You are not obliged to send your children and, if you are living in one of the less crowded areas of your city, you may prefer to keep them at home.
2. Arrangements have been made· to send the children from the schools with their teachers and with other helpers who will look after them, but mothers who have children too young to go to school may go with them in the school party.

3. The Government will supply free transport for persons going with the school party, and will provide both food and lodging for those who cannot afford to pay.
4. If you are sending more than one child, tell the oldest child to take his younger brothers and sisters with him and keep them close to him all day. They will all live together or close beside each other.
6. Each child should wear his warmest clothes and overcoat and should bring –
One change of underclothing and stockings, if possible.
Night clothes and tooth brush, if possible.
Enough food to last a day.
A tin cup.
A gas mask in its box.

A Glasgow magazine reported:

Source 10.13
At the schools where evacuation did not begin until late in the forenoon there was something like a rush on the trains. Many of the children had obviously got together their belongings in a very short time. The persons least affected by the partings were the children themselves. Most of them were happy and gay, as if they were going away on a picnic.

Mothers of Glasgow, standing outside city schools or walking with the evacuation processions to the stations, watched red-eyed with tears but bravely quiet, struggling to hide their feelings as their children disappeared behind the station barriers to the waiting trains. 'See you soon' was all that most of them said.

(Whyte & Berry, *Glasgow Observed*).

Isobel Cameron took her Glasgow pupils to Perth. She recalled:

Source 10.14
We'd no idea where we were bound until after the train left Parkhead Cross, and then we were told 'Perth'. What a journey! Hundreds of mothers, weans and bawling infants packed like herring, and no toilet on the train! Things were that dire by the time we got to Auchterarder we'd to get the train stopped. But just think on yon wee platform at Auchterarder with its *one* toilet and dozens of weans dancing desperate on that train. What could you do?

'Everybody out! Boys . . . all go and perform down that side of the train. Girls . . . come on now . . . down the other side!'

At Perth we were herded into the ice-rink all labelled. It was like a slave-market, us all lined up in rows and a wee man with a bellowing voice and two lists in his hand, one of hosts and one of Glasgow children. Oh what an uproar of greetin' and girnin' from tired weans, away from home . . . maybe forever for all they knew!

(Blair, *Tea at Miss Cranston's*)

Source 10.15 _____

Evacuees leaving from Costorphine station

In September 1939 120 000 Glasgow children left for rural parts of Scotland. By Christmas over three-quarters of them were back home. Many were homesick and their parents' worries faded as the bombers failed to arrive. In 1941, when German aircraft launched serious raids on Scotland, a new flow began as evacuee children once more left the big cities.

In the cities emergency air raid shelters were built. Bob Crampsey's family in Glasgow used a:

Source 10.16 _____

Seven-arched brick structure in the back green. Ours was cold and dank. We hung mats across the door to keep out the cold [and] allow us to light torches. We sat, jerkins and trousers pulled over pyjamas. We drank tea and ate sandwiches of the bread that was growing steadily darker as the war progressed.

(Crampsey, *The Young Civilian*)

To live through a raid was a terrifying experience. Janet Purvis survived the Clydebank blitz where:

Source 10.17 _____

Thousands were bombed out their houses and ever so many people lying injured. But the queer funny wee thing that I remember so vividly was the sight of all the folks' budgies bombed out their cages and fluttering about in a frenzy . . . green and blue and yellow. It was bizarre really in all that devastation, and I can see those budgies yet. But the real job was to see to the injured and set up canteens to feed people in whatever bits of building were still standing until other arrangements were made for them.

(Blair, *Tea at Miss Cranston's*)

Source 10.18 _____

Serving the needy in wartime

Source 10.19 _____

A Clydebank family whose home has been destroyed by bombs

Source 10.20

The notice warns that the penalty for looting may be death

After a raid, as Willie Green of Clydebank recalled:

Source 10.21

Anyone who stayed unless they were necessary, was really a handicap. And one of the trage-dies, you know, there was a certain amount of looting. Yes, I've heard of people who got stuff stolen. Men were re-fixing the houses, you know, wee simple things were stolen, like the wee tumblers out o' Woolworth's, the wee tumbler stands, the wee things that cost six-pence, things like that were all gettin' removed. It's surprisin', people'll take things.

(Ed. Billy Kay, *Oddyssey, The Second Collection*, 1982)

QUESTIONS

1 Use the evidence in the sources to make up a government poster asking women to volunteer for various kinds of work and explaining why they were needed. (K.U)

2 Use sources 10.13, 10.14 and 10.15 to compile a letter home from an evacuee who has left Glasgow and arrived in a rural area. (K.U)

3 Look at source 10.20. Do you think a newspaper of the time would have been happy to print this? Give reasons for your answer. (E.2)

Daily life

Very little new building went on in the War so that housing conditions worsened. Wages rose, and though taxes rose too the average working-class income had gone up by 9% (after tax) by 1944. Middle-class incomes fell 7% because of taxations. Wartime meant all sorts of shortages. The result, Bob Crampsey saw was:

Source 10.22

We stood in queues. Shawlands queues consisted of middle-aged women, dutiful wee girls and the Crampsey boys. We didn't mind queuing much, except on Saturday mornings when it badly affected our football. The rationed foods were easy, the trick was to know when the unrationed but scarce commodities – liver, chocolate biscuits, would be coming in.

Queues often formed on the merest breath of rumour and where coupons had to be clipped or cancelled, serving took an eternity. There were Saturday mornings in the City Bakeries queue in Regwood Street where all life came down to getting half a dozen cream [artificial] cookies. Initially we made ill-advised attempts to get 18 cream [artificial] cookies but this was thwarted by indignant shouts of 'Those three are brothers.'

(Crampsey, *The Young Civilian*)

The government introduced rationing:

Source 10.23

Bert Murray, in Aberdeen, noted a common level of rations:

Source 10.24 ———————————
Tea – ¼ lb [113 g] per month – adults only.
Sugar – 2 lbs [900 g] per month – family of four.
Milk – ½ pint [300 ml] per day per child.
Milk – 1 pint [600 ml] every third day – adults.
Condensed Milk – small tin per month.
Syrup – small tin per month.
Bread – one large per week.
Small loaf extra if available.
Bacon – ½ lb [225 g] per month – adults.
Eggs – one per person every thirteen weeks.
Flour – 2 lbs [900 g] per month.
Butter – ½ lb [225 g] per month.
Margarine – ½ lb [225 g] per month.
Meat or Mince – ½ lb [225 g] per week adults and children over ten.
Cooking Fat – ½ lb [225 g] per month.
Potatoes – quarter stone [1.5 kg] weekly when available.
Fruit or Sweets – none.
Turnip or other Vegetables occasionally.
Soap for all purposes – one bar per month.
Butchers had whale meat sometimes – not very appetizing. An occasional bone to make soup or broth and fish from time to time helped the diet.
Although Ration Books and clothing coupons were necessary, many problems were created, with loss of tempers. Everybody should have been the same, yet if you had cash, there were ways and means of getting extra.

(Murray, *3 Score Years and 10*)

Lord Woolton, the Minister of Food, urged his staff to invent recipes and rhymes to persuade the housewife.

Source 10.25 ———————————
Those who have the will to win
Cook potatoes in their skin
For they know the sight of peelings
Deeply hurts Lord Woolton's feelings.

(Ed. T. Barker *The Long March of Everyman*, 1975)

Source 10.26 ———————————
Everybody in wartime had her own particular shortage which was intolerable. With some it was sugar, with others tea, while some people felt a constant craving for bananas and oranges. With my little niece it was what she called 'shell eggs'. She hummed joyously as she extracted each spoonful.

(Weir, *A Toe on the Ladder*)

All sorts of items, like furniture and bicycles, had to be made to a basic 'utility' standard. Clothes were rationed and the government even controlled fashion styles.

Source 10.27 ———————————
Jackets. No double-breasted jackets; not more than three pockets, no slits or buttons on cuffs; not more than three buttons on front; no patch pockets; no half belt, no fancy belts and no metal or leather buttons.
Waistcoats. Plain, single-breasted only, no collar; not more than two pockets; not more than five buttons; no back straps and no chain hole.
Trousers. Maximum width of trouser bottoms nineteen inches [48 cm], plain bottoms – no permanent turn-ups; not more than three pockets; no side or back straps; no extension waist bands; no pleats; no elastic in waist bands.
General. No zip fasteners and no raised seams.

(*The Times*, 19 March 1942)

A magazine carried out a survey, asking people to choose their main grumble about wartime life.

Source 10.28 ———————————

Main grumbles	Town	Country
Blackout	100	100
Food	66	68
Fuel, petrol	44	50
Evacuation	37	64
Prices	42	39
Lack of amusements	30	21
Transport	38	14
Lack of news	36	21

(*New Statesman*, 13 January 1940)

QUESTIONS

1 Does the ration mentioned in source 10.24 provide a healthy diet or might wartime shortages cause ill-health?
(E.2)

2 Notice the replies in source 10.28 where town and country dwellers differed. Why do you think they differed on these particular topics? (E.1)

Social reform

Conscription once more showed up the poor state of the nation's health. The Ministry of Food used the rationing system to insist on calcium, iron, minerals and vitamins being added to certain foods. The evacuation scheme shocked some well-to-do families who saw, at first hand, the health, clothing and behaviour of children from poor working-class city housing. Moreover, the huge national effort the War demanded encouraged discussion about and publicity for plans to create a better post-war Britain.

A planning group that included Conservatives produced this statement for the Ministry of Information:

Source 10.29 ——————————————

Wartime conditions have already compelled us to make sure, not only that the rich do not consume too much, but that others get enough. The needs of war production call for new measures for improving the housing, welfare and transport of workers. The evacuation scheme should [lead to] improvements in our educational system and social services. The wartime measures to protect the standard of living point the way to a planned population policy. The mobilisation of manpower should spell the end of mass unemployment. War measures for rationalising the distribution of various products should lead to a remodelling of distribution as a whole, so as to transform increased productivity into increased consumption on a higher standard.

(P. Addison, *The Road to 1945*, 1975)

A Motherwell inhabitant reported:

Source 10.30 ——————————————

Promises for better housing and higher living standards were being made by politicians. Tuberculosis was still a scourge in the towns and cities. Better housing was the answer. Tenement properties were to be demolished and replaced by housing schemes.

(Stirling, *Motherwell at War*)

During the War the government carried out reforms. The Labour ministers were especially interested in these improvements, but there were Conservatives, too, who were enthusiasts for social reform.

Source 10.31 ——————————————

Social Reforms during the War
1940. Price rises made it difficult for the elderly to manage. The powers of the Unemployment Assistance Board were widened; extra payments were made to the elderly.
1940. The Emergency Hospital Scheme. The government reserved beds in all hospitals and paid for military and civilian personnel to be cared for there if they were sick or injured.
A free immunisation scheme for diphtheria was introduced. Deaths from this illness fell in Britain from nearly 3000 in 1938 to 818 in 1945.
1941. The Means Test was abolished.
1941. Emergency Milk and Meals Act. Extra high-vitamin foods were provided for mothers and young children, e.g. milk, orange juice and cod liver oil.
School milk and meals were subsidised. In 1940 130 000 British children took school meals: by 1945 there were 1 650 000.
1942. The Beveridge Report. This plan proposed a complete scheme of care for people in need; the old, the sick, and the unemployed.
1943. A ministry to supervise insurance was set up.
1943. Town and Country Planning Act. This led to the creation in 1945 of a separate Ministry. In Scotland the Scottish Office controlled this work.
1944. Education Act. This was mainly the work of a Conservative, R. A. Butler. It proposed free secondary schooling for all, up to the age of 15.
1945. Family allowances were agreed. Extra money was to be paid to families with two or more children.

In 1941 the TUC pressed the government to reform the health insurance system. The minister in charge of such matters was the Labour MP, Arthur Greenwood. He appointed Sir William Beveridge to head a committee. Beveridge had a long career of being involved in social reform. His Report appeared in December, 1942 and rapidly became a bestseller. The public bought 630 000 copies, all told. The Beveridge Report went far beyond simply looking at health insurance. He explained in the Report:

Source 10.32 ——————————————

The Plan for Social Security is put forward as

part of a general programme of social policy. It is one part only of an attack upon five giant evils: upon the physical Want with which it is directly concerned, upon Disease which often causes that Want and brings many other troubles in its train, upon Ignorance which no democracy can afford among its citizens, upon the Squalor which arises mainly through haphazard distribution of industry and population, and upon the Idleness which destroys wealth and corrupts men, whether they are well fed or not, when they are idle. The purpose of victory is to live into a better world than the old world; each individual citizen is more likely to concentrate upon his war effort if he feels that his government will be ready in time with plans for that better world . . .
No satisfactory scheme of social security can be devised except on the following assumptions:
(a) Children's allowances for children up to the age of 15 or if in full-time education up to the age of 16;
(b) Comprehensive health services available to all members of the community;
(c) Maintenance of employment, that is to say avoidance of mass unemployment.

(In A Beattie, *English Party Politics*, 1970)

Beveridge proposed there should be a Minister of Insurance. He suggested that all those in work should pay a standard weekly amount of money into the insurance scheme: from this fund all people in need would be paid standard amounts without any sort of means test. Beveridge was a Liberal. Whilst his scheme was intended to protect the whole population from the hardships of life, he did not think payments ought to be generous.

97 Labour and 22 Conservative and Liberal MPs voted (unsuccessfully) that the Report should be put into operation as soon as possible.

From all over Britain the government received reports that showed the popularity of Beveridge's plans. A Ministry of Information report noted, in March 1943:

Source 10.33
The following notes have been written on the attitude of the Clydeside Workers to the Beveridge Plan, reports from other areas show similar points of view.

Interest in the Beveridge Plan on its publication was really tremendous. For a week or two the war news tended to take a back seat and one report says: 'There has been possibly more widespread discussion on this than on any single event since the outbreak of the War.' The publicity given to the scheme by the radio and Press together with the explanatory pamphlets on the subject, which appeared almost overnight, aroused a quite remarkable enthusiasm.

Practically everyone approved of the underlying principles, and hopes ran high that the Plan would be put into operation as soon as possible. Soldiers writing home spoke of their pleasure at the Scheme.

To the critics who inquired 'Can we pay for it?' the impatient reply was given, 'We can always pay for wars, this one costs £15 million a day. We will just have to afford the Beveridge Plan.'

(R. C. Birch, *The Shaping of the Welfare State*, 1974)

The Labour Party's victory in the 1945 election may well have been helped by the voters' hopes that it really would bring in the Beveridge Report.

The end of the War
The War ended in 1945. Bob Crampsey's memories of this are much like those of people from all over the country. He wrote:

Source 10.34
We were given a holiday of course and in a spontaneous starburst of joy and relief, street parties were organised. Tables were dragged out into the middle of the road, covered with paper. Our piano was commandeered. Every house contributed sandwiches, vast teapots came out of retirement, groups played for dancing and of course the neighbouring children did turns and the adults sang. These parties were to run for the rest of the summer and indeed beyond, they became Welcome Home parties for men who had been prisoners-of-war. Close-mouths would be hung with Union Jacks and any bunting that miraculously might have survived since the Coronation of 1937 and Welcome Home Bill, Alec, Jock, Stevie, would be chalked on paths and build-

ings. The thin, returned men would accept this three-day spotlight uncomplainingly before returning to that civilian obscurity in which they would live out the rest of their lives.

(Crampsey, *The Young Civilian*)

Source 10.35
A Glasgow tenement welcomes home the victors

The War had altered many people's attitudes about daily life and work. A woman who had carried out very responsible war work said:

Source 10.36
I am beginning to see I'm a really clever woman in my own line, and not the 'odd' or 'uneducated' woman that I've had dinned into me . . . I feel that, in the world of tomorrow, marriage will be – will have to be – more of a partnership, less of this 'I have spoken' attitude. They will talk things over – talking does do good, if only to clear the air. I run my house like a business: I have had to, to get all done properly, everything fitted in. Why, then, should women not be looked on as partners, as 'business women'?

(Marwick, *Women at War*)

An elderly inhabitant of a Scottish glen believed the War altered life in the remoter areas. He said:

Source 10.37
The young folk got out into the world, they saw how the rest of the world lived. They got their first taste of real money. They might have gone to Glasgow to the shipyards, to Corby to the steelworks there, or to Aberdeen to work in a factory. In the long run I doubt very much if they were any better off. They might have had a bit more money in their pockets, a modern home, but from what I got to hear about some of them they never seemed to be able to settle down.

(Grant, *Strathalder,*)

The Labour politician, Douglas Jay, suggested:

Source 10.38
In terms of income, in terms of food, in terms of jobs and hours of work, in terms of taxation, there was a tremendous levelling and the fact that it worked did have great effect on public opinion. People felt that if these things could be done in wartime why shouldn't they be done in peacetime.

(P. Addison, *Now the War is Over*, 1985)

QUESTIONS

1 From the evidence in this section what would you say was the most important reason for the demand for social reform that developed in wartime? Give reasons for your answer. (E.2)

2 What sort of reforms do you think the people living in the building in source 10.35 might have wanted most? (E.2)

3 What do you think might have been the purpose in Ministry agents sending in reports like source 10.33? (E.1)

4 How has Beveridge tried to persuade his readers that his proposals are essential? (E.1)

5 'Postwar Britain could never return to its pre-war condition'. Gather evidence from any sources that seem helpful to answering this question and write an account based on them. (K.U)

Difficult Years, 1945–51

The return of peace

Source 10.39
An officer tries on a civilian suit on being demobbed, 1944

The first months of peacetime seemed to Molly Weir to be very happy:

Source 10.40
No air raids. No blackout. No dangerous separation. The simplest pleasures were a matter of rejoicing, coming into the house and being able to switch on a light without having to think of enemy bombers. Street lamps, 2 eggs in one week. An extra half pint of milk. Enough coupons to buy a pair of summer shoes.

(Weir, *A Toe on the Ladder*)

To some the Attlee Government had the chance to carry out enormous changes because it inherited wartime powers. The journalist J. L. Hodson expressed this sort of feeling in his diary:

Source 10.41
We've given coal-miners a minimum of five pounds a week; we've opened up shipyards that had been derelict; we've made wasteland fruitful, and cultivated millions of acres that lay idle. Our evacuation exposed hideous sores in the form of children under-nourished and ill-brought up; I hope we shall be sensible enough to profit by the exposure. Our heavy taxation and our rationing of foods has, willy nilly, achieved some levelling up of the nation; fewer folk have gone hungry and fewer have gorged themselves; the poor have been a trifle better-off and the rich a little less rich.

(Addison, *The Road to 1945*)

In Glasgow Mary Liverani noticed how important the Labour victory seemed to her father. He listened to the election results on the radio:

Source 10.42
Every little while when the man on the radio said that Labour had got another seat, my father would thump his right fist into his left hand. 'C'mon Attlee' he was shouting, 'ye wee smasher, gie it tae the old swine.'
What he wanted from his political system was economic redress; 7 beds for 7 heads and he wanted the heads lying in a row, not alternating with feet. He wanted parklands for us to play in, instead of dark closes. The Labour Party was going to realise his pastoral dream. We would be turned out to graze on the new housing estates.

(M. R. Liverani, *The Winter Sparrows*, 1975)

But the winter of 1946 to 1947 was very severe. Shortages continued. Rationing remained – indeed it became more severe.

Source 10.43

Anthony Bailey was a schoolboy at this time. He recalled:

Source 10.44

Hugh Gaitskell, Minister of Fuel and Power, attempted to persuade us all to save fuel by not bathing often; he said, 'Personally, I have never had a great many baths' – a statement I found sympathetic. Meanwhile our food rations got smaller. There was less meat in 1945 than in 1944; powdered eggs disappeared for a time early in 1946 until shipments from North America arrived. The Ministry of Food advertised such recipes as sardine omelette, for which powdered eggs were suitable, if available. The Ministry suggested putting nasturtium leaves in salad. Bread rationing was finally introduced in July 1946 and lasted for two years; the weekly ration was two large loaves for adults, one for children under six years of age. The so-called white bread was light gray, roughly the colour of the paper in books then being published, on the reverse of whose title pages one read 'Produced to authorised wartime economy standards.'

(A. Bailey, *England First and Last*, 1985)

Source 10.45

Dundee women protest about the difficulty of daily life in the 1950s

" To make sure of your share "

BREAD RATIONING

On and after July 21st, 1946, bread, flour, cakes, buns and scones will be rationed in one scheme and measured in **BREAD UNITS (BU's)**. This will allow you as much freedom of choice as possible. **BU** values will be as follows:

BREAD: 1 small loaf (14 oz.) — 2 BU's
1 large loaf (1 lb. 12 oz.) — 4 BU's
FLOUR: 1 lb. — 3 BU's ; 3 lb. — 9 BU's
CAKES, BUNS, SCONES: ½ lb.—1 BU ; 1 lb. —2 BU's

You can spend your **Bread Units** *where* you choose, on *what* you choose of these flour foods, and *when* you choose within each 4-week period, but remember they have to last for the whole period.

HOUSEHOLD WEEKLY RATION

This table shows you which are your BU coupons and how many **BU's** your household can spend each week without borrowing from next week's allowance. BU's for any 4-week period can be spent only within that period.

	COUPON VALUES IN BU's							Total BU's per week
	Already in Ration Book ★					Extras obtained as below		
	L	M	F	J	G	BUX	BUY	
Child under 1	1	1						2
Child 1–5	1	2	1					4
Child 5–11	1	2		5				8
Adolescent 11–18	1	2		5		4		12
Normal Adult	1	2			6			9
Expectant Mother (including Green Book)	1 1	2 1			6			11
Manual Worker (Woman)	1	2			6		2	11
Manual Worker (Man)	1	2			6	4	2	15

★ L and M coupons are all in Ration Books—pages 19-23; G Coupons in General Book, J in Blue Book, F in Green Book—pages 39-40 in each case.

ADOLESCENTS (11 to 18.) Take or send the Blue Ration Book to the Food Office to get the extra coupons.

MANUAL WORKERS. Employers will obtain the extra coupons for those eligible. Self-employed manual workers should apply to the local office of the Ministry of Labour and National Service.

WORKERS 'ON THE JOB' Canteens will be given special allowances to provide adequate meals (including packed meals) for workers on heavy manual work. Such workers without canteen facilities who receive the special cheese ration will receive further sets of coupons BUX and BUY through their employers to provide packed meals from home.

For women it was a great struggle to be fashionable.

Source 10.47

After the War clothes were still on ration for a year or two. I used to swap and barter with my mother. She'd accumulate sweet coupons, so I'd barter with her with my clothes coupons for her sweets.

Clothes were usually made of cotton, wool or rayon, there were few man-made fabrics at that time. Silk stockings were a rare luxury. Some girls would paint their legs.

You couldn't really be fashion conscious because of the shortages which continued for about four or five years. For a long time there wasn't enough material to care about fashions. But in 1947 the 'New Look' came in, that was basically long clothes, skirts were only about 4 inches [10 cm] off the ground. I suppose that was a reaction against the enforced skimpiness of war clothes. It was after the War when the idea of mail order goods appeared. Great Universal Stores suddenly popped up, they had catalogues which people could run from the home.

(Ed. J. Hubbard, *We Thought it was Heaven Tomorrow*, 1985)

Between 1949 and 1950 conditions slowly improved. Clothes rationing ended in 1949. Imported foods gradually returned – sometimes to great excitement. In 1946 in Motherwell:

Source 10.48

. . . when it was announced that bananas would be on sale weeks were spent at Elder and Fyffe's depot preparing for the big day. This was going to be their first consignment since December, 1940. There were children who had never *seen* a banana. The citizens were kept well-informed of the progress of the bananas towards Motherwell. The possibility of the cargo ship being diverted to Liverpool because of a tugboat strike, struck fear into the hearts of the townsfolk. The ripe bananas, 4 for $\frac{1}{2}$d [0.2p approximately], found their way finally to the shops, where the queues were so lengthy that the police were called upon to control them. It was reported that a youngster, determined to preserve a golden memory of the fruit, broke into another store in Park Street and ate 13 bananas!

(Stirling, *Motherwell Post War*)

Housing

The War totally wrecked 7000 Scottish houses, damaged many more and left great numbers in a poor state of repair for lack of skilled workers and materials. By 1945 there was a desperate housing shortage, indeed around 6800 people in Scotland found temporary shelter in churches, halls and former army camps. The shortage led to events like this (reported in the *Daily Telegraph*, 2 September 1946):

Source 10.49

Squatters poured into the ATS camp at Craigentinny, Edinburgh, over the weekend. The camp was commandeered in an 'after darkness' raid last Thursday. About sixty families, comprising nearly 300 people, including children, are now living there.

The Secretary of State for Scotland supervised the housing situation. A short-term answer was to provide 'prefabs'. These were factory-built units assembled on site. 30 000 of them were put up in Scotland. Their life-span was meant to be ten years; a number were lived in for 30 years.

Source 10.50

The government reckoned Scotland needed at least 469 000 new homes.

1945–51 Numbers of houses built in Scotland

Local authority	New Town	Scottish Special Housing Association	Private
1945	1 351		77	141
1946	3 321		490	499
1947	8 919		1854	1354
1948	16 615		2932	1541
1949	20 004	60	4116	1102
1950	20 989	158	3167	782
1951	17 971	120	2906	1145

The government also planned to create at least six new towns in Central Scotland. Planning on East Kilbride started in 1947 and on Glenrothes in 1948. Local authorities began to be influenced by housing styles developed elsewhere, especially in France. The result was the appearance, by the 1950s, of houses like these in Edinburgh:

Source 10.52

Tenants for the first completed section of Edinburgh Corporation's 8-storeyed block of labour-saving sun-trap flats at Westfield will be moving into their new homes within the next few weeks. All the houses are being equipped with panelled radiators. A small electric elevator is provided in each unit. The sun balconies for each apartment overlook a bowling green.

(*Edinburgh Evening News*, 14 May 1951)

Social reforms

Despite the economic troubles of the time, Labour pushed ahead with its promised programme of reforms. James Griffiths piloted through Parliament the 1946 Insurance Act that carried out the main points of the Beveridge Report.

Source 10.53

Insurance Reform

1946 26 shillings (£1.30) a week for a single person, 42 shillings (£2.10) for a married man at times of old age, unemployment (up to 180 days) and illness.

1946 Compensation for people injured at work – 45 shillings (£2.25) a week, a further 16 shillings (80p) if married. Maternity grants and allowances. Death grant £20. Payments to Widows. No means test. Standard weekly contribution for those in work.

1948 National Assistance Board to help those for whom insurance did not do enough [e.g. pensioners whose pensions did not keep up with the rise in the cost of living]. Old age pensions were paid to men over 65 and women over 60. The government found this expense was soon eating up two-thirds of all insurance spending.

Beveridge had also suggested a National Health Service. Aneurin Bevan had the task of bringing it about. Hospital doctors were not difficult to win over; their hospitals so clearly needed re-organising and developing. Once Bevan had promised that they could continue to treat private patients, they did not resist the state takeover. Family doctors were less easily persuaded.

Source 10.54

Dr Charles Hill, secretary of the British Medical Association, opposed the setting up of the NHS. Popular opinion did not agree with the BMA

The pressure of public opinion, and Bevan's readiness to alter the way doctors were paid and treated (so that they did not simply feel like employees to be ordered around as the government saw fit) eventually succeeded. The NHS came into operation in July 1948.

The service was enormously popular. Alice Law remembered how, immediately the NHS had been created, her mother:

Source 10.55

. . . went to the optician's, obviously she'd got the prescription from the doctor, she went and she got tested for new glasses, then she went further down the road . . . for the chiropodist, she had her feet done, then she went back to the doctor's because she'd been having trouble

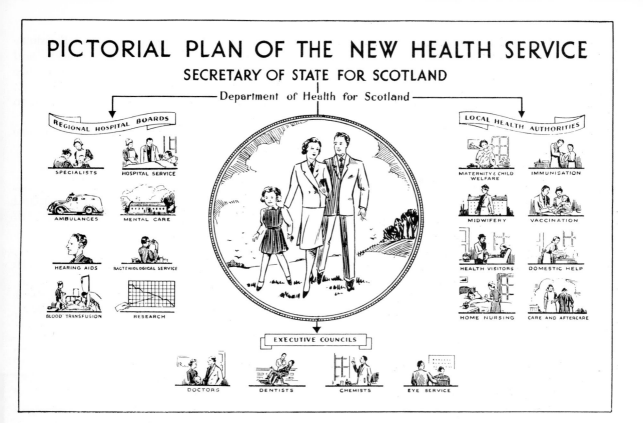

PICTORIAL PLAN OF THE NEW HEALTH SERVICE
SECRETARY OF STATE FOR SCOTLAND
Department of Health for Scotland

REGIONAL HOSPITAL BOARDS

SPECIALISTS · HOSPITAL SERVICE · AMBULANCES · MENTAL CARE · HEARING AIDS · BACTERIOLOGICAL SERVICE · BLOOD TRANSFUSION · RESEARCH

LOCAL HEALTH AUTHORITIES

MATERNITY & CHILD WELFARE · IMMUNISATION · MIDWIFERY · VACCINATION · HEALTH VISITORS · DOMESTIC HELP · HOME NURSING · CARE AND AFTERCARE

EXECUTIVE COUNCILS

DOCTORS · DENTISTS · CHEMISTS · EYE SERVICE

Source 10.56

with her ears and the doctor said . . . he would fix her up with a hearing aid, and I remember, me mother was a very funny woman, I remember her saying to the doctor on the way out, 'Well the undertaker's is on the way home, everything's going on, I might as well call in there on the way home!'

(Addison, *Now the War is Over*)

British dentists had expected 4 million patients a year. Twice that number turned up for treatment. Within three months the amount of prescriptions virtually doubled. The NHS proved increasingly expensive. In 1951 the Labour Government, faced with costly defence policies, too, started to charge patients for prescriptions that had at first been free. Bevan resigned.

Source 10.57
Clues to improving health in Glasgow
1910–14, 9% of Glasgow school children had rickets, 1950–54 – 0.3%
1924 – 87% of Glasgow children were reported as having unsound teeth.

1944 – 51% reported, 1954 – 33%
In 1950 average heights of 13 year old Glasgow girls were four inches (10 cm) more than in 1910; average weight was over a stone (6 kg) more.

Source 10.58
David Kirkwood, MP for Dumbarton, visiting a day nursery in 1951 where children received welfare food

1 Do any words in source 10.52 suggest the author was in favour of flats? Give a reason for your answer. (E.1)

2 What do you think is the point of view of the artist of source 10.54? Did he favour the NHS? (E.1)

3 Use source 10.56 to explain what Local Authorities provided as health care. (K.U)

4 The authors of sources 10.41 and 10.42 expected a great deal of reform. Do you think they were right to do so? (E.2)

5 a) Use source 10.51 to explain the sort of housing the Attlee Government made its priority. (K.U)

   b) How might this have helped the Conservatives win the election in 1951? What sort of change might Conservatives have promised? (E.2)

More Recent Times – since 1951

A more comfortable life

The governments of the fifties and sixties supported the NHS and the new insurance schemes. The whole system of rationing had gone by 1954. World trade expanded. The result was a period sometimes called 'the age of affluence'.

Source 10.59
Clues to greater wealth in Britain

1951–8	– Average wages rose 20% in real value
1950	– 2 307 000 cars and vans: 1960 – 5 650 000
1959	– first stretch of motorway – M1 – opened
1956	– 8% of households had refrigerators: 1962 – 33%

By 1961 – 75% of families owned a television. Spending on furniture, electrical goods and durables: in 1951 £526 million: in 1959 £888 million
Spending on alcohol: in 1951 £843 million, in 1959 £1195 million.

(Marwick, *British Society since 1945*)

Ian Jack recalled:

Source 10.60
I was born in 1945 and grew up in the Scotland of the 50s. Average Britons became better fed, better housed, better paid. Mothers buy washing machines.

(Jack, *Before the Oil Ran Out*)

The fifties saw a shopping revolution beginning – the coming of self-service. One Tesco shop assistant remembered:

Source 10.61
The customers hated it. They wouldn't pick up a basket. They were very suspicious. They didn't want to buy very much, and they felt belittled, I think, at having a basket with perhaps two Oxos in, and a small bread loaf. And people hated the way there was nobody to talk to them. People didn't feel they'd done a proper morning's shopping, if they hadn't had all these conversations which took up the assistant's time. And so the boss tried it for about a year and then it had to be closed and he reopened it later on.

(Overy & Pamagenta, *All Our Working Lives*)

Source 10.62
The changing face of postwar shopping

However, supermarkets soon succeeded. It was the small local shops that suffered. They could not match the low prices in supermarkets. More shopping began to take place at big centres, often not in the middle of towns.

An elderly inhabitant of Kelso looked back at another of the changes of Scottish life in these years. He said:

Source 10.64 ———————————
Life in the town has changed a lot. People are better off, much better off even though there's so much unemployment. For example everybody now has a washing machine in their house – I should know, I used to mend them. So Kelso's 'Steam' or public wash-house probably won't ever come back into use. Inside the Steam were wooden stalls each containing two wash-tubs. You could pay extra and have your clothes spun in a centrifuge and dried in a press on hot rails. Then they were aired on a private drying green before we carried them home in a big basket. Across the road there was Lizzie Tillcock's laundry where you could get your clothes ironed. And there were other women in the town who took in washing just to make ends meet.

(A. Moffat, *Kelsae*, 1985)

Source 10.63 ——
In the late 50s and early 60s most of the old steamies vanished to be replaced by laundrettes

In Aberdeen Bert Murray noticed yet another sign of the increasing wealth of ordinary people:

Source 10.65 ━━━━━━━━━━━━━━━━━━━━
Styles of dress and footwear have changed dramatically from the early days, when you carefully preserved your only suit and only pair of boots or shoes, your best shirt, and 'Darned' your socks, jersey or pullover.

'Darning' made me realise that very few people carry out these repairs nowadays. In fact I find that many young people don't know what the word means. Probably we have reached the age when so many things are disposable, 'the throw away age'.

We still have a small stock of darning wool and needles kept over the years, and old habits die hard, I still darn my socks . . .

Modern housing, labour saving devices, fridge, freezers, radio, television, video, calculators, computers, cars, air travel, hover craft and so on. The patchwork quilt is now Scandinavian, or electric blanket, carpets replacing linoleum in most cases, settees, armchairs, taking the place of the old wooden ones. Gas and electric cookers, plus so many other things, long may progress continue.

(Murray, *3 Score Years and 10*)

An expert who studied the lives of men working in factories, between 1958 and 1959, reported that a typical factory worker of this period was very different from one of 30 years earlier:

Source 10.67 ━━━━━━━━━━━━━━━━━━━━
He wants his own car, more gadgets. There is no more of 'What was good for my father is good for me'. He seeks his pleasures at home more than ever. His main hobby is decorating his home.

(Breach and Hartwell, *British Economy and Society*)

For people able to remain in work, life became increasingly prosperous after the sixties. The kinds of things people now buy for their homes provide some evidence of greater wealth.

The Conservative Government elected after 1979 felt that to help those who were not prospering, it had to consider changing its policies. Those who could afford it were encouraged to make more effort to save for their own old age or time of illness. Charges for some aspects of health care (like spectacles, dental treatment and prescriptions) increased.

Source 10.66 ━━━
Percentage of households with central heating, telephones and certain household appliances

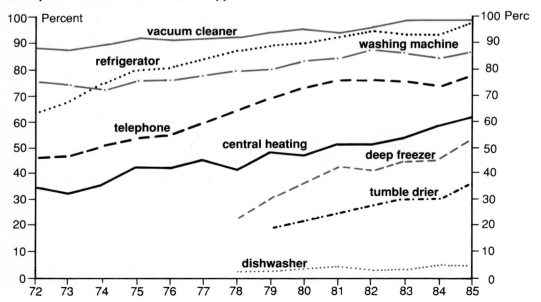

Percentage of private households with central heating, a telephone and certain household appliances

Source 10.68

Old age pensioners receive a free butter allocation from the EEC

In 1984 Ian Jack came away from a visit to Glasgow wondering if its people wouldn't, increasingly, fall into two groups. One group would have well-paid jobs; the other would be without work. He contrasted their lives:

Source 10.69

In future the Glaswegian will come in two types. Here is a day's timetable for each.

The Aspirer:

7.30 Rise: muesli and orange juice
8.00 Jog
9.30 Office: work on new software deal
13.00 Meet Roddy, Fergus and Diarmid in Gertrude's wine bar. Discuss scheme to open print shop in disused railway signal cabin.
15.00 More work on software deal
17.00 Shopping. Shiver while eating hot croissant and watching immitation of Marcel Marceau
19.30 To see Scottish Opera's new production of *Rigoletto* updated to the Gorbals of 1935
22.30 Supper with lawyer friends at Cafe de Paris
23.50 Home; remember to adjust burglar alarm

The Non-aspirer:

11.00 Rise: Wonderloaf and PG Tips
12.00 Dress
13.00 Watch TV
15.00 Watch 'Willy Wonka and the Chocolate Factory' for the 4th time
18.00 Meet pusher, buy £5 bag
22.00 Wonder what happened during the past 3 hours
24.00 Steal car for burglary to finance more £5 bags.

The division exaggerates, but the evidence tends in that direction.

(Jack, *Before the Oil Ran Out*)

QUESTIONS

1 Look at sources 10.62 and 10.63
   a) What main changes do the sources show? (K.U)
   b) Can anything be said in favour of the way of life shown in the older pictures? Explain your answer. (E.2)

2 Find and list any other pieces of evidence you can find that show people became better off in the years after 1950. (K.U)

3 Look at source 10.68. Consider these two statements
   a) 'This picture shows the elderly are much better clothed, fed and looked after than they used to be.'
   b) 'This shows how poor the elderly are for they need to be given free EEC butter.'
   What do you think? (E.1)

4 What do you think the author of source 10.69 thinks about the situation he is imagining? Do you think he approves of it? Give reasons for your answer. (E.1)

Housing

In 1951 there was still a great shortage of housing. Many people still lived in slums.

More new towns were developed at Cumbernauld (1956), Livingston (1962), and Irvine (1966).

QUESTIONS

How was the housing problem tackled? How successful were the authorities in providing satisfactory homes for all? Look through the following sources in order to write a report 'Housing since 1951' that answers the above questions. Make notes on all the useful information you can find before writing your answer.   (E.2)

Source 10.71
Cumbernauld New Town

Source 10.70

	Local authority	New Town	SSHA	Private
1957	24 239	951	3136	3 513
1962	16 245	1576	967	7 784
1967	27 092	3941	2189	7 498
1972	16 335	1519	1739	11 835
1977	9 335	3167	2042	12 132
1982	2 342	729	645	11 530
1985	1 983	201	622	13 869

(T. Begg, *50 Special Years*, 1987)

Source 10.72
Outline plan of Cumbernauld New Town.

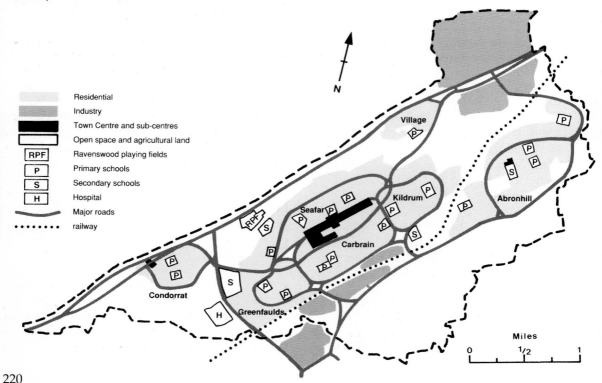

Source 10.73 _____

Cumbernauld was designated in 1956 and by 1978 it had [a] population of 50 000. A garage or parking space is provided for a large proportion of the houses. The pedestrian is equally well served with a network of footpaths which cross all motorways and roads by bridge or underpass. The town centre contains shopping and public services. Entertainment is well catered for in a cinema and bingo hall. Adjacent to the centre the Sports Centre offers modern sports facilities. Uniform housing schemes are a blot on the landscape. In Cumbernauld there is a rich variety of design.

(*Official Guide to Cumbernauld*, 1978)

As well as new towns, the cities developed programmes of clearing older housing and moving people to huge new estates on their outskirts. The *Glasgow Herald* reported on 14 February, 1952:

Source 10.74 _____

Glasgow is to have at Drumchapel a self-contained township of 30 000 persons. It will have its own town centre, a central shopping area and communal services. The houses will consist of flats of 2, 3 and 4 storeys.

Source 10.75 _____

Postwar high-rise housing

All the cities began to build blocks of flats. Glasgow, especially, developed this form of housing, indeed it pursued this policy more vigorously than any other European city. By the late 1970s 65 000 Glaswegians lived in high-rise blocks. A 1968 survey of the views of people who moved into Glasgow flats reported:

Source 10.76 _____

Many families were almost awed with their high flat when they first saw it and they continued to point out its attractions even when they had been there for some years. Its brightness, airiness and modernity were a fantastic contrast to the gloomy places so many had lived in previously. To have a bathroom outweighed even the dream kitchen or the under-floor heating. A mother pointed to her 3-year-old who, accustomed to being washed in the sink, would splash about for ever in this lovely shiny bath. They showed the snow-white toilet next to the bath and some recalled the horrors they had known, maybe a murky, unlighted den off a stone passage outside the house. The snugness of one's home matters a lot in a Northern climate, and comfort was a word constantly in use by people of all ages.

(P. Jephcott, *Homes in High Flats*, 1971)

Jimmy MacGregor, who had been brought up in a Glasgow tenement, commented:

Source 10.77 _____

The life of the tenements ended quite suddenly. In the 1950s, an idealistic and over-enthusiastic town council embarked on a scheme of slum clearance, as it was called. Great areas of old buildings were razed, and the people decanted into the high-rise estates which have been such a social disaster. The whole project was well intentioned but based on modernist architectural theories developed on the Continent incompletely applied and inadequately adapted to Glasgow, with its cold and wet climatic conditions, summer or winter.

The whole process of change took place in a startlingly short space of time, and when the old tenement environment disappeared, it took with it communities that never had the chance to regroup. The tenement single ends, the wee corner shops, the coal-fired black grates are now in museums visited by people who are still young enough to have lived with and used all these things. The surviving tenement buildings have been sandblasted to rich russet, yellow, cream, and honey colours. They're refurbished, much cosseted, and occupied by a quite different kind of person.

('Story of Scotland', *Sunday Mail*)

Source 10.78

. . . Glasgow has built the tallest residential flats, a soaring 31-storey block 300 feet [91. m] high at Balornock's Red Road site. At a cost of £6¼ m the Corporation have built 1350 houses, 73 lock-ups and 252 car spaces – 'birdcage room' for 4500 people. These towering blocks, like many others in the city, would almost seem designed to be the monumental slums of the twenty-first century. Glasgow's skyscrapers are littered with notices banning children from playing; the lifts small, inadequate, and often do not work . . . Loneliness is intensified by the fact that mothers dare not let their three- or four-year-olds downstairs unaccompanied. Children, when they first go to school, are sometimes withdrawn. They do not fit in; the seeds of isolation and mental trouble have already been sown.

(Arthur Foster, *Illustrated London News*, 9 December 1967)

Jimmy Reid was also brought up in a tenement. He wrote:

Source 10.79

In the post-war years the politicians and planners committed a further crime when they demolished some of the slums. For they moved the people to huge dormitory housing schemes, with no attempt to preserve the community, or give it the facilities from which a new community could flourish. Billy Connolly aptly describes them as 'deserts wi' windaes'.

In those days, Govan life was rough and tough but there was that all-important community. In the tenements where I was raised, it would just not be possible for an old pensioner to die and lie unnoticed for weeks.

(J. Reid, *Reflections of a Clyde-built Man*, 1976)

Glasgow's housing convener admitted in 1975:

Source 10.80

Too often we have failed to create communities. Many developments have been rightly described as bleak and windswept. Probably too many tower blocks have been built without adequate supporting services. Housing designs have lacked variety.

(*Farewell to the Single End*, 1975)

The following verses were written to try and show children's feelings about tower blocks.

Source 10.81

I'm a skyscraper wean, I live on the
    nineteenth flair
An I'm no' gaun oot tae play ony mair
For since we moved tae oor new hoose I'm
    wastin' away
'Cos I'm gettin wan less meal ev'ry day
Oh ye canna fling a piece frae a 20 storey flat
700 weans'll testify tae that
If it's butter cheese or jelly, if the breid be
    plain or pan
The odds against it reaching us are 99 tae
    wan'.
We've wrote away tae Oxfam tae try and get
    some aid.
We've a' joined together an' formed a 'piece'
    brigade
We're gonny march tae London tae demand
    our Civil Rights
Like 'Nae mair hooses ower piece flingin'
    height'.

(A. McNaughton, *The Jeely Piece Song*, Scotia Kinnaird)

A journalist reported on the Easterhouse estate in Glasgow:

Source 10.82

The people who went there were often those in the most urgent need of re-housing – such as large families and the unemployed. So by the 1970s the estates had already become recognized as poor and overcrowded. Often half the population were under 15. For years there were few shops, pubs or services. They are solidly working class. There are often vast and green open spaces which are put to little use. Neighbours can hear each other through the walls.

(A. Broadbent, *New Society* 14 June 1985)

Another journalist reported on the work of the government-funded Scottish Special Housing Association. It studied some of the blocks of flats and:

Source 10.83

undertook improvements which included the installation of a warden call system, a new entry phone system. The Association believes tower blocks can be satisfactory homes for elderly people, childless couples and single people. A detailed survey [had] found widespread dissatisfaction and a high level of vandalism. With SSHA [help] each block formed a tenants' committee. It was agreed that a community hall be built and a seven days a week caretaker system be introduced. Almost everyone now agrees that the tower block building boom was a social economic and architectural mistake. Tower block flats were more expensive than houses and their running costs have proved higher.

(Guardian, 2 March 1988)

New housing was provided in smaller places, too. An inhabitant of Alloa noted:

Source 10.84

If we turn our attention now to more everyday dwellings, we will see some quite extraordinary improvements in the quality of housing. All the old slum dwellings have been cleared from the centre of the town, and the population has been moved to the brighter council estates on the outskirts of the town. All of these changes led to a far greater quality of housing in the town, and subsequently, they must have meant a far greater quality of life.

(J. Scott, Alloa in the 1920s, 1987)

The Conservative Government after 1979 brought in laws allowing council tenants to buy their homes. In 1973 32% of Scottish houses were owner-occupied; by 1987 42.3% were owner occupied. By 1988 the government was allowing private landlords to take over whole areas of council property – after a vote on the issue by tenants.

Health

Changes in living and working conditions played their part in affecting people's health. So too did changes in health care and the development of new forms of treatment, such as antibiotics and replacement surgery. A vigorous campaign was waged against tuberculosis in particular. Glasgow's records for this disease show that its people were the greatest sufferers from it in Britain. In the later 1950s, throughout Scotland, letters were sent out to encourage people to come for examination.

Source 10.85
A healthy diet?

However, Scots continued to suffer illnesses where diet played a part. By the 1980s the emphasis was as much on diet and exercise to prevent disease as on diseases themselves. It was also becoming clear that man's own activities caused health problems. Vehicle exhaust fumes, for example, led to a campaign to use lead-free petrol.

Source 10.86
Clues to health in Scotland in recent times

Expectation of life in 1950–52
   64.4 years for men
   68.7 years for women
Expectation of life in 1984–86
   70 years for men
   76 years for women.

The death rate of infants (up to 1-year old).
1940 – 78.3 per 1000 live births
1950 – 38.6 per 1000 live births
1960 – 26.4 per 1000 live births
1969 – 21.1 per 1000 live births
1980 – 12.1 per 1000 live births
1986 – 8.8 per 1000 live births

Numbers suffering from certain selected diseases

	1961	1965	1970	1975	1980	1985
Tuberculosis	8 653	2033	1 602	1270	943	560
Scarlet fever	1 613	1438	793	430	1343	649
Measles	16 040	6263	25 988	5619	6644	4595
Dysentery	5 310	7083	3 032	1206	854	512

The cost of the Scottish health service

1948–9	£ 28 508 000
1960–61	£ 97 962 000
1970–71	£ 226 781 000 (13.1% of public spending)
1986–87	£2 081 844 000 (16.1% of public spending)

Selected causes of death – numbers of cases

	1961	1969	1986
Heart disease	21 373	21 558	22 021
Cancer	11 033	12 446	14 455
Pneumonia and bronchitis	4 312	5 494	4 056
Cerebrovascular diseases (i.e. strokes)	10 657	10 939	8 505

(*Scottish Health Statistics*, 1969, 1985, 1988)

Equality?

Source 10.87

In 1958 the economist, Professor Titmuss, wrote:

Source 10.88
The typical working-class mother of the 1890s, married in her teens or early twenties and experiencing ten pregnancies, spent about fifteen years in a state of pregnancy and in nursing a child for the first year of its life. Today, for the typical mother, the time so spent would be about four years. [This is] a revolutionary enlargement of freedom for women brought about by the power to control their own fertility. At the beginning of this century, the expectation of life of a woman aged twenty was forty-six years. Approximately one-third of this life expectancy was to be devoted to childbearing and maternal care in infancy. Today, the expectation of life of a woman aged 20 is fifty-five years. Of this longer expectation only about 7 per cent of the years to be lived will be concerned with childbearing and maternal care in infancy.

(Breach and Hartwell, *British Economy and Society*)

The large number of household gadgets that became commonly available from the 1950s greatly eased the burden of housework. Men played an increasing part in household tasks.

Moreover, the decline of the old heavy industries and the growth of services and new light industries provided jobs for women especially. Part-time work was increasingly available. By 1981 48.5% of married women under 60 years old in Scotland had jobs.

Source 10.89 ———————————————

Changes in the status of women

1942 The TUC supported equal pay for equal work.

1955 Equal pay was agreed for teachers, civil servants and local government officials.

1958 Women could enter the House of Lords – as life peeresses.

1964 The Succession (Scotland) Act. Upon divorce, the money and goods to be allowed each of the former partners would be decided by the Law courts.

1967 Abortion Act. Abortion was made much easier to obtain.

1970 Equal Pay Act. Equal pay for equal work was brought in for all sorts of employment.

1975 Sex Discrimination Act. All employment and education must be equally open to men and women. An Equal Opportunities Commission enforced the law.

1975 Employment Protection Act. Women could not be dismissed for becoming pregnant but had to be allowed maternity leave.

1976 Divorce Reform Act. Divorce was decided simply on the grounds that the marriage had totally failed – for whatever cause.

1979 Britain's first woman Prime Minister – Margaret Thatcher.

1984 Equal pay was required for work of equal value i.e. comparisons could be made with other sorts of jobs to establish a fair rate of pay for work that was exclusively done by one sex.

QUESTIONS

1 Look at source 10.86. Suggest reasons why most people's life expectancy increased and why infant mortality fell. (E.2)

2 How successful was the campaign to cure TB? (See source 10.86.) (K.U)

3 a) What illnesses became more common 1960–88? (K.U)
   b) Why do you think this has happened? (E.2)

4 Why was it easier for women to go out to work in the post-war years? Use source 10.88 and your own ideas. (K.U)

11 Political Change

The sources in this chapter deal with the political changes that have affected Scottish affairs since 1939. During this period there were further alterations in who had the right to vote.

Source 11.1
Changes in who had the right to vote

1948 Representation of the People Act

This act abolished plural voting i.e. the use of two votes by certain people – one in their place of residence, the other in their place of business or at the university where they were educated.

1969 Representation of the People Act

The minimum age for voting was reduced from 21 to 18 years of age.

Women had voted on the same terms as men since 1928. This did not, however, lead to there being as many women as men in Parliament.

Source 11.2
Numbers of female candidates and MPs in general elections

	Cands	M.P.'s		Cands	M.P.'s		Cands	M.P.'s
1935	67	9	1959	81	25	1974 (Oct)	161	27
1945	87	24	1964	90	29	1979	206	19
1950	126	21	1966	81	26			
1951	77	17	1970	99	26			
1955	92	24	1974 (Feb)	143	23			

A student of this topic concluded that for many women MPs:

Source 11.3
. . . even before they go to work they may have to arrange breakfast, do household chores, get children ready and off to school and a husband out to work. Before she starts on a job outside, a woman has generally done a job inside the house. And after work, or in the lunch hour, she is shopping and planning meals ready for the evening. More than any single factor – like child care itself, or house-work – it is the general organisation of the life of a family that takes up a major part of most women's energy . . . It is clearly necessary for an MP to be able to give his or her whole-hearted attention to the job. It was in this context that one of the early women MPs remarked that a wife is the most valuable asset in politics. And a wife is just what a woman doesn't have.

(Elisabeth Vallance, *Women in the House; A Study of Women Members of Parliament*, 1979)

During these years both Conservative and Labour Parties enjoyed periods in power.

Source 11.4

British Governments since 1939

To May 1940 National Government
Prime Minister Neville Chamberlain. This Ministry was dominated by Conservatives and did not include the Labour Party or the Independent Liberal Party.

May 1940–July 1945. Wartime Coalition Government
Prime Minister Winston Churchill.
The Labour Party joined this government and occupied several senior posts, especially in home affairs.

July 1945–October 1951. Labour Governments
Prime Minister Clement Attlee.
This was the first Labour Ministry to have a clear overall majority. The 1945 election gave Labour a majority of 142 over all other parties. The 1950 election cut this majority to 5.

October 1951–May 1955. Conservative
Prime Minister Winston Churchill.
The election of 1951 gave the Conservatives an overall lead of 17 – though more people (230 000 more) voted Labour than Conservatives. By this time the tiny Liberal Party had shrunk to a mere six MPs.

May 1955–October 1959. Conservative
Prime Minister Anthony Eden, 1955–7 (January), Harold Macmillan, 1957–9. Churchill retired. The Conservatives increased their lead over other parties in the election. Ill health, made worse by difficult and unsuccessful foreign policies in the Middle East, led Eden to resign.

October 1959 – October 1964. Conservative
Prime Minister Harold Macmillan, 1959–October 1963. Alex Douglas Home 1963–4. The Conservatives increased their lead in the 1959 election from an overall majority of 59 to one of 100. Macmillan had to retire because of illness. His successor lost the 1964 election to Labour.

1964–74. Labour
Harold Wilson led the Labour Party to victory. He won a further election in 1966, increasing his Party's hitherto narrow majority.

1970–4. (February). Conservative
Edward Heath was the new Prime Minister. A clash with the miners, leading to big power cuts, led Heath to call an election to secure fresh support.

1974–9. Labour
The Labour Party had four more MPs than the Conservatives, but no overall majority. In October 1974 a new election increased Labour's lead over the Conservatives to 42, but still left it without a really safe overall majority. In 1976 James Callaghan replaced Wilson.

1979–? Conservative
Margaret Thatcher led the Conservatives to victory and went on to win further elections in 1983 and 1987.

The Labour Party's Rise to Power 1945

Labour had briefly held power twice during the inter-war years but it never had an overall majority. In 1945 it finally won a clear majority in the House of Commons.

QUESTIONS

Why did Labour win the 1945 election?

a) Look through the following sources and note down all the reasons you can find. (K.U)

b) Think back over the work you have done in earlier chapters. Are there any more reasons you can add? (K.U)

c) Use these notes to write an answer to the question, adding any further ideas of your own. (E.2)

d) Notice the authorship of each source. Which do you think is the most helpful to you? (E.1)

Source 11.5
Clement Attlee campaigning in the 1945 election which brought Labour to power

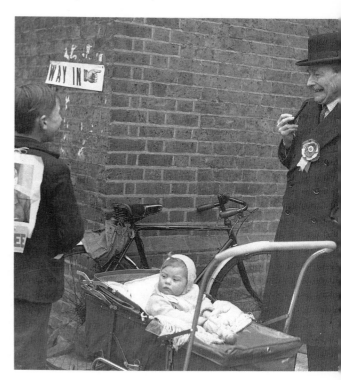

The next source was written by a Conservative MP.

Source 11.6 ――――――――――――
There was unquestionably a profound and burning determination in the electorate never to go back to 1939. The Labour Party's re-actions to the Beveridge Report, which had aroused unparalleled public interest and excite-ment, was undoubtedly more positive and immediate than those of our leaders, and this gave the impression that the Tory Party was not equally interested in wide measures of social reform. I am convinced that the great majority of Labour voters elected the Govern-ment to 'get things done', to build schools, houses, hospitals, and factories, and to provide full employment. No doubt they expected too much to happen too quickly, but in this they were encouraged by Labour propaganda.

(Sir David Maxwell Fyfe in Beattie, *English Party Politics*)

The following source comes from an interview with an ordinary voter.

Source 11.7 ――――――――――――
One thing the nineteen thirties hadn't been was a land fit for heroes. As the War progressed we knew that once it was over there would have to be changes.

It was in the election campaign that Churchill really slipped up. He made a speech, and he said that if the people voted Labour, they'd be voting for the Gestapo. He must have lost a lot of his own supporters with that, they knew that Labour people had fought as hard as anybody, as politicians in the coalition, and as soldiers and workers. But it wasn't Churchill that put Labour in with a landslide, it was the times. The fact was that only a Labour Government could start to put the country on its feet again. People don't realise, but in many ways the coalition had acted on some principles of socialism. You had to have planning, you had to have negotiations, you had to have a people that co-operated and worked together, all pulling together to beat a common enemy. At some level I think that everybody knew that the country couldn't stand a free-for-all after the War.

(Hubbard, *We Thought it was Heaven Tomorrow*)

Part of a speech by Churchill in 1945:

Source 11.8 ――――――――――――
A socialist policy is abhorrent to British ideas of freedom. No socialist government conducting the entire life and industry of the country could afford to allow free, sharp, or violently worded expressions of discontent . . . they would have to fall back on some form of Gestapo.

(In A. Sked and C. Cook, *Post War Britain*, 1979)

Source 11.9 ――――――――――――
Leading Conservatives worry that Churchill is going to use the old scare tactics in an election.

This next source comes from the work of an historian:

Source 11.10 ――――――――――――
When asked [in opinion polls] what they thought would be the question most discussed in the election campaign, most people named housing as the biggest issue, with jobs, social security and nationalisation following. The priorities listed by Churchill in his broadcasts were markedly different . . . he spoke of the completion of the War against Japan, de-mobilisation, the re-starting of industry, the re-building of exports and the four-year plan of 'food, work and homes'. Meanwhile Labour made much of the housing issue . . . Labour put the material needs of the average family above all else in its campaign.

(Addison, *The Road to 1945*)

Party Fortunes after 1950

In 1950 Labour's huge majority was cut down to a mere handful by an election. One of the ministers, George Strauss thought:

Source 11.11 _____

The parliamentary party had exhausted itself. It had introduced an immense programme of reform – the National Health Service was only one – including the nationalisation of a large number of industries. A tremendous programme. They had exhausted themselves, physically and mentally. The ministers had nothing new to offer. They devised various strange schemes – nationalising insurance, and sugar, and so on – without really very much thought; just trying to think up something attractive.

(Thompson, *The Day Before Yesterday*)

The Conservatives were able to attack Labour for keeping controls and much of the rationing system. A Labour voter believed that the government:

Source 11.12 _____

Got bashed a lot for inefficiency. But remember the press is predominantly Tory and so all the big newspapers like the *Express* built up this image of a colossal incompetent and inefficient government. And occasionally Labour played into their hands – you got weird things like the Groundnut scheme in the headlines for months in 1947.

(Hubbard, *We thought it was Heaven Tomorrow*)

But before finally losing office, the Attlee Government organised a celebration to relieve the post-war gloom. This 'Festival of Britain' came 100 years after the Great Exhibition of Victorian Times. It took places on a site in London.

For 13 years (1951–64) Conservative governments ruled Britain. The Labour politician Anthony Crosland explained the Conservative success as follows:

Source 11.13 _____

I think Labour lost the '59 election for one basic reason. That from 1951 to 1959, when the Conservatives were in, there was something like a 20 percent increase in real living standards, as compared with a zero increase from '45 to '51 for post-war reasons. Before that you had war; there was virtually no increase. And of course the inter-war period showed only the slowest possible increase. I think it's that one, simple, basic fact.

(Thompson, *The Day Before Yesterday*)

The Conservatives kept the popular social reforms of 1945 to 1948. As a contemporary writer noted:

Source 11.14 _____

Under a Conservative Government there has been no mass unemployment. There has been no depression. There has been no increase in human misery. The pot-bellied cartoon capitalist has ground very few faces. Indeed he has provided a few million television screens to which working-class faces have been glued.

(Beattie, *English Party Politics*)

The Conservatives' grip on power eventually weakened as signs of economic difficulties began to appear in the early 1960s. An attempt to join the EEC failed. Security scandals shook the government. Meanwhile, Harold Wilson united the Labour Party which had been suffering from divisions over what sort of defence and economic policies to follow. For eight years from 1964 Labour was once more in power. However, economic troubles did not disappear.

Source 11.15 _____

Shipyard workers discuss strike action in Dundee

The Wilson Ministry tried to tackle what it saw as one of the main reasons for these troubles. Its proposals for better relations between employers and workers, to try and reduce strikes and improve productivity, included the following complaints about the existing system:

Source 11.16

. . . our organised system of collective bargaining has not got to grips with a number of economic and social problems . . . it has often failed to provide for effective and acceptable collective bargaining. Too often employees have felt that major decisions directly concerning them were being taken at such a high level that the decision makers were out of reach and unable to understand the consequences of their actions. Decisions have been taken to close down plants without consultation. Outdated social distinctions between hourly-paid employees and those on staff conditions have perpetuated. Some employees have opposed the spread of collective bargaining to new sections of the work force. Unions too have often failed to involve their members closely enough in their work. Many employers' relations with unions have been greatly complicated by the large number of unions that may have members in a single factory.

The combined effect of such defects is to increase the feeling of many employees that they have no real stake in the enterprise for which they work.

(In *Place of Strife*)

But union opposition prevented any reform from taking place. In 1970 the Conservatives returned to power. Their leader, Edward Heath, successfully led Britain into the EEC. But the government's efforts to control the economy and the unions led to a huge struggle with the miners. When Heath called an election to seek new support for his policies, he failed to win enough seats. Labour returned to office, with a very inadequate majority. In 1979, under the leadership (since 1975) of Margaret Thatcher, the Conservatives swept back to power. They promised to attack the power of trade unions and run the economy in new ways, including selling off several nationalised industries and cutting income tax.

Source 11.17

Margaret Thatcher, leader of the Conservatives since 1975

Political Fortunes in Scotland

The post-war elections in Scotland produced results shown in source 11.2. The period saw the emergence of the Scottish National Party to a level when it began to win seats in Parliament.

The SNP was the result of a 1934 merger between the National Party of Scotland (1928) and the Scottish Party (1930). The party did poorly in elections until the War. Then its vote in by-elections began to grow. Tom Johnston, commented the head of the BBC,

Source 11.18

. . . is very bothered by English ministers who do things affecting Scotland without consulting him. He thinks there is a great danger of Scottish nationalism coming up.

(In C. Harvie, *No Gods and Precious Few Heroes*, 1981)

Johnston used the evidence of a growing Scottish desire for greater control of Scottish affairs. He won more power for the Scottish Office. In the post-war years the SNP struggled in vain for many years. The nationalist limelight was-stolen, till the 1950s, by the 'Scottish Covenant' movement organised by the ex-SNP member, John MacCormick. The movement he led signed a Covenant in 1949. This asked for home rule for Scotland. 2 million people eventually signed this document. MacCormick and his followers won national attention in 1950 when they seized the Stone of Destiny from Westminster Abbey. The Conservative Government of the 1950s replied to this pressure by increasing the authority of the Scottish Office. They gave it control of electricity (1954) and roads (1956). In the early sixties its powers were further widened. By 1977 the Secretary of State for Scotland supervised the country's affairs from Edinburgh with 11 000 civil servants directly under his control.

Source 11.19
The powers of the Scottish Office, 1978

Home and Health Department:	National Health Service
	Law and order
Scottish Education Department:	Social Work
	Libraries
	Arts
	Education (except universities)
Department of Agriculture and Fisheries:	Crofting
	Forestry
	Fisheries
	Agricultural price supports
Scottish Development Department:	Local government
	Housing
	Roads
	Transport
Scottish Economic Planning Department:	New towns
	Electricity
	Tourism
	Highland developments
	Industrial incentives
	Economic planning
Lord Advocates' Department and Crown Office	Legal matters

(J. G. Kellas, *Modern Scotland*, 1980)

Source 11.21
SNP successes in by-elections
April 1945, R. D. McIntyre won Motherwell
1967, Mrs W. Ewing won Hamilton
1973, Mrs Margo MacDonald won Glasgow Govan
1988, J. Sillars won Govan

This is how the *Scotsman* reported one SNP successs:

Source 11.22
The rising tide of Scottish Nationalism sensationally swept Labour out of Hamilton last night. A Labour majority of 16 756 at the General Election was transformed by Mrs Winifred Ewing into a 1799 Scottish Nationalist triumph. The Tories lost their deposit in the Scottish seat. The message is plain for all Scottish MPs. Mrs Ewing becomes the only Scottish Nationalist MP at Westminster but all three of the other parties have been told that they ignore Scottish Nationalist aspirations at their peril.

Mrs Winifred Ewing (SNP)	18 397
A. Wilson (Labor)	16 598
I. Dyer (Conservative)	4 896

A jubilant Mrs Ewing, a 38-year old Glasgow solicitor, said 'Hamilton has made history for Scotland tonight. We will have a full-time home based Government by 1970'. She left the hall to a fantastic reception from hundreds of young supporters who had waited more than three hours in teeming rain.

(*Scotsman*, 3 November 1967)

Source 11.20
Scottish election results in general elections

	Labour	Conservative	Liberal	SNP	Communist
1945	37 MPs	27	—	—	1
	3 ILP MPs	—	—	—	—
1950	37 MPs	32	2	—	—
1951	35 MPs	35	1	—	—
1955	34 MPs	36	1	—	—
1959	38 MPs	31	1	—	—
1964	43 MPs	24	4	—	—
1966	46 MPs	20	5	—	—
1970	44 MPs	23	3	1	—
1974 Feb.	40 MPs	21	3	7	—
1974 Oct.	41 MPs	16	3	11	—
1979	44 MPs	22	3	2	—
1983	41 MPs	21	8	2	—
1987	50 MPs	10	9	3	—

(The ILP merged with Labour in 1947)

The SNP's influence helped push to the fore the question of whether Scotland should have its own Parliament. The Liberal Party had been in favour of Scotland managing its own internal affairs as long ago as the 1880s. By the 1970s the SNP was campaigning for complete independence.

In 1973 a Royal Commission suggested the setting up of a Scottish Assembly with ministers drawn from it and responsible to it and finance coming from a grant that an independent board would decide.

The Labour Party was divided as to whether it favoured home rule for Scotland, but, in response to the rise of the SNP it put forward a proposal for setting up a Scottish Assembly with fairly limited powers. The Assembly's Ministers would control housing, education (though not universities) transport, (though not railways), law and local government. Some Scottish Labour supporters of devolution, angry at the limited nature of the plan, broke away and formed the Scottish Labour Party in 1976.

On 1 March 1979 a vote of all Scottish people (a referendum) took place to see if they favoured the proposals. The government had decided that over 40% of the Scots electorate must vote 'Yes' to make the plan come into operation.

A majority of those voting supported the plan. But since they amounted to only 32.85% of the total electorate – well short of the government's 40% minimum – the plan was not put into operation.

In the 1979 election SNP support fell away. However, the party has continued to campaign actively. The debate it has encouraged led to both Liberal and Labour Parties, by the late 1980s, committing themselves to some form of home rule for Scotland.

QUESTIONS

1 Compare sources 11.4 and 11.20. In which years did Scotland elect a majority of MPs who belonged to the party which was in overall power in Britain? (K.U)

2 In which Regions did the majority of those voting in the referendum oppose devolution? (K.U)

3 In which three Regions was support for devolution strongest? (K.U)

4 Can you suggest any reasons for these differences? (E.2)

Source 11.23 _____

Devolution Referendum, 1 March 1979

The question voters were asked was: 'Do you want the provisions of the Scotland Act 1978 to be put into effect?'

	Yes	%	No	%	Turnout %
Borders	20 746	40.3	30 780	59.7	66.4
Central	71 296	54.7	59 105	45.3	65.9
Dumfries and Galloway	27 162	40.3	40 239	59.7	64.1
Fife	86 252	53.7	74 436	46.3	65.3
Grampian	94 944	48.3	101 485	51.6	57.2
Highland	44 973	51.0	43 274	49.0	64.7
Lothian	187 221	50.1	186 421	49.9	65.9
Strathclyde	596 519	54.0	508 599	46.0	62.5
Tayside	91 482	49.5	93 325	50.5	63.0
Orkney	2 104	27.9	5 439	72.1	54.1
Shetland	2 020	27.0	5 466	73.0	50.3
Western Isles	6 218	55.8	4 933	44.2	49.9
Scotland	1 230 937	51.6	1 153 502	48.4	62.9

(*Scottish Government Yearbook*, 1980)

12 Scottish Culture

The author of a recent book on Scotland wrote:

Source 12.1
Since the 1960s Scottish nationalism has been at the fore of Scottish life and the old questions have been raised regarding the place of Scotland within the United Kingdom. Is Scottish society essentially different from that in England?

(Kellas, *Modern Scotland*)

The sources in this section deal with the forces that have been changing Scottish society and Scots' knowledge of their own and the wider world. The years since the 1930s have been a time of great changes in Scottish society. To many people looking back, life in Scottish towns and villages in the 1950s seemed much more cut off from the wider world than it is today. Trevor Royle remembered that:

Source 12.2
The traditional Lammas Fair in St Andrews

Source 12.3
In the 1950s St Andrews was a very different sort of place than the busy town it is today. There was a train service but no Tay Road Bridge and the motor car had not then gained its universal ascendancy. It was a curiously remote town, not quite the same as the rest of Fife and yet firmly set on the edge of the rich farmlands of its Howe. Its history overshadowed the locality and everywhere one looked were the symbols of Scotland's past, a heritage so rich that it was easy to forget that St Andrews had languished for two centuries, a poor, church-ridden fishing town like many another East Coast neighbour.

(T. Royle, *Jock Tamson's Bairns* 1977)

To Christopher Rush, the changes he saw in St Monans, Fife, were a matter of concern:

Source 12.4
The old fishing ways and the men who followed them are pale shadows of the past. It has all been broken up – their community, their art of the story, their feeling for the sea. The faces in the firelight have faded into the garish light of the TV screen and of what is sometimes called progress. The folk culture is now embalmed in the Anstruther Fisheries Museum, the saddest place in the East Neuk. The fishing is going, the boatyards are strangely silent.

(C. Rush, *12 Months and a Day*, 1985)

An opinion poll of 1980 asked people to say how they thought life had changed.

Source 12.5
86% thought people had become more aggressive.
76% thought people had become less polite.
72% thought people were less honest.
56% thought people were less kind.
67% thought people were more knowledgeable.
82% thought people were more open-minded (MORI polls).

A Changing Population

Source 12.6
A Scottish Sikh community

Modern Scotland contains considerable numbers of people who have come from other parts of Britain and the world.

Source 12.7
Country of birth of immigrants living in Scotland in 1981

England	297 784
Northern Ireland	33 927
Irish Republic	27 018
Asian Commonwealth countries	20 258 (including 9097 from India)
Canada	8 547
African Commonwealth countries	7 475
Australia	4 775
Caribbean lands	1 547
Foreign African lands	5 962
USA	12 227
Pakistan	6 459
Middle East	3 081
Italy	4 789
Germany	11 073
Poland	5 083

(Census, 1981)

In the late 1940s large numbers of people from the West Indies and from India and Pakistan began to come to Britain. At the time there were plenty of jobs and the newcomers readily found work. By the 1960s this was no longer the case. British governments began to introduce laws to control the numbers of people coming to settle here.

Source 12.8

Controlling immigration – and its results
From the late 1940s large numbers of people from India, Pakistan and the West Indies came to Britain.
1958 – outbreaks of race rioting in London and Nottingham.
As the economy began to show signs of trouble, large numbers of extra workers in Britain were not thought necessary.
1962 – Commonwealth Immigration Act.
A limited quota of ordinary immigrants was established. Free entry was not allowed. Holders of British passports from the white dominions remained free to come in.
1965 – The controls were tightened.
1965 – Race Relations Act. It was made illegal to discriminate against anyone, in a public place, for racial reasons.
1971 – Only those born in Britain, or with a

Many newcomers had a struggle at first, before settling down. The authors of the following two sources are Italians who settled in Scotland. Mrs Lucchesi came not long after the War. She explained:

Source 12.9 a) ————————————
Italy was very down at that time and the only way that they [Italians] could come over here was to do four years on the farms. After that they were free to take on any work they wanted. The women, they could come over if they were doing domestic work in hospitals or somewhere like that. There was quite a big community here, in fact in Galston they called it 'Little Italy' because right round the farms there was an awful lot of Italians. But after the four years they started getting shops through other Italians telling them there's a shop going to be let and so on . . .

Mr Ioannone:

b) ————————————————
The farm I went to, it was just like slavery the way ye work there. The Scotchman, the boss, had a two son. All the job they no want to do, I had to do. When I'd overtime to do they just paid me two shillings [10p] an hour when everybody else a paid three shillings [15p] or four shillings [20p] an hour! After the four years, after that, I start a myself a business, I started with the ice-cream van and after a couple of years wi' the fish and chips and now I have this wee grocery business.

(Kay, *Odyssey*)

The children of these new arrivals sometimes found that the way of life they were part of in Scotland might differ from the way of life their parents thought was suitable. A girl whose family came from Pakistan explained:

Source 12.10 ————————————
My parents are Muslim but they haven't insisted that I should be a Muslim. Some Muslim parents, you probably know, are very strict. They insist that their daughters are Muslim and they want a say in who the daughter marries – a big say.

My father says: 'If you can't hear, you have to feel.' That means that you can only learn by your own experience. I respect him for his views. He tried hard to get his two daughters to become Muslim like himself but when we wouldn't he accepted it.

I was taught Christianity at school.

(T. Crabtree, *Teenagers*, 1980)

Source 12.11 ————————————
Chinese and Indian restaurants in Edinburgh

The Scottish population changed not only because of incomers, but because Scots continued to leave their native land. In 1987 an article in the *Glasgow Herald* stated:

Source 12.12 ————————————
Year after year we continue to experience a drain of talent both overseas and south of the Border. Official projections show England, Wales and Northern Ireland continuing to gain population with only Scotland seeing a population decline. In previous generations it was our high birth rate which succeeded in preventing our population declining. With falling birth rates we cannot now expect even to keep our population static.

(*Glasgow Herald*, 2 Dec. 1987)

The crofting counties, especially, lost many of their young people. James Hunter came from and works in this area. He wrote:

Source 12.13 _____
Despite almost 90 years of officially inspired efforts, the crofting problem is with us still . . . crofters' living standards are, in many respects, still below those prevailing elsewhere in Britain. . . . Intense emotional attachment to the land . . . is still fairly prevalent among crofters. [But] unaccompanied by the living standards and amenities of the south, crofting life has, during the past 30 or 40 years, become increasingly unattractive to a large proportion of the younger population. The steadily widening educational opportunities have provided these same young people with an alternative to crofting. The crofting community has been impoverished as talent, energy, enthusiasm and leadership have been drained from it . . .

In the years since 1945 the prosperity of crofters has generally continued to increase. New and larger grants are available for housing. Electricity, roads and other services have been provided. The crofter, as the Crofters Commission has observed, is:

'utterly bored with the romantic conception of his life . . . He prizes his Gaelic culture, but not to the extent of being treated as a museum piece.'

Throughout the crofting areas there is a need for more and better jobs.

(J. Hunter, *The Making of the Crofting Community*, 1976)

The weakening of the crofting areas has had an impact on the survival of Gaelic.

Since 1891 a society, An Comunn Gaidhealach, has worked to keep the language alive. At its annual Mod competitions are held in piping, singing and poetry.

Total number: 79 307 (1.64% of total population)

☐ 0–0.9	
▨ 1.0–4.9	% of total
▦ 5.0–9.9	Gaelic speakers
▪ 10.0–15.0	

Source: Census Scotland 1981

1 Why do you think so many people were keen to come to settle in Britain? (E.2)

2 Note two difficulties mentioned in the sources that immigrants might face. (K.U)

3 What is the main reason (source 12.12) that explains Scotland's declining population? (E.2)

4 Is the author of source 12.13 happy with the situation he sees in the crofting counties? Mention those parts of the source that support your answer. (E.1)

5 Look at map 12.14. Why do you think there are quite a large number of Gaelic speakers in the Glasgow area? (E.2)

Source 12.14 _____

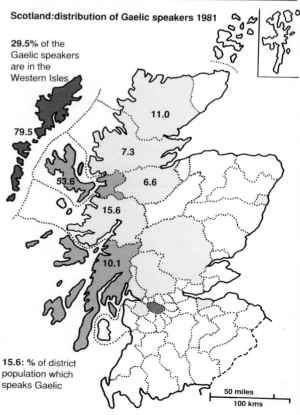

Scotland:distribution of Gaelic speakers 1981

29.5% of the Gaelic speakers are in the Western Isles

15.6: % of district population which speaks Gaelic

50 miles
100 kms

236

Youth

In 1944 an Education Act planned secondary schooling for all children. The Attlee Government put it into operation in 1946. In 1947 the school leaving age was raised to 15. These were bold steps for, at the time, Britain was short of workers and of money. The reforms meant spending on training more teachers and building more schools.

Source 12.15

Goldenhill Primary School in Clydebank was opened in 1955 to replace the old school which was blitzed. Until the new school opened the pupils were accommodated in huts

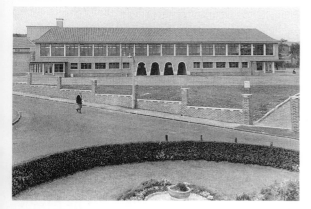

The new secondary system involved making children sit an examination at the end of the primary school stage. A minority went to 'senior secondary' schools, or followed 'senior secondary' academic courses in the secondary schools that served smaller towns.

Mary Liverani took this examination in Glasgow:

Source 12.16

This was the exam that decided the rest of your life: what kind of job you'd get, whom you'd marry, where you'd live and how many children you'd have. It was the exam that got you out of or barred your exit from the tenements. If you got an S1, S2 or S3 pass you went to Bellahouston Academy. Those who did't get an S pass went to Lambhill Street Junior where you studied sewing and cooking and office work or woodwork if you were a boy.

(Liverani, *The Winter Sparrows*)

These separate types of secondary schooling were criticised as being unfair to many children. In 1965 the Scottish Education Department issued Circular 600. This asked local authorities to end their selective system. Instead, children were to go to comprehensive schools. In 1972 the school leaving age was raised to 16. Increasing numbers of children stayed on after the age of 16. More higher educational opportunities were provided including a new university at Stirling (1964) and the separating of Dundee from St Andrews to form a university in its own right (1967).

Source 12.17

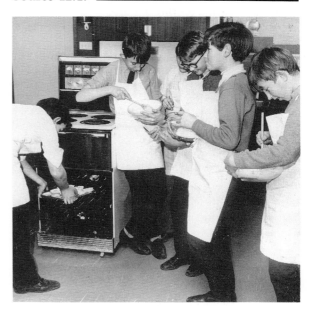

The increase in the numbers of older pupils at schools and of students in higher education helped to contribute to the idea of teenagers being a separate section of society. So too did the growth in the earning power of those teenagers in work. This development was signalled by the appearance in the 1950s of attempts to provide special kinds of clothes and entertainments for the young. In 1953 there first appeared a style of clothing that earned the wearers the title of 'Teddy boys'. Other fashions followed in subsequent years. All were very much aimed at the young. At around the same time a new type of music burst upon the scene, helped by the invention of the long-playing vinyl record. Valve-powered record players able to take a stack of discs, replaced wind-up gramophones. Radios became cheaper and more portable. Some adults did not like these developments. An Ayr girls'-school head told parents:

Source 12.18 _____
If you as parents allow your daughters to become part of the immoral teenage cult so prevalent today, even if it is only in outward appearances, then you can blame yourselves if the rot creeps in and one day you find their minds have been contaminated.

(P. Laurie, *The Teenage Revolution*, 1965)

A reporter from Aberdeen's *Evening Express* went to see the film *Rock Around the Clock* which stirred up a great deal of teenage excitement in 1956. He reported:

Source 12.19 _____
I sat through two performances of Bill Haley and his Comets. As a film it is rubbish. As a box office draw it is terrific. Almost 20 [youths] left their seats and held hands, flailing their arms and legs about. They were politely ignored by the management – but the sound was turned off if they became too bad. As the film neared its climax more and more youths joined the jiving in the aisles.

(*Evening Express* 11 September 1956)

In many cinemas youngsters behaved far more vigorously whilst watching this film than Aberdonians seemed to have done. One youth reported:

Source 12.20 _____
I'd read in the paper that there was this film and kids were tearing up the cinemas, so I went to the cinema and, sure enough, as soon as it started off, with one accord the audience leapt to its feet and started bopping about in a way I'd never seen before in my life.

(P. Everett, *You'll Never be 16 Again*, 1986)

Some cinemas had their furniture wrecked.
    In Orkney Alan Bold was a teenager in 1956. He remembered:

Source 12.21 _____
In January 1956, something exciting happened: the emergence of a voice that gave a massive, pulsating V-sign to the school, to the street, to

urban defeatism. Elvis Presley's 'Heartbreak Hotel' was released and I became an instant convert to rock. My new escape would be to ape Elvis. Parents and teachers – the dreaded 'them' – hated him and I liked him all the more for that.
    I managed to get a cheap guitar and slicked my hair in Elvis fashion. He became my God, something to believe in. Pictures of Elvis – cut from magazines – became instant icons and I scrutinised them religiously. For the first time I put my mind to something: becoming the greatest local authority on Elvis Presley. I remember clearly standing at the bottom of the stair and impressing the girls.

(Royle, *Jock Tamson's Bairns*)

Source 12.22 _____
The Beatles during their first visit to Edinburgh

Britain soon produced its own musical idols for the young. The whole upheaval seemed to a writer of the time, to be:

Source 12.23 _____
'Americanisation' – a brash, standardisation mass-culture, centred on the enormously increased influence of television and advertising, a popular music more marked than ever by the hypnotic beat of jazz and the new prominence given to teenagers and the young.
    Above all, with the coming of this new age, a new spirit was unleashed – a new wind of essentially youthful hostility to every kind of established convention and traditional authority.

(C. Booker, *The Neophiliacs*, 1969)

Source 12.24

A fashionable dance of the 60s – the Twist

The changes were also marked by the setting up of places where teenagers could meet socially. A fifties teenage girl recalled:

Source 12.25

No, girls couldn't go in pubs, and when the coffee bars came out it was an absolutely heaven-sent opportunity – total emancipation for fiteen- or sixteen-year-old girls to be able to go out and sit for the evening and sip coffee and see fellas.

One minute there were none, and then there was perhaps one, and that one became so popular that there would be hundreds of people outside on the pavement waiting to get in. The juke-box would be in the cellar and there would be this thump coming through the pavement, and you were quite happy to mill about outside, with several hundred other people, just for the chance to get in there and sip not-very-good coffee for ten minutes and then be shoved out again. But then, very rapidly, lots more opened, and then they divided up into places for various types of people. There were very sophisticated ones above a department store, then real rock'n'roll ones.

(Everett, *You'll Never be 16 Again*)

Once established this 'pop culture' did not go away, though it took different forms at different times. By the 1970s, a writer of the time noted:

Source 12.26

Way-out clothing of the more agreeable sort began to disappear; decorative arts we had so suddenly and unexpectedly become good at faded; Flower Power withered as a colder, harsher social climate set in. Fashions became severe or sinister. Skinheads and punk rockers had no ambition to be hailed as Beautiful People. Serious-minded young women added karate to their yoga course, feeling that they needed its defensive skills.

(N. Shrapnel, *The 70s*, 1980)

A journalist surveying trends since the fifties wrote:

Source 12.27

I think one of the things to lament, perhaps, about the teen boom of the fifties through the seventies is that it force-fed a couple of generations with false expectations. It made them seem to themselves more important than they really are. What can teenagers do? Not very much. What can teenagers know? Not very much. They might have tons of charm and potential, and that's really where the interest in teenagers lies, it's in their potential. That's what's sad about teenagers out of work today: they're not getting a chance to fulfil that potential. I don't know what the answer is. In the fifties and sixties they were over-indulged to the point of stupidity. They didn't deserve it. They were only kids. But they were a market and it was essentially a market force. And I'm afraid when you take away the market, you take away the interest. That's why it's finding its own level again. It's rather sad.

(Everett, *You'll Never be 16 Again*)

The years from the 1950s were a time when girls gained greater freedom to run their own lives. One observer of these years thought:

Source 12.28

There are signs that some girls are tending towards more independence in their dealings with men, and that they will not be content to sign over their lives to their husbands on marriage. Having experienced the satisfactions of nice clothes, hairdo's and make-up, they are determined to remain smart and in control of events after they have married; they are not prepared to be bowed down with lots of children, and they will expect their husbands to take a fuller share than their fathers in the running of the home.

(Laurie, *The Teenage Revolution*)

During the 1960s oral contraceptives became widely available; in 1967 local authorities were given power to set up clinics to provide contraceptive advice and services.

QUESTIONS

1 Why did the author of source 12.16 think the examination she mentions was so important? (K.U)

2 In what way does source 12.17 show how education had changed since pre-war years? (E.2)

3 Did the author of source 12.19 approve of what he saw? Give reasons for your answer. (E.1)

4 What reasons do you think made possible the 'pop revolution' described in this section? (E.2)

The Changing Media
Reading habits

By the 1940s the average Scot learned about events in the wider world from the many local and national newspapers of the time, from BBC's two radio channels and from newsreels in the cinema. For those able and ready to devote time to reading serious detailed books Penguin produced a range of studies of all sorts of topics. Strict censorship laws applied that were not just a result of the War. They controlled theatre performances, films and books and magazines. By the forties children had a wide range of comics from which to choose. Bob Crampsey was a keen reader of comics, in wartime Glasgow.

Source 12.29

The Beano brought out a comic strip entitled Musso da Wop ('He's a big a da flop'). Riddles abounded such as 'Why does Musso never change his socks? Because he smells defeat' . . . . We bought the *Hotspur* and *Adventure*. The stories were well written. Many involved public schools. There were sagas of the football field [including] Cast Iron Bill. He was a goalkeeper who had never conceded a single goal. Occasionally all seemed lost with Bill helpless on his back and the ball sailing towards an empty net. But thanks to a sudden Force 8 gale [or] a passing sniper who shot the ball Bill's charge was preserved intact.

(Crampsey, *The Young Civilian*)

Source 12.30
The Beano Comic

The War years brought American servicemen to Britain. It also brought other influences, as this witness recalls:

Source 12.31 ────────────
American comics flooded in; new heroes like Superman. And jazz records we learned to listen to the American way, clicking our fingers and if possible chewing gum.

(R. Westwood, *Children of the Blitz*, 1985)

By 1945, Bob Crampsey believed, British people were:

Source 12.32 ────────────
. . . infinitely more Americanised. It was not only that we had heard many more American radio programmes than we would normally have done, or even perhaps seen more films. What was vastly different was that we had met actual Americans, for every second girl one heard of seemed to be awaiting clearance to rejoin boyfriend or husband in the United States. We knew a lot more about them and they knew a little more about us.

The 'pop revolution' of the fifties and sixties led to yet more new publications.

Source 12.33 ────────────
Suddenly there were magazines like *Honey* and *Rave* and comics, *Valentine* and *Roxy*. I especially liked *Valentine* because it had the Beatles in. After that they turned glossy and the middle pages were always a big poster of somebody like Paul McCartney or the Yardbirds or the Small Faces.

(*You'll Never be 16 Again*)

Amid the changes of more recent years, including the coming of 'tabloid' newspapers, some influences changed little. *The People's Friend*, for example, continued to provide the sort of view of Scotland noted by Bob Crampsey:

Source 12.34 ────────────
It could scarcely have been further removed from real Scottish life of the 1940s. [In] the stories . . . the women were of impregnable virtue. The heroes were dependable and quiet. *The People's Friend* took absolutely no notice of the hundreds of thousands of Catholics, Episcopalians, Jews and Nonconformists who

dwelt in Scotland even then. I glanced at one the other day and almost nothing had changed.

(Crampsey, *The Young Civilian*)

In the 1950s and 60s, however, there were considerable changes in what people could read.

Source 12.35 ────────────

Sir John Colville witnessed this time of change:

Source 12.36 ────────────
In 1952 films and books were sternly censored. Glossy magazines published photographs of nude ladies, but few existed for that sole purpose and the photographs were demure by subsequent standards. Homosexuality was illegal.

If the new way of life [in the late 50s], the rise of affluent society and impatience with old-fashioned values have had much to do with the changes that have taken place, the abolition of censorship cannot be disregarded. It began in [1959] when a Court of Law upheld a claim by the publishers of the [complete] edition of *Lady Chatterley's Lover* by D. H. Lawrence, until then banned, that the book was not obscene. This was the charter of the permissive society.

(Colville, *The New Elizabethans*)

Some Scottish writers were alarmed by the way English and foreign influences seemed to threaten the existence of a distinctive Scottish language and literature. The poet, Hugh MacDiarmid, explained:

Source 12.37 _____
If I am asked when I think I got my first idea about Scotland, I can only reply that I don't think I was ever unaware of it. At school we were punished if we lapsed into Scots. Apart from one or two of the love songs of Burns we got nothing at all at school about Scottish literature . . . I am generally credited with having been instrumental in changing all that. Courses in Scottish literature have been established in most of our universities.

(K. Miller, *Memoirs of a Modern Scotland*, 1970)

His fellow writer, Maurice Lindsay, noted of MacDiarmid:

Source 12.38 _____
He spoke of Scotland as if its liberated reawakening was politically imminent. Round him he gathered a group of young writers dedicated to [restoring] the Scots language through poetry.

(M. Lindsay, *Thank you for having me*, 1983)

Other notable Scottish contemporaries of MacDiarmid included William Soutar, Robert Garioch, Edwin Muir, Lewis Grassic Gibbon, Neil Gunn, Fionn MacColla and James Bridie.

QUESTIONS

1 Compare a modern comic with source 12.30. What changes can you find?
(K.U)

2 Why do you think Scots people have read – and still read – magazines like the one described in source 12.34?
(E.2)

3 Photo 12.35 was taken just after the trial mentioned in 12.36. Can you tell it was taken at this time simply from studying the picture?
(E.1)

4 Photo 12.35 was taken just after the trial mentioned in studying the picture?
(E.1)

The cinema and television

Throughout the 1940s cinema-going remained very popular. During the War years, a man who lived at the time recalled:

Source 12.39 _____
Much of our limited understanding of war was learned in the cinema. And never have children enjoyed their films so much . . . *One of our Aircraft is Missing, Target for Tonight, Ships with Wings, A Yank in the RAF* – these were some of the films we watched . . . In black and white and sometimes gory colour we watched the glory of war unfolded. Always our bombs dropped on target, always our planes limped home. The officers were all decent and the men were cheeky but gallant. German soldiers were all oafish – particularly sentries who never heard saboteurs until they were cracked on the skull – and German officers were monocled sadists who clicked their heels crisply in the presence of superior monocled sadists.

(N. Longmate, *The Home Front,* 1981)

The cinema continued to flourish until the 1950s. It then met such severe difficulties that many cinemas closed. The development of better quality sound and pictures were not enough to halt this decline.

Source 12.40 _____
An unsuccessful attempt by an old cinema to adapt to modern times

The reason behind this decline was the arrival in Scotland of television. The transmission of television programmes began again in 1946. The coverage of Britain was rapidly extended, reaching Scotland by 1952. Even though television at this time offered viewers only one (BBC) channel, it was enough to stop people from going as often to the cinema. In 1955 ITV was established, with STV being the first company to offer a Scottish service. In 1952 there were 41 000 sets in Scotland. By 1962 there were 1 119 000 and in following years the numbers increased.

Source 12.42 _____

Percentage of private households with television and video   **Scotland**

```
Percent                                                    Percent
100 ┐                                                    ┌ 100
 90 ┤         television                                 ├  90
 80 ┤                                                    ├  80
 70 ┤         colour television                          ├  70
 60 ┤                                                    ├  60
 50 ┤                                                    ├  50
 40 ┤                                                    ├  40
 30 ┤                                            video   ├  30
 20 ┤    black and white                                 ├  20
 10 ┤    television only                                 ├  10
  0 ┴────────────────────────────────────────────────┴   0
    72  73  74  75  76  77  78  79  80  81  82  83  84  85
```

Television helped to destroy the remains of old-fashioned music hall and many small repertory theatres too. The number of TV channels increased – Channel 4 opened in 1982. By 1989 technology had reached the point of offering viewers a whole range of channels transmitted by satellite. Television spread into the educational system, too. In 1957 the BBC began to transmit school programmes in Scotland.

Source 12.43 _____

Modern technology in use in the classroom

Television altered people's lives. In 1988 an official report observed:

Source 12.44 _____

While people today are healthier and wealthier, an analysis of leisure activities suggests they are also lazier. By far the most popular pastime is watching television. The average person over the age of four watches 27 hours a week.

(*Guardian*, 6 Jan. 1988)

Arguments began as to whether television brought an improvement to people's lives. The following are differing views expressed on this issue by people living in the sixties, seventies and eighties.

Source 12.45
The individual now, whether he wishes or not, has got disasters being brought to him, from all over the world. I still think that probably the news is the most powerful aspect of television for the adult population; for the children I am beginning to think the violent programmes [matter most].

Source 12.46
Years ago we used to entertain ourselves, with the piano, you see, and the gramophone. And there was always a party, you know, you could go to of a weekend – somebody was having a party which . . . you made your own entertainment, which really and truly was better entertainment than what you get on the television today.

Source 12.47
It is an absurd upper-middle-class fantasy to imagine that if only people [would] turn their televisions off they would all start reading Solzhenitsyn or attending lectures on the Late Renaissance. Most people deprived of their TV pick up the *Sun* or listen to Radio 1. It is sometimes suggested that in the days before TV 'took over' there was a golden age when families clustered around the piano and made their entertainment, when voters [took part] in public meetings instead of being fed political messages by the telly; when the factory worker rushed out after supper to attend lectures. Yet the figures for people 'doing their own thing' whether jogging or gardening – attending evening classes or ballroom dancing – have gone up during the television age, not down.

(C. Dunkley, *Television Today and Tomorrow*, 1985)

QUESTIONS

1 In what ways was the cinema used to shape people's views during wartime? (K.U)

2 Do you think it was right to do this? (E.2)

3 In what ways do the authors of 12.45, 12.46 and 12.47 differ about the impact of television? (E.1)

4 Which view do you prefer? Give a reason for your answer. (E.2)

A Scottish culture?

The past century has been a time when Scotland has been opened up to all sorts of outside influences. To one Scottish writer, (Tom Scott):

Source 12.48
The Scotland of today is no longer Scotland, it is 'Scotshire' a county in the north of England.

(Miller, *Memoirs of a Modern Scotland*)

Source 12.49
The Edinburgh Festival

The writer, Maurice Lindsay, welcomed the setting up of the Edinburgh Festival in 1947. But the event brought yet more outside influences into Scotland. He wrote:

Source 12.50 —————————————————
It is impossible to exaggerate the impact the Festival made upon us. Here, in prim grey Edinburgh, civilization had once again found courage to reassert itself. There were those who argued that the introduction of such a concentration of alien music and drama must have a [harmful] effect on the native product. 40 years on such fears can be seen to have been unfounded. We have enjoyed Scottish Opera and the Citizens Theatre; seen Scottish plays and heard music by Thea Musgrave and Iain Hamilton [Scottish composers].

(Lindsay, *Thank you for having me*)

Another writer commented on the cultural changes in Scotland's biggest city:

Source 12.51 —————————————————
Things are beginning to stir again culturally in Glasgow. New art galleries are springing up. More and more buildings are cleaned. There's the growing success of the Scottish Opera Company to add to the concerts of the Scottish National Orchestra [and] the Citizens' Theatre. New pubs, new restaurants, new hotels have multiplied and Glasgow has found itself liking Chinese, Indian, Italian food.

(Edwin Morgan, *New Statesman*, 13 Aug. 1965)

Maurice Lindsay welcomed such developments. He did not think much of Scotland's main orchestra of the immediate post-war years:

Source 12.52 —————————————————
Scotland's acceptance of a second-rate orchestra coupled with a preference for musicians with a [foreign] name led to the appointment of a succession of second-rate conductors. A campaign had to be fought for the acceptance of a Scottish conductor. This was achieved in 1959 with the appointment of Alexander Gibson. This gifted man has done [much] for Scottish music-making, not only in building up the Scottish National Orchestra to international concert giving, but also in the creation of Scottish Opera.

(Lindsay, *Thank you for having me*)

The 1970s and 1980s have been a time of increasing interest in Scotland's past. Civic societies, local authorities and the National Trust have tried to preserve and restore Scottish buildings. Museums have been improved and extended and new ones established. To some people, like the academic, James Kellas, a separate Scottish identity clearly exists. He explained it as follows:

Source 12.53 —————————————————
At the time of the Union the culture of Scotland was inherently strong. Kirk, school and law court were thriving institutions, popularly supported. This culture proved [strong] throughout the succeeding years of the Union . . . There is a Scottish Football League, a National Trust for Scotland, a Scottish Opera, a Scottish Television. The visitor who settles in Scotland soon becomes amazed at the more subtle parts of Scottish life. His children have to be educated in a Scottish way. His dealings with his solicitor bring him face to face with Scots law. Scotland has 1/10 of the population of England and is subject to a constant process, or threat, of assimilations. To some this poses no problems. To others anglicisation represents the loss of a valued style of life.

(Kellas, *Modern Scotland*)

Source 12.54 —————————————————
The opening of the General Assembly in 1971

The writer, Trevor, Royle has complained of:

Source 12.55 ───────────────

. . . the grim nationalism of many Scots who keep alive a selfish feeling for their country. It is too easy to summon up the half-true romantic spirit of long lost battles or football matches, the two blending together against the Auld Enemy. By learning about the real past . . . it may be that Scots at school today will have a greater compassion for other parts of the world.

(Royle, *Jock Tamson's Bairns*)

Postscript

Many of the sources in this book are memories of the past provided by older people. Are they always accurate? An Aberdeen journalist suggested that such memories tend to show an ideal past.

Memory Lane was an ideal place to live. Its pavements were clean and safe, even after dark and the generous neighbours cared and shared the little they had with you. Housewives got more for their pennies and a more friendly efficient service. Life was lived at a slower pace and there was always time for a natter over the fence. Streets were filled with carefree laughing children who played mischievous games. Families had more time for day trips to the seaside.

(*Evening Express*, 30 Nov. 1988)

Other critics complain that some of our museums give a far too kindly and romantic view of our past. How can we know what the past was really like? How accurate are your memories of your early life? How can the student of the past really understand the time being studied? Is it ever possible to really know what the past was like?

Further reading

The clearest, fullest and most readable general history of this period is T. C. Smout, *A Century of the Scottish People*, 1986.

The best way to explore the period more fully is to read the books from which source extracts have been obtained. Some of the best of these books which are still currently available, are listed below.

E. Sillar, *Edinburgh's Child*, Edinburgh, 1961
M. Weir, *Shoes Were for Sunday*, London, 1970
A. Blair, *Tea at Miss Cranston's*, London, 1985
L. Derwent, *A Breath of Border Air*, 1975, London
R. Glasser, *Growing up in the Gorbals*, London, 1986
Billy Kay, *Odyssey*, Edinburgh, 1980
Bob Crampsey, *The Young Civilian*, Edinburgh, 1987
Amy Stewart Fraser, *The Hills of Home*, London, 1973